LONGMAN'S GUIDE TO THE

Advanced Placement Examination in European History

Mildred Alpern

Longman

New York

**Longman's Guide to the Advanced
Placement Examination in European History**

Copyright ©1993 by Longman Publishing Group.
All rights reserved.
No part of this publication may be reproduced,
stored in a retrieval system, or transmitted
in any form or by any means, electronic, mechanical,
photocopying, recording, or otherwise,
without the prior permission of the publisher.

Longman, 10 Bank Street, White Plains, N.Y. 10606

Associated companies:
Longman Group Ltd., London
Longman Cheshire Pty., Melbourne
Longman Paul Pty., Auckland
Copp Clark Pitman, Toronto

Acquisitions editor: Lyn McLean
Production editor: Linda Moser
Text design: David Levy
Cover design: Joey DePinho

ISBN 0-8013-0943-3

6 7 8 9 10 -ML- 99 98 97

For Nubs, who shares my past—
and August, who is our future

CONTENTS

Chapter 8   Industrialization and the "Isms"   84

Chapter 9   The Age of Nationalism: 1850-1900   98

Chapter 10   Russia: From Peter the Great to Nicholas II
in the Early 1900s   110

FOREWORD

This book has been designed for Advanced Placement (AP) European History students to use as a supplement to their textbooks and class notes. It will help them, systematically review and prepare for the annual Advanced Placement European History Examination, which is administered each May to approximately 30,000 students in over 2,000 schools worldwide. However, it should be noted that the College Board Development Committee for Advanced Placement European History does not endorse any one course design or supplementary materials, and prides itself on preparing a syllabus and an examination that accommodate a great diversity of approaches.

The reader will quickly see that Mildred Alpern is a firm believer in the empowerment of students to "do" history, i.e., to make it interesting and to make it their own. She seeks to have students become critical readers of historical writing and documents, to teach them to analyze carefully and evaluate everything they read, and finally, to have them write cogent and well-reasoned responses to a variety of essay questions. Ample samples of classroom-tested thematic and document-based essay questions with student responses are provided. They cover a wide variety of topics across the chronology.

The author of this book is in a unique position to prepare this review book. She has been an active and involved Advanced Placement European classroom teacher for almost a quarter of a century. She has taught an extremely successful and popular AP European History course at Spring Valley Senior High School, Spring Valley, New York, for many years. She has also served with the national team of European history professors and teachers responsible for evaluating the essays written by AP European history students. She has chaired the College Board committee of college history professors and high school history teachers charged with the responsibility for producing the course syllabus and the annual examination. Serving as a consultant to the College

Board, she has also taught numerous workshops around the country instructing AP European History teachers how to improve their courses. She co-authored a widely-read monthly column in Perspectives, the newsletter of the American Historical Association, which provides survey course history teachers at both the secondary and collegiate levels with access to the latest scholarship and new teaching materials.

Lawrence Beaber, Consultant
AP European History Development Committee
College Board Division
Educational Testing Service
Princeton, New Jersey

PREFACE

I have been very fortunate to teach a wide range of courses, among them Advanced Placement European History, at Spring Valley Senior High School. Each year's new crop of students has challenged me to rethink my courses and methods in an effort to spark interest and deepen student knowledge and understanding.

I am indebted to the many students over the years whose intellectual and personal growth has made teaching such a rewarding career; to my department chairman, Dr. Donald Elwell; and to my longtime colleague in the Social Studies Department, Mr. Larry Schwartz, for the stimulating collegial and professional atmosphere they have provided. They are models of the finest in teaching in their wisdom and dedication to our young. I am also grateful to the administrators and board members of my district for their support and encouragement in my classroom teaching and professional activities.

Finally, I would like to thank my family–my mother, husband, and children, Merry and Spenser–for the richness they have added to my life.

Mildred Alpern

INTRODUCTION

The Advanced Placement European History examination covers the modern period from approximately 1450 to the early 1970s. It traces themes in political, diplomatic, economic, intellectual, social, and cultural history. The examination is comprehensive in scope and coverage of events and personalities of the past. Thus students are encouraged to master the broad chronological contours of modern European history as well as to have in-depth knowledge of specialized topics. Students must also be familiar with the historian's craft of analyzing and synthesizing primary sources and have experience in this practice.

Currently, the examination is three hours in length:

- one hour and fifteen minutes for 100 multiple-choice questions—half dealing with the period from 1450 to 1789 and the other half with the period from 1789 to 1970
- one hour for a document-based essay that includes a fifteen-minute silent reading and note-taking period
- a forty-five-minute free-response essay selected from six offerings*

---

*In 1994, there will be the following change in the examination format:

- sixty minutes for 80 multiple-choice questions
- the hour-long document-based essay will not change
- two thematic free-response essays will be required, with thirty minutes allotted to each essay. Students will be required to choose one question from each of two different time periods—1450-1789 and 1789-1970. In addition, they must select their questions from two of the following different topics: (1) political/diplomatic, (2) economic/social, and (3) cultural/intellectual.

The essay section of each examination is graded at a national reading by professors and teachers who gather to establish standards for ranking the essays. The multiple-choice section of the exam is machine-graded. On the basis of a composite score, final results are reported on a five-point scale: 5–Extremely well qualified; 4–Well qualified; 3–Qualified; 2–Possibly qualified; 1–No recommendation. With scores of 3 or better, most colleges and universities award credit and/or placement out of introductory courses. And many colleges and universities grant instant sophomore standing to students who have earned scores of 3 or better on three AP exams. There is good reason, therefore, to perform well on the test.

Advanced Placement European History, however, is a curriculum, not a test. It is a course of study designed to parallel college freshmen introductory courses. It is an endeavor that requires skills in reading, writing, recalling, summarizing, assessing, and analyzing–skills that need to be polished and reviewed throughout the year.

Reviewing materials that have been read and studied during the year in preparation for a national exam is a concentrated task different from studying for a particular unit exam. While a year-end review does provide the opportunity to recall what one has learned and to refresh that knowledge on a much larger scale, it also lets one see how developments have unfolded and have been linked to one another over the centuries. It is a chance to see the changes that have occurred and also the continuities that have persisted in patterns of human behavior.

A review must go well beyond dates, events, and personalities. Like the course of study, it must be selective in (1) highlighting trends, (2) illustrating conclusions with representative evidence, and (3) raising questions that challenge one's ability to formulate a compelling answer with clarity. This particular review book represents a distillation of textbook coverage and anthology source materials. It aims to supplement class notes and assignments with these additions:

- overviews of major units

- selected primary sources to aid in answering topic-related and document-based questions

- definitions of major terms, events, and persons encountered in textbook readings

- multiple-choice questions for testing understanding

- essay questions requiring definition of terms, formulation of hypothesis, marshalling of evidence, and defense of a position

- essay writing tips using student models and focusing on common writing problems

The best way to review each chapter is first to read the overview and the included documents, answering the questions framed on these sources. This exercise will sharpen skills in reading and evaluating documents. Next, review the identifications at the end of the chapter. Go on to the multiple-choice questions analyzing why certain answers are wrong. Then, test yourself on the study essay questions by writing out an introductory paragraph that includes your hypothesis. Outline the evidence you would use to substantiate your thesis. Write out a conclusion that reinforces the position you have taken, reflects on counterarguments you may wish to address, or even speculates on the significance of the topic in the larger scheme of human and historical development. Conclusions may be quite diverse, but in all well-written essays they provide a polished ending. Last, study carefully the essay writing tip as a guide to help you develop and refine your own writing style.

Your efforts in these review steps will pay off. The practice you put into each phase will ready you for the similarly related tasks of the AP exam.

PRELUDE

With the collapse of the late Roman Empire, localized and fragmented government or feudalism took its place as urban centers declined. **Feudalism** was a political system whereby lords and their vassals, members of the aristocracy, allied to fight wars. **Manorialism** was the economic base supporting the political arrangement. The serfs who lived on the manor belonged to the feudal lord or vassal and provided the material wherewithal to support the noble class. Society was rigidly hierarchical; one's status was based on birth.

The church was the dominating institution that provided the cultural cement even as its power in Western Europe waxed and waned in struggles with feudal kings. Within the church there was also status ranking, with the higher church authorities drawn from noble families.

By the eleventh century, agricultural production increased and towns began to emerge, contributing to a cultural revival. Universities were built. They fostered the spread of learning dominated by a Christian worldview of a geocentric universe created by God out of the basic elements of fire, earth, air, and water. The Schoolmen who preached Christian philosophy or Scholasticism used concepts of the Greeks in their explanations of Christian teachings. Chaucer and Dante wrote in the vernacular. And the Gothic churches, with their soaring heights and brilliantly colored stained glass Christian scenes, were testimony to the contemplation by medieval people of spiritual ideals.

The cultural and demographic expansions of the twelfth- and thirteenth-centuries were adversely affected by the **Black Death,** or bubonic plague, which decimated almost one third of the European population and gave the reduced laboring force a bargaining chip in wage conflicts with landlords. Other struggles ensued between popes and kings. Christian councils raised challenges to papal authority; so too did the critics **John Wycliffe** (c. 1320-1384) of England and **John Huss** (1369-1415) of Bohemia. The prestige of the church waned even as the Christian religion remained the integrating force in preindustrial Western society.

Into this briefly described setting emerged the period that historians call the Renaissance.

IDENTIFICATIONS

Black Death–The bubonic plague that struck Europe in the mid-fourteenth century and killed from one third to one half of the population before it ran its course after 1600.

Feudalism–A decentralized political system in which lords and their vassals, both members of the aristocracy, allied to fight wars and defend territorial gains.

John Huss (1369-1415)–Czech priest who was burned at the stake for rejecting and questioning certain church doctrines, such as transubstantiation.

Manorialism–The economic base of feudalism; in brief, the economic system in which the serfs worked the fields of the manorial lord and provided the material wherewithal to support the noble class.

John Wycliffe (c. 1320-1384)–English theologian who wrote that Scriptures alone, not papal claims, should be the standard of Christian belief and practice.

LONGMAN'S GUIDE TO THE

ADVANCED PLACEMENT EXAMINATION IN EUROPEAN HISTORY

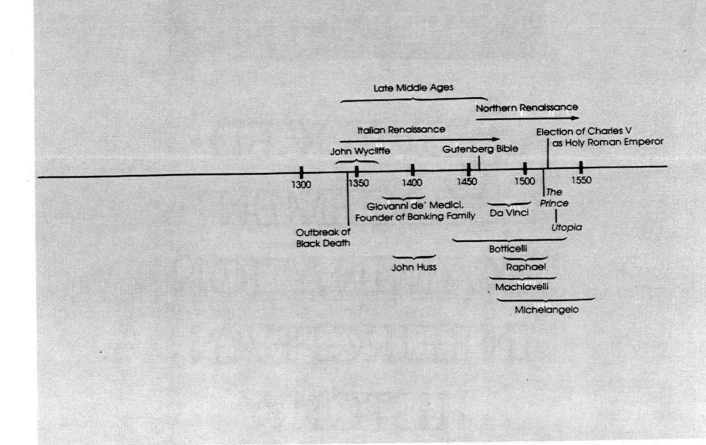

THE RENAISSANCE

How distinctive was the **Renaissance** as a period in European history? The Italian Renaissance, many historians agree, was not a complete break with the outlook and institutions of the Middle Ages; rather, it was an artistic and intellectual transformation of an urban elite, characterized by **rationalism, secularism, individualism,** and **humanism**. A wealthy merchant and banking class enriched by trade and commerce in the cities of Genoa, Milan, and Florence patronized the arts and education. Ruling dynastic families such as the Medicis in Florence and the Sforzas in Milan with their **condottieri**, or mercenary soldiers, defeated their rivals and promoted the signs of their wealth. Building extensive libraries and commissioning artistic masterpieces—from Michelangelo and **Benvenuto Cellini** (1500–1571), among others—these rulers competed with the growing material power of the Catholic church in influence and prestige.

ITALIAN RENAISSANCE

Italy's geographical location as the crossroads of the Mediterranean trade, with abundant seaports where travelers mixed and profits mounted, helps to explain the cultural expansion. But Italy was also the home of the ancient Romans, and relics of Greco-Roman antiquities abounded to inspire imitation. Humanists revered the ancient classical authors like Plato and Socrates and developed educational programs based on their study. According to Castiglione (*The Courtier*, 1528), the court gentleman must be widely educated to paint, sing, wrestle, ride, converse in many languages, speak eloquently, and write skillfully.

Political Theory

In the realm of political theory, Machiavelli (*The Prince*, 1513), revolutionized the science with his pragmatic prescriptions for obtaining and maintaining power. Since men are naturally selfish and corrupt, Machiavelli wrote, the prince must be as cunning as a fox and as ferocious as a lion in his dealings with them. He must be able to manipulate men's emotions and feelings, understanding that it is better to be feared than loved by his people. Christian teachings were irrelevant in the prince's pursuit of power. Political ends justified whatever means, however brutal, the prince employed.

Realism in Art

An artistic breakthrough to realism is found in the works of Michelangelo, da Vinci, Raphael, and Botticelli that illustrate the ways in which Christian and Greco-Roman themes converge. Michelangelo's *David* conveys the Greek ideal of beauty with its classical proportions, anatomical perfection, and glorification of the human body. The biblical David is portrayed as an independent moral agent who embodies reason and free will, and exhibits *virtu,* the striving for personal excellence. The Medicis placed the statue before the city hall in Florence as a symbolic defender of the republic. To the humanists, republican government was a superior form because it invited the participation of citizens in the dialogue of governing on which human progress depended.

Literary Criticism

The humanists studied the Latin classics and literary culture of the ancient world with deep interest. A famous humanist was **Lorenzo Valla** (1407-1457), who used historical criticism to discredit an eighth-century document giving the pope Italy and the entire Western empire. Analyzing the language in the document, he proved that it could not have been written in the fourth century and was, in fact, forged in the eighth century.

DOCUMENT-BASED ESSAY QUESTIONS

Compare the visual and document below and summarize in writing the ways in which they reflect the values of the Renaissance.

FROM "ORATION ON THE DIGNITY OF MAN" BY PICO DELLA MIRANDOLA

"I have set thee," says the Creator to Adam, "in the midst of the world, that thou mayst the more easily behold and see all that is therein. I created thee a being neither heavenly nor earthly, neither mortal nor immortal only, that thou mightest be free to shape and to overcome thyself. Thou mayst sink into a beast, and be born anew to divine likeness. . . . To thee alone is given a growth and a development depending on thine own free will."

FROM MICHELANGELO'S SCENE OF THE MOMENT OF MAN'S CREATION, SISTINE CHAPEL

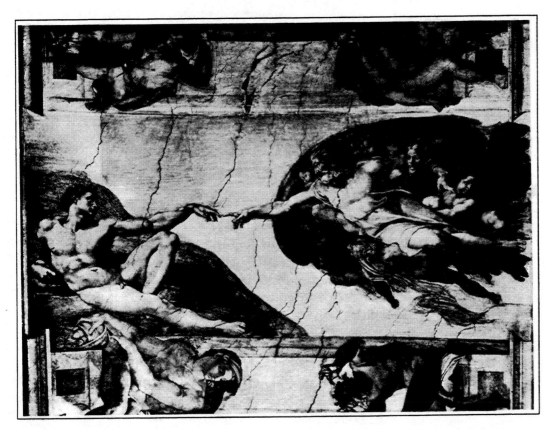

The Bettman Archive.

If there was a Renaissance for the man of wealth and court connections, as historians maintain, was there a similar "rebirth" for women? Use the documents below to guide you in writing an answer to the question. Consider the nature of the document you are using: its author and point of view, the intended audience, how representational the document may be of other contemporary sources, its possible impact, and whether it is descriptive or prescriptive in nature.

FROM THE DESCRIPTION OF DAILY LIFE IN FLORENCE BY J. LUCAS-DUBRETON

Here . . . is a picture of a model household. After their marriage the burgher takes his young wife over the house from top to bottom, from the attic, where grain is stored, to the cellar for wine and wood. He shows her . . . the great chest in the bedroom where valuables are kept, money, clothes and jewels. He does not show her his ledger and account-book. Next, beside her at the tabernacle of Our Lady, he prays to God to give her grace to make good use of all the things which in his bounty he now shares with her; he prays that they may live long together in joy and concord and have many *male* children. For himself, the merchant asks for riches, powerful friends and great honours; for her, a stainless reputation . . . perfect respectability and the virtues of a good housekeeper.

FROM *THE COURTIER* BY CASTIGLIONE

I think that in her ways, manners, words, gestures, and bearing, a woman ought to be very unlike a man; for just as he must have a certain solid and sturdy manliness, so it is seemly for a woman to have a soft and delicate tenderness, with an air of womanly sweetness in her every movement. . . . And I do think that beauty is more necessary to her than to the Courtier, for truly woman lacks much who lacks beauty. . . . I say that, in my opinion, in a lady who lives at court a certain pleasing affability is becoming above all else, whereby she will be able to entertain graciously every kind of man with agreeable and comely conversation suited to the time and place. . . .

NORTHERN RENAISSANCE

Growing prosperity and the printing press carried Renaissance culture to northern and Western Europe, to England and the Low Countries (now Belgium and Holland). The Christian humanists Erasmus (*In Praise of Folly*, 1509) and Thomas More (*Utopia*, 1516) were advocates for the deeply religious character that distinguished the northern Renaissance from its Italian counterpart.

DOCUMENT-BASED ESSAY QUESTION

Using the documents below, compare and summarize in writing the human and social values that More ascribes to the Utopians with those attributed to Pope Julius in the book *In Praise of Folly*. What were the authors seeking to change in their societies?

FROM *UTOPIA* BY THOMAS MORE

Silver and gold, the raw materials of money get more respect from anyone than their intrinsic value deserves—which is obviously far less than that of iron. Without iron human life is simply impossible, just as it is without fire or water—but we could easily do without silver and gold, if it weren't for the idiotic concept of scarcity value. And yet kind Mother Nature has deliberately placed all her greatest blessings, like earth, air, and water, right under our noses, and tucked away out of sight the things that are of no use to us.

To get around these difficulties, they've devised a system which is diametrically opposed to ours. Plates and drinking-vessels, though beautifully designed, are made of quite cheap stuff like glass or earthenware. But silver and gold are the normal materials, in private houses as well as communal dining-halls, for the humblest items of domestic equipment, such as chamber-pots. They also use chains and fetters of solid gold to immobilize slaves, and anyone who commits a really shameful crime is forced to go about with gold rings on his ears and fingers, a gold necklace round his neck and a crown of gold on his head. In fact they do everything they can to bring these metals into contempt. This means that if they suddenly had to part with all the gold and silver they possess—a fate which in any other country would be thought equivalent to having one's guts torn out—nobody in Utopia would care two hoots.

It is much the same with jewels. There are pearls to be found on the beaches, diamonds and garnets on certain types of rock—but they never bother to look for them. However, if they happen to come across one, they pick it up and polish it for some toddler to wear. At first, children are terribly proud of such jewelry—until they're old enough to register that it's only worn in the nursery. Then, without any prompting from their parents, but purely as a matter of self-respect, they give it up—just as our children grow out of things like dolls and lucky charms.

FROM *IN PRAISE OF FOLLY* BY ERASMUS

Persons: POPE JULIUS II.; FAMILIAR SPIRIT: ST. PETER.
Scene: GATE OF HEAVEN.

JULIUS: What the devil is this? The gates not opened! Something is wrong with the lock.

SPIRIT: You have brought the wrong key perhaps. The key of your money-box will not open the door here. You should have brought both keys. This is the key of power, not of knowledge.

JULIUS: I never had any but this, and I don't see the use of another. Hey there, porter! I say, are you asleep or drunk?

PETER: Well that the gates are adamant, or this fellow would have broken in. He must be some giant, or conqueror. Heaven, what a stench! Who are you? What do you want here?

JULIUS: Open the gates, I say. Why is there no one to receive me?

JULIUS: Will you make an end of your talking and open the gates? We will break them down else. You see these followers of mine.

PETER: I see a lot of precious rogues, but they won't break in here.

JULIUS: Make an end, I say, or I will fling a thunderbolt at you. I will excommunicate you. I have done as much to kings before this. Here are the Bulls ready.

PETER: Thunderbolts! Bulls! I beseech you, we had no thunderbolts or Bulls from Christ.

JULIUS: You shall feel them if you don't behave yourself. . . .

Summary Trends   For ordinary people, the subject matter of social history, life had greater continuity with the past. The natural rhythms of sunrise, sunset, and the seasons regulated work in the villages. In towns and cities, craft guilds dictated the rules for work and regulated the quantity and quality of goods produced. Christianity played a dominant role in daily life, sanctifying the occasions of birth, death, and marriage and providing the religious basis for frequent festivals. Life, however, was hard. Drinking was widespread among the poor. Hangings and mutilations were public events. Marriages were frequently arranged to consolidate property. And while divorce did not exist, annulments occasionally occurred.

In the Italian city-states, political warfare ensued. Powerful states dominated weak ones, resulting in chaos and invasion by foreign powers. In England, France, and Spain, however, new monarchical dynasties, also known as the **new monarchs**, emerged (Tudors in England, Valois in France, Hapsburgs in Spain) by suppressing rebellious nobles and relying on middle-class civil servants to administer royal affairs. European power began to shift from the Mediterranean to the Atlantic coasts.

MULTIPLE-CHOICE QUESTIONS

1. During the Renaissance, Italy
   a. was administered by a consortium in Rome
   b. enjoyed relative peace and tranquillity
   c. was under attack by Turkish warlords
   d. was organized similarly to the Holy Roman Empire
   e. was dominated by several powerful city states

2. Which was not a characteristic of the Renaissance?
   a. emphasis on individuality
   b. confidence in human rationality
   c. the emergence of merchant oligarchies
   d. the development of social insurance programs
   e. emulation of classical writers

3. The northern Renaissance differed from the Italian Renaissance in its
   a. growth of religious activity among common people
   b. earlier occurrence
   c. greater appreciation of pagan writers
   d. decline in the use of Latin
   e. pagan themes in art

4. In his analysis of statecraft, morality was irrelevant. What worked was good; what failed was bad. His textbook is considered a classic in the practice of tyranny. The author of this political tract was
   a. Castiglione
   b. Erasmus
   c. Cellini
   d. Machiavelli
   e. Lorenzo de Medici

5. Which of the following was a major source of study for Renaissance humanists?
   a. original classical manuscripts
   b. medieval history
   c. Scholastic debates
   d. diplomatic correspondence
   e. parish census data

6. Europeans influenced by Italian Renaissance thought believed that
   a. humans should be satisfied with their ascribed status
   b. religious devotion was the key to a fulfilling life
   c. striving for *virtu* was ignoble
   d. individuals could shape their own destiny
   e. good manners were untrustworthy guides to character

7. Commissioned paintings during the fifteenth and sixteenth centuries
   a. concentrated exclusively on ways to enrich Christian worship
   b. ignored mythological and classical themes
   c. presented subjects in indeterminate space
   d. were executed in coeducational training studios
   e. ensured prestige and high status for the artist

8. Thomas More's *Utopia* promoted the view that
   a. men are inherently evil and untrustworthy
   b. monied wealth ensures happiness
   c. social institutions needed reform
   d. ethical principles rarely apply to politics
   e. learning could not improve human character

9. To the enterprises of banking and trading they added silk and wool workshops in their home town of Florence. When deposits of alum, necessary to fix dyes, were

found at a site near Rome, they entered into an agreement with the papacy and others to exploit them. The entrepreneurs described here were from the ruling family of

   a. Charles V
   b. the Medicis
   c. the Sforzas
   d. the Borgias
   e. Pope Pius II

10. The emergence of strong monarchs in the fifteenth and sixteenth centuries, like the Tudors in England, was the result of all of the following EXCEPT
   a. improvements in their armies
   b. the linkage of government policy with commercial interests
   c. the use of arbitrary judicial methods like the Star Chamber
   d. the strengthening of aristocratic power
   e. the avoidance of expensive foreign wars

PRACTICE ESSAY QUESTIONS

Use the questions below to practice essay writing. For each question write an essay that includes an introductory thesis, a body of supporting and/or illustrative data, and a conclusion.

1. "What captivated the Italians of the Renaissance was a sense of man's tremendous powers, the rich potentialities of human nature, the free and unfettered creative play of talent in every field." Assess the accuracy of this quotation as a summation of the period in history labeled the Renaissance. Refer to specific individuals and examples to support your answer.
2. To what extent does the Renaissance represent the birth of modernity in the Western world?
3. How and in what ways did the printing press foster the spread of the Renaissance to other parts of Europe? What classes of people did its output influence?
4. Compare the Christian humanism of Erasmus and Thomas More with the Italian humanism of Castiglione and Machiavelli.
5. Assess the degree to which economic rather than social and political factors gave rise to the Italian Renaissance.
6. Why did the middle class support the new monarchs and why did the nobility oppose them?

ESSAY-WRITING TIPS: MODELS OF AN OPENING PARAGRAPH

Below are two models of an opening paragraph in student essays assessing the statement "What captivated the Italians of the Renaissance was a sense of man's tremendous powers, the rich potentialities of human nature, the free and unfettered creative play of talent in every field." Read the models and write a paragraph explaining which is a better introduction to the essay question. Compare your evaluation with the one that follows on the next page.

Paragraph A

The Renaissance was a new beginning for Italians. Renaissance means rebirth and Italy was the center of the new talent. Artists changed their style of painting and Machiavelli wrote *The Prince*. Men were more interested in human things and turned their attention to this world from the spiritual world. So the Renaissance was a time when men began to discover their talents and develop their powers. Castiglione described the ideal court gentleman and Cellini criticized a sculpture because it wasn't lifelike. Even church leaders bought works of art and had the artists sign their names to show the wealth of the church.

Paragraph B

The Renaissance is a useful label for the approximate period 1400-1600 in Western Europe. In certain respects, the Renaissance was a new beginning for an elite group of urban citizens in Italy. While not a dramatic break in their concerns with the here-and-now, interest in secular affairs developed appreciably. In art, philosophy, political theory, and education, themes indebted to the classical world emerged. Wealthy bankers and traders promoted this rebirth and enjoyed the rich discoveries. Yet the impact was narrow. For the common man and for most women, the "sense of man's tremendous powers" probably had little meaning. Their roles in society were set and unchanging.

Evaluation

Paragraph B tries to deal with the accuracy of the quotation: "What captivated the Italians of the Renaissance was a sense of man's tremendous powers, the rich potentialities of human nature, the free and unfettered creative play of talent in every field" and its validity as a summary for the period known as the Renaissance.

First, it considers the Renaissance as a label for the time period. Second, while it agrees to some extent with the quotation, it notes possible exceptions to the educated and wealthy Italians who shared in the intellectual and artistic changes of the time. Finally, it sets up the categories—art, political theory, education, and philosophy—that the body of the essay will explore.

Paragraph A, on the other hand, apart from asserting that the Renaissance was a new beginning, fails to consider the legitimacy of the term *Renaissance* for the historical period in early modern European history. Moreover, it includes the illustrative data that properly should make up the body of the essay in a series of paragraphs focusing on art, etiquette, and political theory.

Paragraph B is the better paragraph.

IDENTIFICATIONS

Benvenuto Cellini–A goldsmith and sculptor who wrote an autobiography, famous for its arrogance and immodest self-praise.

Condottiere–A mercenary soldier of a political ruler.

Humanism–The recovery and study of classical authors and writings.

Individualism–The emphasis on the unique and creative personality.

New Monarchs–The term applied to Louis XI of France, Henry VII of England, and Ferdinand and Isabella of Spain, who strengthened their monarchical authority often by Machiavellian means.

Rationalism–The application and use of reason in understanding and explaining events.

Renaissance–The period from 1400 to 1600 that witnessed a transformation of cultural and intellectual values from primarily Christian to classical or secular ones.

Secularism–The emphasis on the here-and-now rather than on the spiritual and otherworldly.

Lorenzo Valla (1407-1457)–A humanist who used historical criticism to discredit an eighth-century document giving the papacy jurisdiction over Western lands.

Virtu–The striving for personal excellence.

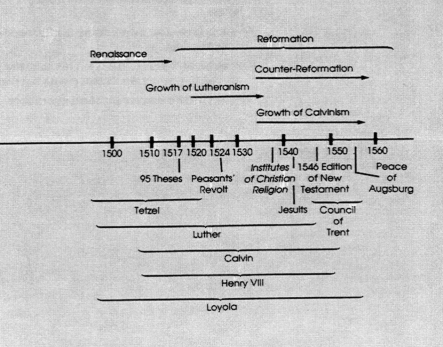

THE PROTESTANT REFORMATION AND THE CATHOLIC COUNTER-REFORMATION

CHAPTER 2

LUTHERANISM

Criticism of abusive practices of the Catholic church, such as **simony**, **nepotism**, and **pluralism**, mounted in the sixteenth century. But it was the specific practice of selling **indulgences**, papal pardons for sins, that aroused the wrath of **Martin Luther** (1483-1546) and led to the religious split in western Christendom. In 1517, Martin Luther, a German priest, posted his ninety-five theses, or principles, on the church door at Wittenberg castle, near the university where he lectured. His attack centered on the doctrine that faith alone, not good works (which included the purchase of indulgences) ensured salvation. He also believed that final authority on debatable religious issues lay in the word of God, as revealed in the Bible and as interpreted by the individual. Luther's challenge to the papal hierarchy and to the Holy Roman Emperor **Charles V** (1519-1556), fearful of disintegration of his authority within the empire, resulted in Luther's excommunication at the German Diet of Worms in 1521.

Supporters of Luther

Luther's plea for church reform, however, won him supporters:

1. German princes such as Frederick of Saxony, who saw the benefit of converting to the Lutheran religion. The princes could keep the taxes flowing to Rome for their own territorial power and the church lands as well.

2. Townspeople with commercial interests who felt constrained by the church's restrictions on **usury** (lending money for interest) and sought flexible business practices.
3. German peasants who took literally Luther's dictum that a Christian man is the most free lord of all, subject to none. The peasants wanted freedom from manorial dues and obligations. Luther, however, rejected their concept of secular liberty. He insisted that they obey the civil authorities, if not the religious ones. Society required civil obedience to avoid chaos.

The German princes who supported Luther confiscated the rich church lands and opposed Charles V. The struggle between princes and emperor resulted in the Peace of Augsburg (1555), whereby the princes could determine the religion of their own territory and their subjects within it.

CALVINISM

Calvinism, the revolutionary edge of Protestantism in the second half of the sixteenth century, became the international form of the movement. It spread from Geneva, the **theocracy** of **John Calvin** (1509–1564), to France, England, Scotland under **John Knox** (1505–1572), the Netherlands, and the New World. In his tightly organized writings, known as the *Institutes of the Christian Religion*, Calvin made explicit the notion of predestination, the idea that eternal salvation is determined by an omniscient, omnipotent, and inscrutable God.

Protestantism and Capitalism

According to Max Weber, a German sociologist, Calvinism, with its concept of serving God through one's calling or vocation, helped shape the spirit of capitalism. Weber has written: "The ideal type of the capitalist entrepreneur . . . avoids ostentation and unnecessary expenditure, as well as conscious enjoyment of his power, and is embarrassed by the outward signs of the social recognition which he receives. . . . His manner of life is...distinguished by a certain ascetic tendency. . . . He gets nothing out of his wealth for himself, except the irrational sense of having done his job well."

THE CATHOLIC COUNTER-REFORMATION

In order to salvage its eroding power, the Roman Catholic Church undertook its own reform and sought countermeasures against Protestantism. The mid-century Council of Trent forbade the sale of indulgences, pluralism, and simony and insisted on strict morals, behavior, and dress of clergy. In matters of doctrine, the council insisted that salvation could be assured through faith *and* good works.

A new teaching order, the **Jesuits**, led by Ignatius Loyola (1491-1556), reaffirmed obedience to the decrees of the pope and to the hierarchy of the church. The church further sanctioned the revival of the **Inquisition**, a medieval court that tried heretics and punished the guilty. And to prevent exposure to dangerous ideas, the church provided an **index**, or list of prohibited books. Finally, in an effort to win back adherents, the church commissioned many Catholic painters to turn their talents to religious art. For example, Caravaggio, Bernini, Rubens, and El Greco painted religious scenes that were theatrical, sensuous, and dynamic. The classical harmony of the Renaissance gave way to the extravagance and passion of **baroque** art.

THE ENGLISH REFORMATION

In spite of efforts to check the spread of Protestantism, the Catholic church was unsuccessful in preventing England's withdrawal from its fold. But in the case of England, the reason was personal and political rather than religious. Henry VIII (1509-1547) became infatuated with Anne Boleyn. He sought to dissolve his marriage to Catherine of Aragon so that he could marry Boleyn. This dissolution was accomplished when he broke with the church and declared himself the Supreme Head of Church and Clergy of England (1534). Insistent on recognition of his title, he beheaded the famous chancellor **Sir Thomas More** (1478-1535) for refusing to acknowledge publicly his supremacy.

DOCUMENT-BASED ESSAY QUESTION

Considering the factors that contributed to the Protestant Reformation, compare the following documents for a motive that can be identified as one of the causes of the Protestant Reformation. Summarize in writing the motive found in both documents and justify your selection based on your explanation of the source.

ACCOUNT FROM THE SON OF AN EYEWITNESS, 1591

As soon as the [English] king's commissioners entered within the gates, they called the abbot and other officers of the house and caused them to deliver up to them all their keys, and took an inventory of all their goods, both within doors and without; for all such beasts, horses, sheep, and such cattle as were abroad in pasture or grange places, the visitors caused to be brought into their presence, and when they had done so, turned the abbot with all his convent and household forth of the doors.

FROM THE WRITINGS OF ULRICH VON HUTTEN, A GERMAN NOBLEMAN

Now, if all these [the council of the most holy members of the Roman curia] who devastate Germany and continue to devour everything, might once be driven out, and an end made of their unbridled plundering, swindling and deception, with which the Romans have overwhelmed us, we should again have gold and silver in sufficient quantities, and should be able to keep it. And then this money . . . might be put to better uses. . . .

MULTIPLE-CHOICE QUESTIONS

1. Which of the following did Luther reject?
   a. the priesthood of all believers
   b. justification through faith alone
   c. the Bible as the final authority of God's word
   d. the spiritual life as superior to the secular one
   e. financial payment for remission of sins

2. Calvin's theology is noteworthy for its
   a. toleration of other religious sects
   b. profile of a merciful and forgiving God
   c. concept of the Elect
   d. well-turned Latin phrases
   e. acceptance of a women priesthood

3. The Reformation in Germany resulted in
   a. a unified German state
   b. political fragmentation
   c. Italian control of Austria
   d. the abolition of Catholicism
   e. secular freedom for the peasantry

4. Which of the following is not considered a cause of the Protestant Reformation?
   a. increased lay interest in purifying church practices
   b. northern Renaissance scholars' interest in early biblical texts
   c. the reform decrees of the Council of Trent
   d. nationalist movements in the Holy Roman Empire
   e. the taxing policies of the Roman Catholic Church

5. The true center of this artistic style was in Rome, from which the Catholic Reformation radiated and its climax came during the seventeenth century in the work of the sculptor and architect Lorenzo Bernini. This artistic style is
   a. surrealist
   b. Gothic
   c. classical
   d. mannerist
   e. baroque

6. "You may obtain letters of safe conduct from the vicar of our Lord Jesus Christ, by means of which you are able to liberate your soul from the hands of the enemy, and convey it by means of contrition and confession, safe and secure from all pains of Purgatory, into the happy kingdom.... Are you not willing, then, for the fourth part of a florin, to obtain these letters?" The author of this passage would most likely have agreed with which of the following statements?
   a. The pope has supreme power.
   b. The Bible is the source of truth.
   c. A sinner can repent only through the heart.
   d. Salvation is through faith alone.
   e. Giving to the poor earns God's grace.

7. The country that prevented the spread of Protestantism within its borders and remained the supreme defender of Catholicism is
   a. Sweden
   b. France
   c. Poland
   d. Spain
   e. Ireland

8. "Neither oppression nor injustice excuses revolt. . . . the only liberty for which you should care is spiritual liberty; the only rights you can legitimately demand are those that pertain to your spiritual life." The social group most likely to agree with this quotation from Luther in the sixteenth century would be
   a. peasants
   b. merchants and townspeople
   c. bourgeoisie
   d. nobles
   e. artisans

9. The significance of the Reformation lies in its
   a. destruction of the unity of the Christian world
   b. support of democratic political systems
   c. widespread toleration of diverse religious sects
   d. reconciliation of Christian principles with pagan values
   e. direct impact on the development of capitalism

10. All of the following are Protestant sects EXCEPT
    a. Presbyterians
    b. Huguenots
    c. Jansenists
    d. Anabaptists
    e. Episcopalians

PRACTICE ESSAY QUESTIONS

Use the questions below to practice essay writing. For each question write an essay that includes an introductory thesis, a body of supporting and/or illustrative data, and a conclusion.

1. It has been said that Erasmus laid the egg that Luther hatched. Evaluate the accuracy of this statement.
2. To what extent do you agree or disagree with the following statement? "Although he intended to conserve the original church, Luther was no conservative. He was a revolutionary radical."
3. What factors explain the success of the Reformation in the sixteenth century?
4. How did the Reformation in England differ from its counterpart on the Continent?
5. What strategies did the Roman Catholic Church use to achieve religious unity in the sixteenth century, and why did its efforts fail?

ESSAY-WRITING TIPS: INTEGRATING DOCUMENTS

On the basis of the following four documents, explain the causes of the Protestant Reformation. Be sure to use all the documents.

DOCUMENT 1

Julius II. Exclusus. A Dialogue

PERSONS:—POPE JULIUS II.; FAMILIAR SPIRIT: ST. PETER.

SCENE:—GATE OF HEAVEN.

JULIUS: What the devil is this? The gates not opened! Something is wrong with the lock.

SPIRIT: You have brought the wrong key perhaps. The key of your money-box will not open the door here. You should have brought both keys. This is the key of power, not of knowledge.

JULIUS: I never had any but this, and I don't see the use of another. Hey there, porter! I say, are you asleep or drunk?

PETER: Well that the gates are adamant, or this fellow would have broken in. He must be some giant, or conqueror. Heaven, what a stench! Who are you? What do you want here?

JULIUS: Open the gates, I say. Why is there no one to receive me?

JULIUS: Will you make an end of your talking and open the gates? We will break them down else. You see these followers of mine.

PETER: I see a lot of precious rogues, but they won't break in here.

JULIUS: Make an end, I say, or I will fling a thunderbolt at you. I will excommunicate you. I have done as much to kings before this. Here are the Bulls ready.

PETER: Thunderbolts! Bulls! I beseech you, we had no thunderbolts or Bulls from Christ.

JULIUS: You shall feel them if you don't behave yourself. . . .

From In Praise of Folly, *Erasmus.*

DOCUMENT 2

. . . Know that the life of man upon earth is a constant struggle. We have to fight against the flesh, the world and the devil, who are always seeking to destroy the soul. In sin we are conceived,—alas! what bonds of sin encompass us, and how difficult and almost impossible it is to attain to the gate of salvation without divine aid: since He causes us to be saved not by virtue of the good works which we accomplish, but through His divine mercy; it is necessary then to put on the armor of God.

You may obtain letters of safe conduct from the vicar of our Lord Jesus Christ, by means of which you are able to liberate your soul from the hands of the enemy. . .

Do you not know that when it is necessary for anyone to go to Rome, or undertake any other dangerous journey, he takes his money to a broker and gives a certain per cent—five or six or ten—in order that at Rome or elsewhere he may receive again his funds intact, by means of the letters of this same broker? Are you not willing, then, for the fourth part of a florin, to obtain these letters, by virtue of which you may bring not your money, but your divine and immortal soul safe and sound into the land of Paradise?

Excerpt from sermon, 1515, by Tetzel, a friar

DOCUMENT 3

21. Thus those preachers of indulgences are in error who say that by the indulgences of the Pope a man is freed and saved from all punishment.

24. Hence, the greater part of the people must needs be deceived by this indiscriminate and high-sounding promise of release from penalties.

32. Those who believe that, through letters of pardon, they are made sure of their own salvation will be eternally damned along with their teachers. . . .

43. Christians should be taught that he who gives to a poor man, or lends to a needy man, does better than if he bought pardons. . . .

Selected theses, Martin Luther, October 31, 1517

DOCUMENT 4

. . . We see that there is no gold and almost no silver in our German land. What little may perhaps be left is drawn away daily by the new schemes invented by the council of the most holy members of the Roman curia. What is thus squeezed out of us is put to the most shameful uses. Would you know, dear Germans, what employment I have myself seen that they make at Rome of our money? It does not lie idle. Leo the Tenth gives a part to nephews and relatives (these are so numerous that there is a proverb at Rome, ''As thick as Leo's relations''). A portion is consumed by so many most reverend cardinals (of which the holy father created no less than one and thirty in a single day), as well as to support innumerable referendaries, auditors, prothonotaries, abbreviators, apostolic secretaries, chamberlains and a variety of officials forming the elite of the great head church.

Now, if all these who devastate Germany, and continue to devour everything, might once be driven out, and an end made of their unbridled plundering, swindling and deception with which the Romans have overwhelmed us, we should again have gold and silver in sufficient quantities, and should be able to keep it.

Ulrich von Hutten, German nobleman

CAUSES OF THE PROTESTANT REFORMATION

The two essay samples below are provided to contrast (1) introductory paragraphs and (2) topic sentences that integrate and clarify the relationships among the four previous documents on the Reformation. Read the essays and write a brief paragraph that evaluates whether there is a cohesive fit between the introductory paragraph and the topic sentences that appear in all capital letters within each essay.

Essay A

WHAT CAUSED THE PROTESTANT REFORMATION WAS ERASMUS, TETZEL, LUTHER, AND ULRICH VON HUTTEN. EACH OF THEM PLAYED A PART IN THE REFORMATION.

FIRST, ERASMUS CAUSED IT BY CRITICIZING POPE JULIUS AND THE WAY HE SPENT THE CHURCH'S MONEY. He portrayed Julius as an arrogant man who thought he could get into heaven with a money key.

NEXT, TETZEL CAUSED IT BY SELLING INDULGENCES AND USING PROPAGANDA TO CONVINCE THE CREDULOUS. He said that an indulgence would ensure entrance into paradise.

THIRD, LUTHER CAUSED IT BY POSTING HIS THESES ON A CHURCH DOOR WHERE EVERYONE COULD READ HIS CRITICISM OF INDULGENCES. He said that believers in the power of bought pardons would be damned.

LAST, VON HUTTEN CAUSED IT BY CONVINCING OTHER CITIZENS THAT THEY SHOULD NOT SEND MONEY TO ROME BUT SHOULD KEEP IT FOR THEMSELVES. He said that the money going to Rome is used to support Pope Leo's nephews and relatives.

Essay B

THE SIXTEENTH CENTURY WITNESSED RELIGIOUS TURMOIL THAT SHATTERED THE CATHOLIC UNITY OF THE WESTERN WORLD. MANY FACTORS CONTRIBUTED TO THE BREAK IN MEDIEVAL CHRISTENDOM. PROMINENT AMONG THEM WERE RELIGIOUS, POLITICAL, AND ECONOMIC CAUSES.

ERASMUS, A CHRISTIAN HUMANIST, ATTACKED CHURCH ABUSES WITH IRONIC WIT. In a play attributed to him, he satirized Pope Julius's unholy concern with money and power. Pope Julius is portrayed as aggressive and insolent, believing that money rather than spiritual knowledge earns access to heaven.

CRITICISM OF PAPAL AUTHORITY WAS CARRIED FURTHER AND MORE OPENLY IN THE WRITINGS OF MARTIN LUTHER. In ninety-five theses that he posted on a church door, he attacked the sale of indulgences, or pardons for sins. Luther claimed that their purchase in no way ensured salvation.

THE STATEMENTS UNDERMINED THE CLAIMS OF TETZEL, A DOMINICAN FRIAR WHO MADE PROMISES INCONSISTENT WITH LUTHER'S RELIGIOUS BELIEFS. Tetzel preached that his indulgences carried the weight of insurance policies—inexpensive in price yet with an eternal and heavenly payoff.

BUT THE ECONOMICS OF THE BARGAIN WAS SERIOUSLY CHALLENGED BY ULRICH VON HUTTEN, A GERMAN NOBLEMAN, WHO RESENTED THE FLOW OF GOLD AND SILVER TO ROME. It is likely that von Hutten was representative of the vast number of Germans who enviously eyed the wealth of the papacy and the political power of the pope's ally, Charles V in Germany. Support for Luther would bring political independence and economic benefits.

Evaluation

Essay A commits the sin of "laundry listing." The content of each document is summarized in sequential and unintegrated fashion. There is no attempt to link the documents or to categorize them in any way.

Essay B, on the other hand, tries to organize the contents of each document within religious, economic, and political categories. The writer *weaves*, rather than *lists*, the information in the documents to explain various causes contributing to the Protestant Reformation. The writer considers individuals as representative of broader social forces in the analysis of each document and points out the connecting relationships among the writers.

IDENTIFICATIONS

Baroque–The sensuous and dynamic style of art of the Counter Reformation. (See Appendix.)

Brethren of the Common Life–Pious laypeople in sixteenth-century Holland who initiated a religious revival in their model of Christian living.

John Calvin (1509-1564)–A French theologian who established a theocracy in Geneva and is best known for his theory of predestination.

Charles V (1519-1556)–Hapsburg dynastic ruler of the Holy Roman Empire and of extensive territories in Spain and the Netherlands.

Council of Trent–The congress of learned Roman Catholic authorities that met intermittently from 1545 to 1563 to reform abusive church practices and reconcile with the Protestants.

Index–A list of books that Catholics were forbidden to read.

Indulgence–Papal pardon for remission of sins.

Inquisition–A religious committee of six Roman cardinals that tried heretics and punished the guilty by imprisonment and execution.

Jesuits–Also known as the Society of Jesus; founded by Ignatius Loyola (1491-1556) as a teaching and missionary order to resist the spread of Protestantism.

John Knox (1505-1572)–Calvinist leader in sixteenth-century Scotland.

Martin Luther (1483-1546)–German theologian who challenged the church's practice of selling indulgences, a challenge that ultimately led to the destruction of the unity of the Roman Catholic world.

Sir Thomas More (1478-1535)–Renaissance humanist and chancellor of England, executed by Henry VIII for his unwillingness to recognize publicly his king as Supreme Head of the Church and Clergy of England.

Nepotism–The practice of rewarding relatives with church positions.

Peace of Augsburg (1555)–Document in which Charles V recognized Lutheranism as a legal religion in the Holy Roman Empire. The faith of the prince determined the religion of his subjects.

Pluralism–The holding of several benefices, or church offices.

Simony–The selling of church offices.

Theocracy–A community, such as Calvin's Geneva, in which the state is subordinate to the church.

Usury–The practice of lending money for interest.

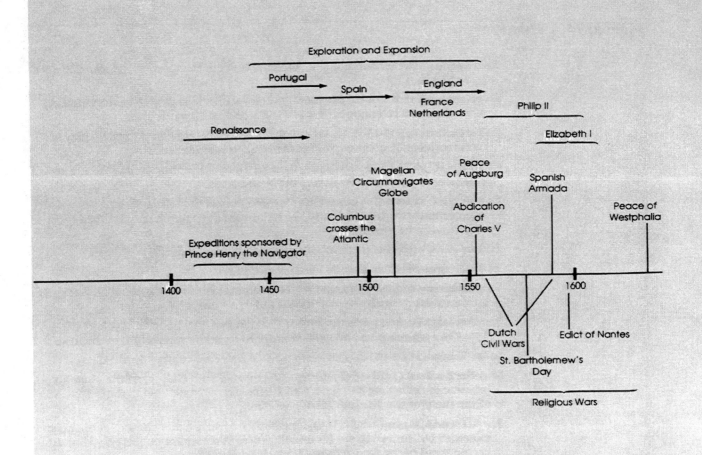

RELIGIOUS WARS AND THE
AGE OF EXPANSION

The Peace of Augsburg failed to solve the religious question in the Hapsburg-ruled territories. While Lutheranism was recognized as a legal religion that the ruling prince could choose for his subjects, Calvinism was not. The issue of Calvinism became especially troublesome in the Netherlands, the seventeen semi-independent provinces under Charles V's rule.

PROTESTANT REVOLT IN THE NETHERLANDS

Charles V had rebuked religious reformers. His successor, **Philip II**, would prove harsher. When Charles V abdicated in 1556, his brother Ferdinand (1556-1564) received Austria and the Holy Roman Empire; his son Philip II (1556-1598), Spain and the Low Countries (present-day Netherlands and Belgium). The militant minority of Calvinists in the Netherlands was a powerful group of merchants, financiers, and working-class people who resented tax hikes and religious repression.

Defeat of the Spanish Armada

Their response was bitter. Calvinists destroyed the art works and libraries of the Roman Catholic churches in their country. Mercenary troops led by the **Duke of Alva** (1508-1582) were called in to put down the rebellion, initiating a ten-year civil war (1568-1578) between Catholics and Protestants, who were united under **Prince William of Orange** (1572-1584). The upshot was

23

division in the Netherlands. The seven northern provinces, highly defensible because of their canals and dikes, secured their independence from Spain. But independence came slowly. English financial and military aid was required. **Elizabeth I** (1558–1603) of England, fearful of Spanish invasion of England after a successful defeat of the Protestant Netherlands, supplied aid. Philip launched his **armada**, or fleet of ships, to the English Channel, where the highly maneuverable smaller English ships and "Protestant" squalls and storms defeated the crescent formation of Spanish ships in 1588. In 1609, Philip II officially recognized the independence of the northern provinces led by Holland under the name of the United Provinces. The ten southern provinces, eventually to become Belgium, remained under the control of the Spanish Hapsburgs within the Catholic fold.

RELIGIOUS WARS IN FRANCE

Religious upheavals affected France also. The **Concordat of Bologna** (1516) had established Catholicism as the state religion; yet abuses existed as church offices were used to pay civil servants. Many peasants and lower-middle-class French searching for salvation adopted Calvinism. For the nobility, however, religion served more as an ideological cloak in a power struggle with the king and his allied nobles. The Catholic Guise and Protestant Bourbon families eyed the throne under a weakening Valois line, with **Catherine de Médicis** (1547–1589) dominating the throne and switching her religious allegiance when to do so was in her interest. The brutal St. Bartholemew's Day massacre of **Huguenots** (French Calvinists) by Catholics in 1572 set off rioting and economic disorder. Assassinations of leading contenders to the throne, as well as the death of Catherine de Médici, enabled the Protestant Henry of Navarre to ascend the throne as **Henry IV** (1589–1610). "Paris is worth a mass," asserted Henry, who converted to Catholicism to become the first in a line of Bourbon rulers and sixteenth-century political leaders more concerned with internal stability than religious certitude. His publication of the **Edict of Nantes** (1598) granted Huguenots the rights of private worship throughout France and public worship in specified towns. They could also hold public office.

RELIGIOUS STABILITY IN ENGLAND

The ideological struggles over religion and the civil wars they unleashed were avoided in England once Elizabeth I ascended the throne in 1558. Tranquillity was maintained until her death in 1603. She said: "I desire to open a window into no man's conscience." In short, she did not want religious divisions of opinion to surface and create disputes. Catholic and Puritan extremes threatened a tenuous stability. Elizabeth, therefore, insisted on external conformity to ensure political order but showed no concern for people's private thoughts. Everyone had to attend the Anglican church under punishment of fine. The church had both Catholic and Protestant elements and was thus comprehensive enough in doctrine and dogma to win the support of most of the loyal English.

RELIGIOUS WARS IN GERMANY

While France, England, Spain, and the Dutch were achieving national unity, Germany was not. Religious issues resurfaced in 1618 with the closing of Protestant churches in Prague, in the kingdom of Bohemia (formerly Czechoslovakia). Enraged Protestants hurled Catholic officials from a castle window, so the story goes. This event known as the **defenestration of Prague** set off the Thirty Years' War. Denmark and later Sweden led by its able king Gustavus Adolphus (1594–1632) entered the war, hoping to thwart Hapsburg ambition to unify all of the German states. France, although a Catholic country, also supported the Protestant camp to reduce the power of the Hapsburg ruler Ferdinand.

Terms of the Peace Treaty

The war dragged on—on German soil—until 1648, when the **Peace of Westphalia** was signed. Each prince, whether Lutheran, Catholic, or Calvinist, had independent sovereign power and could choose the established creed of his territory. Political and religious authority rested in the hands of approximately three hundred German princes. The Thirty Years' War effectively destroyed Germany's economy. Over one third of the population had been destroyed. The peasants were hardest hit. Many became day laborers for nobles and landlords who bought up their landholdings and thus created a new serfdom in the empire.

EXPLORATION AND EXPANSION

While religious and political wars raged on the Continent, adventurous Europeans were discovering new trading routes to the Orient and India and new routes for the exploration and exploitation of a new world across the Atlantic Ocean. They included **Prince Henry the Navigator**, **Francisco Pizarro**, **Hernando Cortez**, **Ferdinand Magellan**, **Christopher Columbus**, **Bartholomew Diaz**, and **Vasco de Balboa**. Governments helped sponsor the voyages, most notably the **Dutch East India Company**, the organ of Dutch conquest and exploration. The mixed motives of seeking glory, finding gold, and proselytizing for God set the Portuguese, Spanish, English, French, and Dutch on their overseas voyages.

DOCUMENT-BASED QUESTION PRACTICE

In the New World, European settlers were faced with a labor shortage and had to remedy the problem. Use the two documents below to write an answer to the following questions:

1. What incentives for Spain did Columbus describe to elicit the financial support of King Ferdinand and Queen Isabella?
2. According to Bartholomew de Las Casas (1474–1566), a Dominican friar, how successful were the Spanish in realizing Columbus's aims? Why or why not?

FROM A LETTER WRITTEN BY COLUMBUS FROM AN ISLAND IN THE AZORES, FEBRUARY 15, 1493

Presently many inhabitants of the island assembled. I saw and knew that these people are without any religion, not idolaters but very gentle, not knowing what is evil, nor the sins of murder and theft, being without arms, and so timid that a hundred would fly before one Spaniard, although they joke with them. They, however, believe and know that there is a God in heaven, and say that we have come from heaven. At any prayer that we say, they repeat, and make the sign of the cross. Thus your Highnesses should resolve to make them Christians, for I believe that if the work was begun, in a little time the multitude of nations would be converted to our faith, with the acquisition of great lordships, peoples, and riches for Spain. Without doubt there is in this land a vast quantity of gold, and the Indians do not speak without reason when they say that in these islands there are places where they dig out gold, and wear it on their necks, ears, arms, and legs, the rings being very large. There are also precious stones, pearls, and an infinity of spices. Here also there is a great quantity of cotton, and I believe it would have a good sale here without sending it to Spain, but to the cities of the Gran Can, which will be discovered without doubt, and many others ruled over by other lords, who will be pleased to serve your Highnesses, and whither will be brought other commodities of Spain and of the Eastern islands.

FROM AN ACCOUNT BY BARTHOLOMEW DE LAS CASAS (1474–1566)

In the island of Hispanola—which was the first to be invaded by the Christians—the immense massacres and destruction of the Indians began. It was the first to be destroyed and made into a desert. The Christians began by taking the women and children, to use and to abuse them, and to eat of the substance of their toil and labor, instead of contenting themselves with what the Indians gave them spontaneously, according to the means of each. Such stores are always small, because they keep no more than they ordinarily need, which they acquire with little labor; but what is enough for three households of ten persons each for a month, a Christian eats and destroys in one day. From their using force, violence, and other kinds of vexations the Indians began to perceive that these men could not have come from heaven.

The Christians, with their horses and swords and lances, began to slaughter and practice strange cruelty among them. They penetrated into the country and spared neither children nor the aged, nor women, all of whom they ran through the body and lacerated, as though they were assaulting so many lambs herded in their sheepfold.

They made a gallows just high enough for the feet to nearly touch the ground, and they put wood underneath and, with fire they burned the Indians. They generally killed the lords and nobles in the following way: they made wooden gridirons of stakes, bound them upon them, and made a slow fire beneath; thus the victims gave up the spirit by degrees, emitting cries of despair in their torture.

And because all the people who could flee hid among the mountains and climbed the crags to escape from men so deprived of humanity, so wicked, such wild beasts, exterminators and capital enemies of all the human race, the Spaniards taught and trained the fiercest boarhounds to tear an Indian to pieces as soon as they saw him, so that they more willingly attacked and ate one than if he had been a boar. These hounds made great havoc and slaughter.

And because sometimes, though rarely, the Indians killed a few Christians for just cause, they made a law among themselves that for one Christian whom the Indians killed, the Christians should kill a hundred Indians.

Economic Trends

It was Las Casas who urged the ending of Indian slavery in the New World and the importation of blacks from South Africa. Charles V heeded his request, and in 1518 the slave trade into the American possessions began, becoming an integral part of European expansion and colonization.

With the new ocean trade routes, power shifted from the Mediterranean to the Atlantic. Italy declined as a major power; Spain, Portugal, England, Holland, and France rose. Spain initially benefited from the influx of gold and silver drawn from the mines in Mexico and Peru. Soon, however, inflation, resulting from silver imports and population increases in Spain, put pressure on governmental budgets. Spanish inflation spread to other European countries, hurting those on fixed incomes and, of course, the poor. Mercantilist principles—an idea that colonies exist for the benefit of the mother country—thwarted the development of manufacturing industries in the American dominions. Yet the price revolution led to an expansion in trade and commerce as increased incomes of merchants and landlords led to increased demand for consumer goods. In terms of trends, the European economy was becoming global and complex, and rivalries among the European powers intense.

MULTIPLE-CHOICE QUESTIONS

1. He is best referred to as a *politique*, because he was willing to set aside religious principles to secure the unity of his nation. This individual is
   a. Charles V
   b. Henry IV
   c. Gustavus Adolphus
   d. Philip II
   e. William of Orange

2. The English defeat of the Spanish Armada resulted in
   a. the French invasion of Spain
   b. the end of silver imports from the New World
   c. growing nationalism in England
   d. the conversion of Spain to Anglicanism
   e. the Spanish loss of overseas empire

3. They waged a successful revolution against foreign domination. Their Protestantism and capitalism enabled them to develop the most advanced commercial and financial techniques in Europe in the early 1600s. These people are
   a. the German princes
   b. English Puritans
   c. French Huguenots
   d. the Dutch
   e. the Bohemians

4. The king's ruling enabled the people of the so-called Reformed religion to live in the towns and districts of the kingdom with freedom to have full liberty of religious conscience. The ruling is
   a. the Peace of Westphalia
   b. the Edict of Nantes
   c. the Concordat of Bologna
   d. the Treaty of Cateau-Cambrésis
   e. the Charter of Liberties of the United Provinces of the Netherlands

5. Gold and silver from the New World brought to sixteenth-century Europe
   a. an end to political rivalries among the commercial nations
   b. a general improvement in living standards among all social classes
   c. respect for the indigenous peoples in the New World
   d. long-range rising inflation
   e. the onset of factory production and improvements in technology

6. All of the following were results of the Treaty of Westphalia EXCEPT
   a. the reduction of the German population through military action and disease
   b. the toleration of the major Protestant churches
   c. the reduction of the role of the papacy in German affairs
   d. the recognition of the independence of the Netherlands
   e. the union of all German-speaking states under a strong emperor

7. Which of the following groups generally benefited from the inflation of the sixteenth century?
   a. merchants
   b. landowning nobility
   c. journeymen
   d. peasants
   e. government officials

8. Mercantilist policy was characterized by which of the following features?
   a. increased importance of guilds in regulating the national economy
   b. the development of international common markets
   c. government subsidies for domestic industries of finished goods
   d. the exportation of raw materials to colonial possessions
   e. balanced budgets in international trade

9. All of the following were features of the commercial revolution EXCEPT
   a. double-entry bookkeeping
   b. maritime insurance
   c. antitrust laws
   d. joint-stock companies
   e. state-sponsored monopolistic trading companies

10. Seeking to benefit from the sixteenth-century rise in prices, English landlords
    a. encouraged tenant farmers to increase their use of common pastures
    b. introduced the system of land enclosure
    c. divided land into strips for tenant farming
    d. codified tenants' rights in formal legal agreements
    e. organized cooperative peasant farming units

PRACTICE ESSAY QUESTIONS

Use the questions below to practice essay writing. For each question write an essay that includes an introductory thesis, a body of supporting and/or illustrative data, and a conclusion.

1. What was the impact of the Peace of Westphalia on the political and religious issues in the Holy Roman Empire?
2. How did the aims and actions of Elizabeth I and Henry IV resolve the religious conflicts in their respective countries, England and France, in the sixteenth century?
3. To what extent were overseas discoveries in the sixteenth century the cause of early modern capitalism?
4. Discuss the buildup of social, political, and economic factors in the fifteenth century that led to the internal decline of Spain after 1600.
5. "The Netherlands' revolt, which began as a struggle against Spain, became part of the international conflict of the age." Assess the validity of this statement.

ESSAY-WRITING TIPS: COMPLETING AN ANSWER

Below is a student response to the essay question: "How did the aims and actions of Elizabeth I and Henry IV resolve the religious conflicts in their respective countries, England and France, in the sixteenth century?" Read the essay and write a brief paragraph evaluating the writer's success and/or failure in dealing with the question.

Student Essay

Elizabeth I of England and Henry IV of France faced religious warfare in their countries. In England, Elizabeth faced the Catholics, who wanted to bring back the church and recognize the pope as the supreme authority. Elizabeth felt forced to have her cousin Mary, a Catholic, killed because she and her supporters were trying to gain control of the English throne.

Elizabeth also gave financial and military support to the Calvinist Dutch in the Netherlands who were trying to break away from Spanish control. If the Spanish under Philip II had conquered the northern provinces, it is likely that he would have invaded England and seized control there.

After the execution of Mary Stuart, Philip II did plan an invasion. In the battle of the Spanish Armada, however, the English fleet was able to outmaneuver the Spanish ships and win the sea battle. Thereafter, Elizabeth continued to support the Dutch. She also tried to satisfy religious extremes in her country by setting up the Anglican church with traditional services conducted in English and run by bishops appointed by Elizabeth.

Henry IV also had to deal with religious dissidents. He was Protestant, and his enemies were Catholic. The struggle was between two noble families fighting to put their candidate on the throne. The ruling regent Catherine de Médicis had Huguenots put to death on St. Bartholemew's Day, when they were in Paris for the wedding of Henry of Navarre (who became Henry IV). Henry escaped death by converting to Catholicism, and, upon ascending the throne, he issued the Edict of Nantes. The legislation allowed most Huguenots to practice their religion in peace and to hold public office. It also allowed the construction of fortified towns in which the Protestant Huguenots could defend themselves if attacked. This edict resolved the religious conflicts and allowed France to develop peaceably.

Commentary

The essay, while dealing with certain actions of Elizabeth I and Henry IV, ignores the aims of both rulers. It fails to answer the question completely. An improved essay would examine their possible motives or aims, describe the setting in which both rulers came to power, and define their actions using the concept of *politique*. It would include some mention of the ideas in the paragraph below:

> In the second half of the sixteenth century, religious issues threatened the stability of England and France. Two rulers, Elizabeth I of England and Henry IV of France, ascended their thrones. They hoped to quell the religious tensions dividing their country. Both rulers were *politiques*, individuals who subordinated religious controversy to the welfare of their state. Their political actions mirrored their aims—to defuse the religious controversies destroying their countries and to govern wisely and well.

Note: There are various ways to organize an essay. One way is to consider and explain the pronounced aims of both rulers in conjunction with the religious problems they faced.

For Elizabeth, it would be important to point out her aim of trying to achieve consensus in a country shaky in religious matters. Hoping to blur the lines of dispute over religious doctrine, she permitted private conscience but insisted on public conformity, opening no "window" into personal beliefs.

For Henry IV, the attributed saying "Paris is worth a mass" helps explain his willingness to convert to Catholicism to maintain the unity of his country. Reference to the struggles between the noble Guise and Bourbon families would suggest how the power conflict entwined with religious ideologies.

Better essays, in addition, have a conclusion. In this case, a student might look ahead to the difficulties that arose when the Stuarts came to power in England and when Louis XIV ascended the throne in France. Being aware how later rulers exacerbated religious tensions would support the conclusion that Henry IV and Elizabeth I *resolved* the religious conflicts in their countries, but only temporarily. After both rulers' deaths, ascending rulers seem to have lacked the commodious political vision characteristic of their predecessors.

Adopting all of the suggestions, the final essay appears below:

> In the second half of the sixteenth century, religious issues threatened the stability of England and France. Two rulers, Elizabeth I of England and Henry IV of France, ascended their thrones when religious tensions ran high. As *politiques*, both rulers subordinated religious controversy to the welfare of the state. Their political actions in their respective countries mirrored their aims—to defuse the religious controversy destroying political stability and to govern wisely and well.

In England, Elizabeth faced Catholics who wished to reconvert the Protestant nation and recognize the pope as the supreme authority. She felt forced to put to death her Catholic cousin Mary Stuart, who was trying to gain control of the English throne.

After the execution, Philip II planned an invasion of England. Not only had he supported Mary Stuart's candidacy for the throne, but he also was embroiled in a war with the Calvinist Dutch in the Spanish Netherlands. Elizabeth had provided financial and military support to the Dutch, who were important trading partners. If the Spanish under Philip II had conquered the breakaway northern provinces of the Netherlands, it seemed likely to Elizabeth that he would attempt to subdue England.

She was right in her predictions. Philip launched an armada, or fleet of Spanish ships, that engaged in battle with an English fleet that outmaneuvered the Spanish and won the sea battle. Thereafter, Elizabeth continued to support the Dutch. She also tried to satisfy the religious extremes in her country by setting up the Anglican church with traditional services conducted in English and run by bishops whom she appointed.

In religious matters, Elizabeth tried to achieve a workable consensus. Hoping to blur the dispute over doctrine, she permitted private conscience but insisted on public conformity, opening no "windows" into personal beliefs.

Henry IV was equally skillful. As a member of the noble Bourbon family engaged in political struggle with the noble Guise family for the throne, Henry understood the way in which Protestant and Catholic religious issues cloaked the contest for the throne. "Paris is worth a mass," he allegedly proclaimed in his conversion from Protestantism to Catholicism, a conversion of practical necessity.

The ruling regent Catherine de Médici sanctioned the massacre of thousands of Huguenots on St. Bartholemew's Day, when they were in Paris for the wedding of Henry of Navarre (who became Henry IV). Henry's conversion saved his life, and the Edict of Nantes, which Henry issued in 1598, saved France. It legislated that Huguenots could practice their religion in peace and also hold public office. In addition, it permitted the construction of fortified towns where the Huguenots could defend themselves if attacked. In short, it quelled religious rebellion within France.

But in both England and France, religious troubles were only temporarily suppressed. With Elizabeth's death in 1603 and Henry IV's assassination in 1610, conflict again surfaced. The Stuart kings in England were Catholic sympathizers and Louis XIV insisted on one faith alongside his single law and his personal rule. Neither Stuart kings nor Louis XIV had so commodious a political and religious vision as their predecessors.

IDENTIFICATIONS

Gustavus Adolphus (1594-1632)—Swedish Lutheran king who won victories for the German Protestants in the Thirty Years' War and lost his life in one of the battles.

Duke of Alva (1508-1582)–Military leader sent by Philip II to pacify the Low Countries.

Armada (1588)–Spanish vessels defeated in the English Channel by an English fleet, thus preventing Philip II's invasion of England.

Vasco de Balboa–First European to reach the Pacific Ocean, 1513.

Catherine de Médici (1547-1589)–The wife of Henry II (1547-1559) of France, who exercised political influence after the death of her husband and during the rule of her weak sons.

Christopher Columbus–First European to sail to the West Indies, 1492.

Concordat of Bologna (1516)–Treaty under which the French Crown recognized the supremacy of the pope over a council and obtained the right to appoint all French bishops and abbots.

Hernando Cortez–Conqueror of the Aztecs, 1519-1521.

Defenestration of Prague–The hurling, by Protestants, of Catholic officials from a castle window in Prague, setting off the Thirty Years' War.

Bartholomew Diaz–First European to reach the southern tip of Africa, 1487-1488.

Dutch East India Company–Government-chartered joint-stock company that controlled the spice trade in the East Indies.

Edict of Nantes (1598)–The edict of Henry IV that granted Huguenots the rights of public worship and religious toleration in France.

Elizabeth I (1558-1603)–Protestant ruler of England who helped stabilize religious tensions by subordinating theological issues to political considerations.

Prince Henry the Navigator–Sponsor of voyages along West African coasts, 1418.

Henry IV (1589-1610)–Formerly Henry of Navarre; ascended the French throne as a convert to Catholicism.

Huguenots–French Calvinists.

Ferdinand Magellan–Circumnavigator of the globe, 1519-1522.

Peace of Westphalia (1648)–The treaty ending the Thirty Years' War in Germany; it allowed each prince–whether Lutheran, Catholic, or Calvinist–to choose the established creed of his territory.

Philip II (1556-1598)–Son and successor to Charles V, ruling Spain and the Low Countries.

Francisco Pizarro–Conqueror of Peru, 1532-1533.

St. Bartholemew's Day (August 24, 1572)–Catholic attack on Calvinists on the marriage day of Margaret of Valois to Henry of Navarre (later Henry IV).

Prince William of Orange (1572-1584)–Leader of the seventeen provinces of the Netherlands.

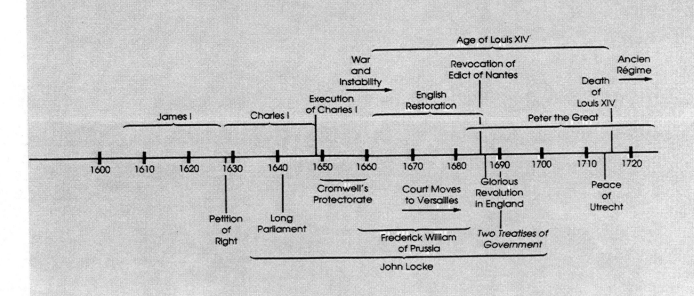

CONSTITUTIONAL
CONFLICTS IN EUROPE

CHAPTER 4

The seventeenth century can be viewed as an age of constitutional conflicts. England and France serve as prototypical models of the power struggles between monarch and nobility that led to vastly different outcomes in each country—**constitutionalism** and **absolutism**. A summary review of the political developments in each country follows.

ENGLAND

In England, two revolutions—**Puritan** and **Glorious**—resulted from clashes between king and Parliament. Parliament was a medieval English institution that sought to defend the ancient liberties that noblemen had wrested earlier from kings.

Upon the death of the childless Elizabeth I, her cousin **James I** (1603-1625), a Stuart, inherited the throne. He boldly asserted the theory of **divine-right monarchy**, proclaiming himself to be God's legal representative on earth. Puritans in Parliament, who comprised many gentry members of the House of Commons, opposed James. His extravagant spending and his intolerance toward the Puritans were among the reasons for their antagonism toward him. Each body, Crown and Commons, asserted rights challenged by the other. Parliament held the purse strings and refused to relinquish control, even forcing **Charles I** (1625-1649), desperate for money, to accept its **Petition of Right** with its writ of **habeas corpus**.

Civil War

The issue came to a head in 1640, when revolution broke out between the aristocracy and the Anglican church hierarchy *and* the **New Model Army** led by **Oliver Cromwell** (1559-1658), a **Puritan** member of Parliament belonging to the gentry. In the ensuing civil war, the forces of Cromwell defeated the king, and Charles I was beheaded. He had arbitrarily forced loans to finance a Scottish war; he had tried to arrest members of Parliament while in session; and he had ignored the principles in the 1628 Petition of Right, which he had earlier signed. A rump Parliament convicted him of treason.

Cromwell ruled sternly during the **Interregnum**. The revolutions had produced extremists, like the **Diggers** and **Levellers**, who called for the abolition of private ownership and the extension of the franchise. Cromwell's military dictatorship and his Puritanical rule collapsed with his death and was quickly followed by the **restoration** of the Stuart kings, who were Catholic sympathizers, in 1660. As a result, Parliament passed the **Test Act** in 1673, requiring all officeholders to be members of the Church of England. Still, **Charles II** (1680-1685) plotted with Louis XIV to convert England back to Catholicism. **James II** (1685-1688) proved no wiser. He appointed Catholics to high government positions. Such affront led leading British citizens, both Whigs and Tories, to join forces and drive James from the throne. **William of Orange** (1672-1702) and Mary, his Protestant wife and the daughter of James II, accepted the invitation tendered by British leaders to ascend the throne upon signing the English **Bill of Rights**. The political theory of **John Locke** (1632-1704) won out over that of **Thomas Hobbes** (1588-1679).

Creation of a Constitutional Monarchy

The document guaranteed individual rights of life, liberty, and property for the aristocratic oligarchy against the absolute power of kings. It undermined divine right theory and signaled a victory for Parliament. By the end of the seventeenth century, England was established as a Protestant state, controlled by gentry burghers and noble lords with power over the king.

FRANCE

In France, the final outcome was different. King **Louis XIV** (1643-1715) consolidated absolute power and brooked no challenge to his authority. He can be viewed as a master state builder who weakened the rival power of the nobility, strengthened the allied power of the bourgeoisie, and thus emerged as absolute king.

The Rule of Louis XIV

Louis inherited the throne at the age of five and, soon after, witnessed an attempt by the nobility to overthrow him. Cardinal Mazarin, his able minister, gathered military forces and quelled the rebellion, known as the **Fronde**. Louis allegedly was never to forget the quick escape of his family. Upon independent rule in 1660, at age twenty-three, he devised policies to prevent further uprisings. Following Cardinal Richelieu's strategies, he appointed able members of the bourgeoisie to the positions of intendant, the chief agent of the king in the local areas of France. In addition, the bourgeoisie benefited from the **mercantilist** policies of Louis's financial minister Colbert (1619-1683), the son of a draper. **Colbert** provided subsidies for the domestic production of silk, improved harbors and roads, and abolished internal tolls that had benefited the nobles.

If the political power of the nobility was waning, their social status neverthe-less remained high. Louis constructed a lavish palace at **Versailles**. Invitations to the court were prized, although the activities there were mainly ritualistic services to the king.

Revocation of the Edict of Nantes

In keeping the nobility under his control at Versailles, Louis XIV emasculated a significant sector of rival contenders to his power. He sought to establish "one king, one faith, and one law." With this aim, he revoked the Edict of Nantes in 1685. Persecuted Calvinists fled France and journeyed to England, Prussia, Holland, and the New World. They brought their skills as artisans to the new countries that welcomed their creativity and diligence.

By the end of the seventeenth century, Louis emerged as chief architect over a nation owing its first allegiance to his absolute rule and supporting his wars of conquest that culminated in the **War of the Spanish Succession** (1701–1713) and the **Peace of Utrecht** (1713). Even the art and literature of the period known as **French classicism**, the official style of Louis's court, ex-hibited the qualities of discipline and control.

Absolute monarchy as it existed in France was in large measure a reflection of the policies of Louis XIV. The same was true for Prussia and Russia under their respective rulers Frederick William, the Great Elector, and Peter the Great.

PRUSSIA

Frederick William (1640–1688), known as the "Great Elector," infused military values into an authoritarian Prussian society. His power stemmed from a standing army and an efficient bureaucracy. Commoners could hold impor-tant positions in his civil government, but only the Prussian nobility, or Junkers, made up the officer caste of his army. Historically, the nobility in their estates controlled finances. But the Great Elector ignored these political rights and without Junker approval collected taxes to build up his army. The nobility was exempt from taxes, socially privileged, and in full control over peasants residing on their land. Taxes fell on the towns, and the nobility, benefiting from the freedom from financial obligations, sided with their Hohenzollern king.

Frederick the Great

A later key figure in Prussian history was **Frederick the Great** (1740–1786). Although artistically inclined and rebellious as a youth, in adulthood he adopted the militaristic values of his predecessors. In 1740, when the Austrian ruler **Maria Theresa** (1740–1780) inherited the dynastic Hapsburg posses-sions, Frederick invaded the duchy of Silesia in violation of an earlier law—the Pragmatic Sanction, which held that the lands of Austria, Bohemia, and Hungary were to remain intact and could pass to a female heir. Maria Theresa lost the battle; Frederick the Great won—and doubled his state's population to six million in the War of the Austrian Succession. Frederick's victory earned him an alignment of the military powers of Austria, France, Russia, and Sweden against his army for the Seven Years' War, fought on Prussian soil. In the Peace of Paris (1763), Frederick was able to keep Silesia and his power status, but he concluded that "the acquisitions which one makes by the pen are always preferable to those made by the sword." He turned his attention to rebuilding the economy and encouraging education.

RUSSIA

The final absolute ruler to be discussed is Russia's **Peter the Great** (1682–1725), who had thirty-five years of war during his forty-three-year reign. Service in the Russian army was compulsory and for life. Peter set up schools to train his officers and bureaucrats drawn from the nobility. Peasants served in the regular standing army or worked in factories and mines.

Peter the Great

Peter's efforts centered on directing the westernization of Russian society. He insisted on the adoption of Western dress and manners by nobles, gentry, and the city population generally. And to glorify his state, he had the city of St. Petersburg built on drained swampland. It was located on the Baltic coast, facing the West. Nobles were required to build their palaces there and live under Peter's watchful eye.

The defeat of Sweden in the Great Northern War had enabled Peter to obtain this territory along the Baltic coast. His war with the Ottoman Turks for access to the Mediterranean, however, was unsuccessful.

In spite of reforms in rebuilding the army, creating a navy, and stimulating exploration, trade, and industry, Peter remained an autocratic czar who widened the gap between the educated upper-class Russians and the exploited peasants who bore the heavy burden of taxation in an onerous system of serfdom.

DOCUMENT-BASED ESSAY QUESTION

Below are two eighteenth-century documents written by Englishmen sixty years apart. Both refer to the process of westernization in Russia. Write a comparison considering the extent to which Peter the Great was successful in westernizing Russia. In your essay explain the obstacles that Peter faced. Point out the standard used by the second author in his assessment of the degree of change and tell whether you agree with the author's standard of westernization.

FROM AN ACCOUNT BY JOHN PERRY, ENGLISH ENGINEER, 1712

About this time the Czar (Peter the Great) came down to Veronize, where I was then on service, and a great many of my men that had worn their beards all their lives, were now obliged to part with them, amongst which, one of the first that I met with just coming from the hands of the barber, was an old Russ carpenter that had been with me at Camishinka, who was a very good workman with his hatchet, and whom I always had a friendship for. I jested a little with him on this occasion, telling him that he had become a young man, and asked him what he had done with his beard? Upon which he put his hand in his bosom and pull'd it out, and shew'd it to me, telling me that when he came home, he would lay it up to have it put in his coffin and buried along with him that he might be able to give an account of it to St. Nicholas, when he came to the other world; and that all his fellow-workmen, who had been shaved that day, had taken the same care.

FROM AN ACCOUNT BY WILLIAM COXE, ENGLISH TRAVELER, 1772

I was astonished at the immensity and variety of Moscow. Wretched hovels are blended with large palaces; cottages of one story stand next to the most superb and stately mansions.

Much has been written concerning the great civilization which Peter I introduced into this country; that he obliged the people to relinquish their beards, and their national dress; that he naturalized the arts and sciences; that he disciplined his army, and created a navy; and that he made a total change throughout each part of his extensive empire. But the pompous accounts of the total change he effected in the national manners, seem to have been the mere echoes of foreigners who have never visited the country. . . . I must own I was astonished at the barbarism in which the bulk of the people still continue. I am ready to allow that the principal nobles are civilized, and as refined in their entertainments and mode of living as those of other European countries. But there is a wide difference between polishing a nation, and polishing a few individuals.

MULTIPLE-CHOICE QUESTIONS

1. When James I of England stated, "That which concerns the mystery of the King's power is not lawful to be disputed; for that is to wade into the weakness of Princes, and to take away the mystical reverence that belongs unto them that sit in the throne of God," he was referring to
   a. the writ of habeas corpus
   b. the theory of divine-right monarchy
   c. the Calvinist concept of predestination
   d. papal supremacy
   e. balance-of-power politics

2. The political theorist who defended absolutism by picturing humans in a state of primitive anarchy, leading lives that were "solitary, poor, nasty, brutish and short" is
   a. Thomas Hobbes
   b. Niccolò Machiavelli
   c. Bishop Bossuet
   d. Jean Bodin
   e. René Descartes

3. A central feature of the English Bill of Rights was its
   a. policy of imprisonment for unpaid debts
   b. insistence on the abolition of rotten boroughs
   c. acceptance by the monarch of parliamentary supremacy
   d. establishment of universal manhood suffrage
   e. allowance for a Catholic to be king of England

4. To strengthen the unity and uniformity of his state, Louis XIV did all of the following EXCEPT
   a. revoke the Edict of Nantes
   b. appoint intendants throughout the country
   c. allow Colbert to draw up a commercial code
   d. have Versailles built
   e. decrease the size of the French army

5. In order to put French finances on a stable footing and make France self-sufficient, Colbert did all of the following EXCEPT
   a. set up the area of the Five Great Farms
   b. build an infrastructure of roads and canals
   c. reduce tariffs on Dutch and English products
   d. promote tax exemptions for manufacturers
   e. establish overseas trading companies

6. Seventeenth-century warfare was increasingly characterized by
   a. mercenary soldiers of fortune
   b. trench warfare
   c. independent infantry and artillery regiments
   d. disciplined standing armies for home and foreign use
   e. privately funded training and provisioning programs

7. Frederick the Great was able to win the support of the nobles in Brandenburg-Prussia by giving them increased control over
   a. commerce
   b. the church
   c. Huguenot immigrants
   d. the peasants
   e. guild policies

8. Peter the Great did all of the following to westernize his country EXCEPT
   a. abolish serfdom
   b. reform traditional dress and manners
   c. build a new capital on the Baltic
   d. recruit engineers and artisans from abroad
   e. provide primary education for Russian children

9. Peter the Great's chief opponent in his quest for a warm-water port was
   a. the Spanish Hapsburgs
   b. the Ottoman Turks
   c. Sweden's royal army under Charles XII
   d. the Mongols of China
   e. the Russian nobles in Kiev

10. What was distinctive about this empire was its scattered territories. They were noncontiguous and therefore needed a powerful army and efficient bureaucracy to maintain them. The empire is
    a. Poland
    b. Austria
    c. Brandenburg-Prussia
    d. Sweden
    e. Russia

PRACTICE ESSAY QUESTIONS

Use the questions below to practice essay writing. For each question write an essay that includes an introductory thesis, a body of supporting and/or illustrative data, and a conclusion.

1. Account for the fact that by the end of the seventeenth century, France was an absolute monarchy and England was a constitutional monarchy.

2. Compare the ways and methods by which the political rulers of France, Prussia, and Russia developed absolute states in the seventeenth century.

3. How glorious was the Glorious Revolution of 1688-1689 in England? What arguments can be made for and against the use of the term?

4. "Louis XIV's chief asset as a political leader was his ability to defuse class tensions in France." Assess the validity of this statement, paying particular attention to the roles of the nobility and the bourgeoisie.

5. How successful was Peter the Great in realizing his dream of a westernized Russia? Consider domestic and foreign policy in your answer.

ESSAY-WRITING TIPS: MULTIPLE CAUSATION AND ORGANIZATION

Below are two essays that were written to answer the following essay question: Account for the fact that by the end of the seventeenth century, France was an absolute monarchy and England was a constitutional monarchy. Read the essays and compare in writing the efforts of each essay to answer the question.

Essay A

When the seventeenth century came to a close, the rulerships of England and France were very different. England had a Parliament in political control, and France had a Bourbon king–Louis XIV–in control. The reason for the difference relates to one factor alone–the personalities of Louis XIV and the Stuart kings from James I through James II.

Louis XIV was an absolute ruler who insisted that France be a unified religious nation under his supreme control. He did everything himself. He ran the council of state, and he limited the power of the nobility to exercise authority. He set up Versailles, where the nobles' attendance was required, and he insisted on their personal attention from morning to night.

He went so far as an absolute ruler to revoke the Edict of Nantes in 1685 which had guaranteed certain religious freedoms to the Huguenots. Many of them fled to England and Holland, where they could live peaceably. Louis also engaged in a series of wars with many of the major European countries to expand France and weaken his Hapsburg rivals. In effect, though, he weakened France and left it in heavy debt when he died. In short, he was an absolute ruler *par excellence*.

England, on the other hand, became a constitutional monarchy owing to the rule of the Stuart kings. All of them–James I, Charles I, Charles II, and James II–fancied themselves divine-right monarchs who refused to listen to Parliament.

Neither the civil war with Cromwell, nor the execution of Charles I in 1649, convinced the latter two that they were subject to parliamentary restrictions. They even plotted to win support from Louis XIV and reconvert England to Catholicism.

England became a constitutional monarchy because these kings refused to listen to warnings from parliamentary leaders. If they had, they could have stayed on the throne. By the end of the century, however, James II was booted off the throne by Whigs and Tories who together decided that he must go. The incident that sparked their decision was the birth of a boy to the wife of James II. His wife was French and Catholic, and the king's sympathies with Catholicism were strong and evident.

In summary, both England and France had different governments at the end of the seventeenth century owing to the rule of their kings. All of them were subscribers to divine-right philosophy which resulted in the different forms of government.

Essay B

By the end of the seventeenth century, Louis XIV ruled supreme in France; in England, Parliament was sovereign. Louis had revoked the Edict of Nantes; William and Mary had signed the Bill of Rights. The Edict sent Huguenots fleeing; the Bill of Rights guaranteed the legal and civil rights of English citizens and also established England as a constitutional monarchy. The extreme differences in the political systems derive from three factors: (1) historical precedents, (2) social class alliances, and (3) political leadership—or its lack.

First medieval parliaments of lords, bishops, burghers, and gentry had checked kings' powers. During the Renaissance, Parliament had controlled finances and approved royal spending. The Stuart rulers ignored historical precedents and proclaimed divine-right rule. In France, however, there had been no medieval parliament and no Magna Carta, either. Nobles often exercised political power in the countryside, but the intendant system, set up by Richelieu and strengthened by Louis, undermined the authority of the provincial nobility. The intendant was the king's representative and his eyes and ears in the local areas.

Second, in examining social class alliances in France, it is necessary to understand the role and origin of the intendants. They were generally of bourgeois origin. In appointing them to key political positions, Louis earned their approval. The bourgeoisie also benefited from Colbert's policies of constructing harbors and roads, setting up a uniform currency, and providing subsidies for domestic manufacturing. For the politically weakened nobility, Louis provided the grandeur of Versailles, the social setting for court intrigue and extravagant dress.

Across the English Channel, social class relationships formed another pattern. Burghers and gentry sat together in the House of Commons and challenged Stuart political, financial, and religious policies. For example, pro-Catholic Stuart kings ignored Puritan calls for religious reform and rebuked the leaders, including one Oliver Cromwell, whose New Model Army later defeated and beheaded the Stuart king Charles I.

Finally, if Louis XIV proved the master state builder in his skillful alliance with the bourgeoisie and his handling of the nobility at Versailles, the Stuart kings proved no match for gentry and burghers in the House of Commons. These two groups formed an aristocratic oligarchy. They subscribed to Locke's political philosophy that kings gain their power from the people who delegate that authority. The king's role then becomes one of safeguarding the natural rights to life, liberty, and property. If the king violates these natural rights, according to Locke, his subjects can overthrow him.

Thus, in examining the different political outcomes for France and England in the seventeenth century, the importance of historical backgrounds, social class relationships, and the political skills of monarchs deserve attention. Each of these factors—and undoubtedly there are others beyond the scope of this essay—contributes to an understanding of the emergence of absolutism and constitutionalism in the two countries.

Commentary It should be evident that Essay A fails to answer the question. It limits its analysis solely to the role of political leaders, who are certainly important but not exclusive to explaining the political outcomes in both countries. Essay B improves the answer by developing a thesis with multiple factors that are analyzed throughout the essay in significant detail.

IDENTIFICATIONS

Absolutism–The theory that the monarch is supreme and can exercise full and complete power unilaterally.

Bill of Rights (1689)–English document declaring that sovereignty resided with Parliament.

Charles I (1625-1649)–Stuart king who brought conflict with Parliament to a head and was subsequently executed.

Charles II (1660-1685)–Stuart king during the Restoration, following Cromwell's Interregnum.

Colbert (1619-1683)–The financial minister under the French king Louis XIV who promoted mercantilist policies.

Constitutionalism–The theory that power should be shared between rulers and their subjects and the state governed according to laws.

Oliver Cromwell (1559-1658)–The principal leader and a gentry member of the Puritans in Parliament.

Diggers and **Levellers**–Radical groups in England in the 1650s who called for the abolition of private ownership and extension of the franchise.

Divine-right monarchy–The belief that a monarch's power derives from God and represents Him on earth.

Frederick the Great (1740-1786)–The Prussian ruler who expanded his territory by invading the duchy of Silesia and defeating Maria Theresa of Austria.

Frederick William (1640-1688)–The "Great Elector," who built a strong Prussian army and infused military values into Prussian society.

French classicism–The style in seventeenth-century art and literature resembling the arts in the ancient world and in the Renaissance–e.g., the works of Poussin, Molière, and Racine.

Fronde–The last aristocratic revolt against a French monarch.

Glorious Revolution–A reference to the political events of 1688–1689, when James II abdicated his throne and was replaced by his daughter Mary and her husband, Prince William of Orange.

Habeas corpus–The legal protection that prohibits the imprisonment of a subject without demonstrated cause.

Thomas Hobbes (1588-1679)–Political theorist advocating absolute monarchy based on his concept of an anarchic state of nature.

Interregnum–The period of Cromwellian rule (1649-1659), between the Stuart dynastic rules of Charles I and Charles II.

James I (1603-1625)–Stuart monarch who ignored constitutional principles and asserted the divine right of kings.

James II (1685-1688)–Final Stuart ruler; he was forced to abdicate in favor of William and Mary, who agreed to the Bill of Rights, guaranteeing parliamentary supremacy.

John Locke (1632-1704)–Political theorist who defended the Glorious Revolution with the argument that all people are born with certain natural rights to life, liberty, and property.

Louis XIV (1643-1715)–Also known as the "Sun King"; the ruler of France who established the supremacy of absolutism in seventeenth-century Europe.

Maria Theresa (1740-1780)–Archduchess of Austria, queen of Hungary, who lost the Hapsburg possession of Silesia to Frederick the Great but was able to keep her other Austrian territories.

Mercantilism–Governmental policies by which the state regulates the economy, through taxes, tariffs, subsidies, laws.

New Model Army–The disciplined fighting force of Protestants led by Oliver Cromwell in the English civil war.

Peace of Utrecht (1713)–The pact concluding the War of the Spanish Succession, forbidding the union of France with Spain, and conferring control of Gibraltar on England.

Peter the Great (1682-1725)–The Romanov czar who initiated the westernization of Russian society by traveling to the West and incorporating techniques of manufacturing as well as manners and dress.

Petition of Right (1628)–Parliamentary document that restricted the king's power. Most notably, it called for recognition of the writ of habeas corpus and held that only Parliament could impose new taxes.

Puritan Revolution–A reference to the English civil war (1642-1646), waged to determine whether sovereignty would reside in the monarch or in Parliament.

Puritans–Protestant sect in England hoping to "purify" the Anglican church of Roman Catholic traces in practice and organization.

Restoration–The return of the Stuart monarchy (1660) after the period of republican government under Cromwell–in fact, a military dictatorship.

Test Act (1673)–Law prohibiting Catholics and dissenters to hold political office.

Versailles–Palace constructed by Louis XIV outside of Paris to glorify his rule and subdue the nobility.

War of the Spanish Succession (1701-1713)–The last of Louis XIV's wars involving the issue of succession to the Spanish throne.

William of Orange (1672-1702)–Dutch prince and foe of Louis XIV who became king of England in 1689.

Scientific Revolution

Renaissance
and
Reformation

Enlightenment

Inquisition
Condemns
Galileo

Scientific Societies

Galileo's
Dialogue

Royal Society
of London

Encyclopedia

French
Revolution

Descartes's
Discourse on Method

Newton's
Mathematical Principles

*The Social
Contract*

Kepler's Laws

1600 1610 1620 1630 1640 1650 1660 1670 1680 1690 1700 1710 1720 1730 1740 1750 1760 1770 1780 1790

Kepler

Voltaire

Montesquieu

Joseph II
of Austria

Galileo

Newton

Rousseau

Descartes

Diderot

Adam Smith

Mary Wollstonecraft

THE SCIENTIFIC
REVOLUTION AND
THE ENLIGHTENMENT

CHAPTER 5

"Nature and nature's laws lay hid in night,
God said, " 'Let Newton be,' and all was light."
Alexander Pope, 1713

A cosmology is a systematic conception of the universe. It is a world view that satisfactorily explains the operation of the universe. From the fourth century B.C. to the sixteenth and seventeenth centuries, the **Aristotelian-Ptolemaic cosmology** prevailed. Accordingly, the cosmos was made up of four elements—earth, fire, water, and air. It was geocentric. The earth, at the center, was enclosed in a series of crystalline spheres in which were embedded stars and planets revolving on cycles and epicycles in circular yet complex patterns. Beyond the spheres lay the empyrean blue where God resided. Motion resulted from angels' hands revolving the crystal orbs. The entire conception accorded with church teachings and Scriptures.

THE SCIENTIFIC REVOLUTION

A revolution took place, in the stretch of time between publication of works by **Nicolaus Copernicus** (1473-1543) and **Isaac Newton** (1642-1727), that shattered the old heavens and substituted the Newtonian cosmology, mathematical and mechanistic in its conception of the universe. Copernicus proposed a heliocentric system that simplified the complex pattern of cycles and epicycles by reducing their number. Tycho Brahe (1546-1601), the Danish astronomer, catalogued the stars. In Germany, Johannes Kepler (1571-1630) formulated planetary laws and theorized that the planets moved in elliptical rather than circular patterns. **Galileo** (1564-1642) formulated terrestrial laws and the modern law of inertia. He used the telescope to discover the four moons of Jupiter and prove that Jupiter was not encased on any crystal orb, and thus he provided evidence for the Copernican theory. These findings brought trouble with church authorities, who placed Galileo under house arrest.

Newton's Synthesis

The final figure in the story is Newton, who published *Mathematical Principles of Natural Philosophy* in 1687. Building upon the work of his predecessors, he formulated a universal law of gravity that embraced heaven and earth in one grand system. Most important, the new system operated in accord with natural laws that were immutable, inviolable, and discoverable through human reason. In his scientific works Newton had stressed experimentation and mathematics; both became the bases for a new methodology for arriving at truth. Subsequently, scientific societies were formed—the **Royal Society** in London and the **French Academy of Sciences**—to share findings and methods.

The Scientific Method

The harbingers of this new scientific method were **Francis Bacon** (1561-1626) and **René Descartes** (1596-1650). Stressing empiricism and deriving his "truths" from experimentation, Bacon was the inductive thinker. Descartes was the deductive thinker. Cartesian rationalism derived "truths" from axioms, deductions, and proofs—like the geometer. His most famous truth, *cogito, ergo sum* ("I think, therefore I am"), rested upon the notion of a rigorous intellect far surpassing the deceiving senses.

Locke's Epistemology

John Locke's (1632-1704) epistemology (the knowledge of how we know what we know) is the bridge between the scientific revolution of the seventeenth century and eighteenth-century Enlightenment. Locke pictured the mind of a newborn as a **tabula rasa**. Sense impressions hit this blank sheet like so many Newtonian particles. Humans, however, because they have the power and capacity to reason, according to Locke, are able to reflect on these sense impressions and form ideas, unaided by Scriptures, traditional beliefs, or authoritative decrees. In short, natural laws could be discovered through the powers of reasoning.

THE ENLIGHTENMENT

Newton's *Principles* and Locke's essay on knowledge shaped the thinking of the philosophes, French scholars (but there were English, Italian, and German thinkers as well) who led the intellectual movement known as the **Enlightenment**. These thinkers subscribed to the belief that humans could discover the natural laws of society, as Newton had discovered the natural laws of the cosmos. Upon discovery, these laws could be used to reconstruct society. The result would be great improvement of the social and individual circumstances of life for all.

The Philosophes

In brief, the **philosophes** were social critics—mainly French, but not exclusively so—who subjected human behavior and social institutions to the critical test of reason. *Sapere aude* ("dare to know") was their motto. Leading philosophes—**Voltaire** (1694-1778), **Montesquieu** (1689-1755), **Denis Diderot** (1713-1784), **Jean-Jacques Rousseau** (1712-1778), **Beccaria** (1738-1794), **Condorcet** (1743-1794), **David Hume** (1711-1776), **Mary Wollstonecraft** (1759-1797), **Adam Smith** (1723-1790)—wrote articles, plays, essays, and encyclopedias attacking arbitrary and capricious rule, status based on birth rather than merit, religious superstitions, unduly harsh criminal punishments, divine-right rule, mercantilism, and gender roles. As fighters for liberal thought and freedom in political, social, and economic spheres (**laissez-faire**), they did not always agree with one another.

DOCUMENT-BASED ESSAY QUESTION

Compare the two documents below in their analysis of socially appropriate behavior for the sexes. In a written essay, explain how both authors make use of natural law and reason to argue their cases. Why do they arrive at such different conclusions?

FROM JEAN-JACQUES ROUSSEAU, *EMILE*, 1762

Men and women are made for each other, but their mutual dependence differs in degree; man is dependent on woman through his desires; woman is dependent on man through her desires and also through her needs; he could do without her better than she can do without him. She cannot fulfill her purpose in life without his aid, without his goodwill, without his respect; she is dependent on our feelings, on the price we put upon her virtue, and the opinion we have of her charms and her deserts. Nature herself has decreed that woman, both for herself and her children, should be at the mercy of man's judgment.

Boys and girls have many games in common. . . . they have also special tastes of their own. Boys want movement and noise, drums, tops, toy-carts; girls prefer things which appeal to the eye, and can be used for dressing-up —mirrors, jewelry, finery, and especially dolls. The doll is the girl's special plaything; this shows her instinctive bent toward her life's work. . . . she is engrossed in her doll and all her coquetry is devoted to it. This will not always be so; in due time she will be her own doll.

FROM MARY WOLLSTONECRAFT, *A VINDICATION OF THE RIGHTS OF WOMAN*, 1792

Women are told from their infancy, and taught by the example of their mothers, that a little knowledge of human weakness, justly termed cunning, softness of temper, *outward* obedience, and a scrupulous attention to a puerile kind of propriety, will obtain for them the protection of man, and should they be beautiful, everything else is needless, for, at least, twenty years of their lives.

I love man as my fellow, but his sceptre, real or usurped, extends not to me, unless the reason of an individual demands my homage; and even then the submission is to reason, and not to man.

I lament that women are systematically degraded by receiving the trivial attentions, which men think it manly to pay to the sex, when, in fact, they are insultingly supporting their own superiority. It is not condescension to bow to an inferior. So ludicrous, in fact, do these ceremonies appear to me, that I scarcely am able to govern my muscles, when I see a man start with eager and serious solicitude, to lift a handkerchief, or shut a door, when the *lady* could have done it herself, had she moved a pace or two.

Political and Religious Theory

In political theory, the philosophes differed also. Voltaire favored enlightened despotism; Montesquieu, a system of checks and balances; and Rousseau, the most politically radical, participatory democracy, with the law derived from the "General Will." The general will was not necessarily the will of the majority. It was a consensus that placed the interests of society before personal ones, a set of moral ideals by which a nation ought to be governed.

Most of the philosophes were adherents of **deism**. A few were atheists. But all called for religious freedom, representative government, legal equality, and free speech and press. They looked back to ancient Greece and Rome for inspiration and delight. They were the first social scientists—the muckrakers of their day.

MULTIPLE-CHOICE QUESTIONS

1. According to the Newtonian world model, the physical universe had all of the following characteristics EXCEPT
   a. asymmetry
   b. rationality
   c. balance
   d. uniformity
   e. harmony

2. Their lives revolved around two poles—the salon and the censor. In one they stimulated the flow of thinking; regarding the other, they disguised their beliefs with acerbic wit. An individual whose life would fit this description is
   a. Bacon
   b. Charles II
   c. Voltaire
   d. Locke
   e. Cardinal Richelieu

3. John Locke's concept of the tabula rasa relates best to
   a. republicanism
   b. empiricism
   c. skepticism
   d. socialism
   e. classicism

4. Which of the following philosophes is correctly paired with one of his or her major works?
   a. Beccaria—*A Vindication of the Rights of Woman*
   b. Rousseau—*Spirit of the Laws*
   c. Voltaire—*Persian Letters*
   d. Diderot—*Encyclopedia*
   e. Smith—*Emile*

5. The Enlightenment can be best described as
   a. a political revolution accompanied by dynastic change
   b. an intellectual revolution indebted to scientific findings
   c. a support system for organized Christianity
   d. a pessimistic view of the limits of human progress
   e. a return to the democratic institutions of ancient Athens

6. Which of the following ideas would Mary Wollstonecraft have probably subscribed to?
   a. Nature, not nurture, shapes our personalities.
   b. Ladies are obligated to act modestly and discreetly.
   c. Careers should be open to persons of talent.
   d. Boys' toys should encourage hardy physical play.
   e. Women should not physically exert themselves.

7. Deism was the eighteenth-century belief that
   a. God actively intervenes in the workings of the universe
   b. there is no God
   c. God does not sanction established churches
   d. certain religions are superior to others
   e. miracles can correct the injustices of life

8. Kepler's heliocentric theory differed from that of Copernicus in that the former
   a. posited elliptical planetary movement
   b. noted the magnetic pull of the moon
   c. based his theories on deduction
   d. won papal approval for his discoveries
   e. discovered the modern law of inertia

9. According to Adam Smith, rational economic behavior was in accord with
   a. governments establishing tariff systems
   b. nations becoming self-sufficient producers
   c. individuals pursuing their own self-interests
   d. individuals mastering entire productive processes
   e. governments promoting socialist economies

10. "There would be an end of everything were the same man or the same body . . . to exercise those three powers, that of enacting laws, that of executing the public resolutions, and of trying the causes of individuals. . . ." The author of this quotation is
    a. Rousseau
    b. Locke
    c. Montesquieu
    d. Hume
    e. Diderot

PRACTICE ESSAY QUESTIONS

Use the questions below to practice essay writing. For each question write an essay that includes an introductory thesis, a body of supporting and/or illustrative data, and a conclusion.

1. "The intellectual revolution of the eighteenth century was indebted to the scientific revolution of the seventeenth century." Explain the connection

between the two, paying special attention to the role of Locke in the process.
2. The philosophes have been described as modern pagans. What was modern about them? What was pagan? How appropriate is this label for their collective efforts and accomplishments?
3. To what extent did the eighteenth-century philosophes achieve unified thinking in their political ideas and social objectives?
4. "The scientific revolution ushered in a new body of thought and a new methodology. In fact, it was two revolutions in one." Support or refute this statement.
5. Rousseau has been described as the most radical philosophe in his thinking. Others have argued that he was conservative. Was he, in fact, a radical or a conservative? Use specific examples to defend your position.

ESSAY-WRITING TIPS: BLOCKING OUT A DBQ (DOCUMENT-BASED ESSAY QUESTION)

In the Advanced Placement examination, students have a fifteen-minute silent reading period. During that time, they are expected to read the question on which the edited documents are framed as well as the documents. They may take notes on the documents they are reading, a practice to be encouraged after an initial skimming of the documents' contents.

Below is a document-based essay question on medical treatment in the seventeenth century. First, read the question, underlining the information that you are seeking. Second, after skimming the documents, set up the categories that you will elaborate in your essay. And third, as you are reading through the documents more closely for the information you will need, jot down the words and phrases that come to mind and that you plan to incorporate in your essay. Do the second and third steps on a separate sheet of paper.

DOCUMENT-BASED ESSAY QUESTION—MEDICAL TREATMENT IN THE SEVENTEENTH CENTURY

Identify at least three methods that preindustrial people used in treating illness and disease and explain what these medical practices indicate about preindustrial attitudes toward human ability to effect change.

Historical Background

Preindustrial people faced epidemic and endemic diseases. Epidemic diseases, such as the plague, struck quickly and unexpectedly, often dramatically reducing town and village populations. Endemic diseases, such as common colds and measles, were constantly present. In preindustrial England, health care was provided by numerous practitioners, including university-trained physicians, surgeon-barbers, druggists, midwives, clergy, ladies of manor houses, and peddlers selling their wares.

DOCUMENT 1

If you would get rid of the ague*, go by night alone to a crossroads, and just as the clock is striking midnight turn round three times and drive a large nail into the ground up to the head. Walk backwards from the nail before the clock has finished the twelfth stroke. The ague will leave you, but will go to the person next to step over the nail.

English folk belief of the 1600s
*A fever marked by chills and sweating that recur at regular intervals.

DOCUMENT 2

As soon as any person shall be found by Examiner, Surgeon, or Searcher to be sick of the plague, he shall be isolated in the same house. The goods and stuff of the infected, their bedding and apparel, and hangings of chambers, must be well aired with fire and such perfumes as are necessary within the infected house, before they be used again.

To every infected house there be appointed two watchmen; one for every day, and the other for the night. These watchmen have a special care that no person go in or out of such infected houses upon pain of severe punishment.

Orders published by the Lord Mayor and Aldermen of the City of London, concerning the infection of the plague, 1665

DOCUMENT 3

``Rules for Blood Letting''
The vein above the thumb is good against all fevers. . . . The vein between the thumb and the forefinger, let blood for the hot headache, for frenzy and madness of wit.

``Rules concerning Blood-letting to be observed''
Also be ye always well advised, and wary, that ye let no blood, nor open no vein, except the Moon be either in Aries, Cancer, the first half of Libra, the last half of Scorpio, or in Sagittarius, Aquarius, or Pisces. . . .

Peter Levens, master of arts in Oxford, and student in physick and chirurgery, The Pathway to Health, 1664

DOCUMENT 4

. . . there was still another madness which may serve to give an idea, of the distracted humor of the poor people at that time. It lay chiefly in the people deceived; and this was in wearing charms, exorcism, amulets, and I know not what preparations, to fortify the body with them against the plague, as if the plague was not the hand of God, but a kind of a possession of an evil spirit; and that it was to be kept off with crossings, signs of the zodiac, papers tied up with so many knots, and certain words or figures in a triangle or pyramid, thus,—

ABRACADABRA
ABRACADABR
ABRACADAB
ABRACADA
ABRACAD
ABRACA
ABRAC
ABRA
ABR
AB
A

Daniel Defoe, A Journal of the Plague Year, 1665

DOCUMENT 5

Scarlet Fever may appear at any season. Nevertheless, it often breaks out toward the end of summer, when it attacks whole families at once, and more especially the infants. The patients feel rigors and shiverings, just as they do in other fevers. Afterwards, however, the whole skin becomes covered with small red sores which last for two or three days and then disappear.

I am hesitant both of blood letting and of enemas, and cautious in the use of cordials (a strong liqueur). They may act as fuel to fever.

The patient should abstain wholly from animal food and from fermented liquors; to keep always indoors, and not to keep always in bed. When the symptoms are departing, I consider it proper to purge the patient with some mild laxative, accommodated to his age and strength. By treatment thus simple and natural, this ailment is dispelled without either trouble or danger. Otherwise, we overtreat the patient and the sick man dies of his doctor.

From Dr. Thomas Sydenham, Medical Observations on the History and Cure of Acute Illnesses, *1676*

DOCUMENT 6

Charles II ``Touching,'' to Cure Kings Evil. Illustration from John Browne's Adenocholradelogia, 1654.

SUGGESTED OUTLINE AND NOTE TAKING
FOR BLOCKING OUT THE ESSAY

Methods	Attitudes
magical	Is there a cause-and-effect relationship?
faith in spirits, ghosts, astrology	Is there a need for "professionals" of some sort?
quarantine	
surveillance	Is the treatment aggressive or nonaggressive?
inhalants	
exorcism	Is the treatment to vary during the course of an illness?
purging	
faith healing	Is the body essentially self-healing?
surgical	
medicinal	
dietary	
self-healing	
disinfection	
confinement	

As you can see, the list of methods is extensive and the questions relating to preindustrial attitudes varied and diverse, yet focusing on human ability to effect change. Some of the methods can be combined—e.g., quarantine, surveillance, inhalants, disinfection, and confinement for document 2. And faith in astrology as well as surgical (bloodletting) are methods prescribed in document 3.

Before you write your essay answer, briefly review your lists and construct a thesis that you know you will be able to defend using your documents. As you note, in all cases, humans believed that they could bring about some change in their illness. However, that role varied from being an active agent to being a docile patient or a willing subject.

Blocking out a DBQ essay in this manner simplifies the forty-five-minute writing process and aids in organizing a well-constructed essay.

IDENTIFICATIONS

Aristotelian-Ptolemaic cosmology–the geocentric view of the universe that prevailed from the fourth century B.C. to the sixteenth and seventeenth centuries and accorded with church teachings and Scriptures.

Francis Bacon (1561-1626)–Inductive thinker who stressed experimentation in arriving at truth.

Nicolaus Copernicus (1473-1543)–Polish astronomer who posited a heliocentric universe in place of a geocentric universe.

Deism–The belief that God has created the universe and set it in motion to operate like clockwork. God is literally in the wings watching the show go on as humans forge their own destiny.

René Descartes (1596-1650)–Deductive thinker whose famous saying *cogito, ergo sum* ("I think, therefore I am") challenged the notion of truth as being derived from tradition and Scriptures.

Enlightenment–The intellectual revolution of the eighteenth century in which the philosophes stressed reason, natural law, and progress in their criticism of prevailing social injustices.

Galileo (1564-1642)–Italian scientist who formulated terrestrial laws and the modern law of inertia; he also provided evidence for the Copernican hypothesis.

Laissez-faire–The economic concept of the Scottish philosophe Adam Smith (1723-1790). In opposition to mercantilism, Smith urged governments to keep hands off the operation of the economy. He believed the role of government was analogous to the night watchman, guarding and protecting but not intervening in the operation of the economy, which must be left to run in accord with the natural laws of supply and demand.

Isaac Newton (1642-1727)–English scientist who formulated the law of gravitation that posited a universe operating in accord with natural law.

Philosophes–Social critics of the eighteenth century who subjected social institutions and practices to the test of reason.

Royal Society of London and **French Academy of Sciences**–Organized bodies for scientific study.

Tabula rasa–John Locke's concept of the mind as a blank sheet ultimately bombarded by sense impressions that, aided by human reasoning, formulate ideas.

Key Authors and Their Works

Cesare Beccaria–*Of Crime and Punishment.*

Condorcet–*Sketch of the Progress of the Human Mind.*

Denis Diderot–*Encyclopédia.*

David Hume–*An Inquiry Concerning Human Understanding.*

John Locke–*Two Treatises on Government; Essay on Human Understanding.*

Montesquieu–*Spirit of the Laws; Persian Letters.*

Jean-Jacques Rousseau–*The Social Contract; Emile.*

Adam Smith–*Wealth of Nations.*

Voltaire–*Philosophical Letters; Candide.*

Mary Wollstonecraft–*A Vindication of the Rights of Woman.*

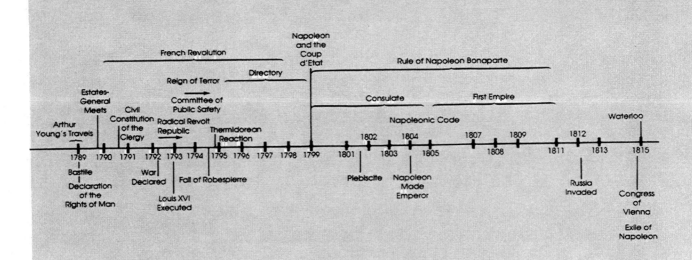

THE FRENCH
REVOLUTION AND THE
ENLIGHTENED DESPOTISM
OF NAPOLEON

CHAPTER 6

THE FRENCH REVOLUTION

May 5, 1789	Estates-General convene at Versailles
June 17, 1789	Third Estate declares itself the National Assembly
June 20, 1789	Oath of the Tennis Court
July 14, 1789	Storming of the Bastille
July-August 1789	The Great Fear in the countryside
August 4, 1789	National Assembly abolishes feudal privileges
August 27, 1789	National Assembly issues Declaration of the Rights of Man
October 5, 1789	Parisian women march on Versailles and force royal family to return to Paris
November 1789	National Assembly confiscates church lands
July 1790	Civil Constitution of the Clergy establishes a national church
	Louis XVI reluctantly agrees to accept a constitutional monarchy
June 1791	Arrest of the royal family while attempting to flee France
August 1791	Declaration of Pillnitz by Austria and Prussia
April 1792	France declares war on Austria

August 1792	Parisian mob attacks palace and takes Louis XVI prisoner
September 1792	September Massacres National Convention declares France a republic and abolishes monarchy
January 1793	Execution of Louis XVI
February 1793	France declares war on Britain, Holland, and Spain Revolts in provincial cities
March 1793	Bitter struggle in the National Convention between Girondists and the Mountain
April–June 1793	Robespierre and the Mountain organize the Committee of Public Safety and arrest Girondist leaders
September 1793	Price controls to aid the sans-culottes and mobilize war effort
1793–1794	Reign of Terror in Paris and the provinces
Spring 1794	French armies victorious on all fronts
July 1794	Execution of Robespierre Thermidorean Reaction begins
1795–1799	The Directory
1795	End of economic controls and suppression of the sans-culottes
1799	Napoleon defeats Austrian armies in Italy and returns triumphant to Paris
1798	Austria, Great Britain, and Russia form the Second Coalition against France
1799	Napoleon overthrows the Directory and seizes power

THE FRENCH REVOLUTION

The French Revolution is a complex phenomenon with several stages and several phases. Supporters see it as a necessary rebellion against tyranny and aristocratic privilege. Critics see it as the unleashing of mob feeling and rabble behavior destructive of order and stability. Its causes were many:

Long range—state inefficiency buttressed by entrenched privilege. Opportunities for social mobility were negligible for the educated and wealthy bourgeoisie. They could not rise in the social scale or hold the highest state offices. Nobles held the highest offices in the church and in the **parlements** (law courts). They were exempt from taxation in the **ancien régime**. In short, they formed a closed and socially privileged caste.

Short range—a government financial crisis. The government was bankrupt. Fifty percent of its expenditure was used to pay interest on the growing debt, and less than 20 percent financed general maintenance of the state (25 percent maintained the military and 6 percent, the upkeep of Versailles).

The First Phase

In order to remedy the problem of debt, Louis XVI agrees to call the **Estates-General**, the national assembly, which had not convened since 1614. The summoning initiates the first act of the revolution, as each estate draws up its **cahier de doléances**, or list of grievances. The subsequent acts are outlined below.

Act I. The nobility insist that Louis XVI call the Estates-General if he wishes to levy a **taille**, or land tax, on those who have been legally exempt from paying taxes. Members of the nobility are intending to reassert their political power, which was lost under Louis XIV, and are resurging under the recall of the **parlements** by Louis XVI. Thus the aristocracy has engineered the first act of the revolution. The Estates-General will convene as it did in 1614 with three separate estates, each having one vote.

Act II. The Third Estate has twice as many representatives as those of the First Estate (the clergy) and the Second Estate (the nobility) combined. They chafe at the arrangement of separate estates with a single vote as an insult to the economic power they hold. On June 20, 1789, representatives of the Third Estate and some liberal nobles having declared themselves the National Assembly, move to a large indoor tennis court where they take the **Tennis Court oath**, swearing never to disband until they have written a new constitution for France. The bourgeoisie have thus engineered the second act, for the king capitulates and orders all representatives to sit in one assembly with one vote per person. In this assembly the bourgeoisie are on an equal social footing with the nobility.

Act III. Unrest is high in Paris. Poor grain harvests and high bread prices increase agitation. Meanwhile, Louis XVI has dismissed some liberal ministers and has begun summoning a mercenary army to Versailles. The Parisian workers, known as **sans-culottes**, think it necessary to arm themselves for impending trouble. They storm the **Bastille**, a fortress where arms and gunpowder are kept. Panic ensues. The governor of the prison and ninety-eight people are killed. Louis XVI recalls his ministers and disperses the troops. The Parisian mob has engineered the third act. They have saved the National Assembly from being dismissed by the king.

Act IV. In the summer of 1789, rumors spread that the aristocrats are hiring outlaws to harm the peasants. The rumors, known as the **Great Fear**, are unfounded. Nevertheless, the peasants burn manor houses and manorial records in a state of uncontrolled violence. Liberal-thinking aristocrats and members of the bourgeoisie meet secretly at Versailles on the **night of August 4** to declare feudalism abolished in France. The peasants have engineered the fourth and final act of the first phase of the French Revolution. No longer will the peasants have to pay fees (**banalités**) to their lord for hunting, justice, or salt. Nor will they be obliged to work on the roads (**corvées**). As religious Catholics they become forces for conservatism and stability.

The crowning act of the first phase of the revolution is the issuance of the **Declaration of the Rights of Man and Citizen** by the National Assembly on August 27, 1789.

The Second Phase

In the second phase of the French Revolution, women march to Versailles in protest over rising bread prices. A constitutional monarchy is established, but Louis XVI is opposed and tries to flee. He is captured and eventually guillotined when the **Committee of Public Safety** is established under **Robespierre** (1758-1794) during the third and radical phase of the revolution. The Legislative Assembly, dominated by the **Jacobins**, has declared war on Louis's allies Austria and Prussia, hoping to save the revolution from conservatives who wish to restore the ancien régime. The assembly is replaced by a National Convention. It decrees a **lévee en masse** to make the resources of the nation available to fight the war. And in the face of economic chaos, it establishes the **law of the maximum**, which fixes prices on bread and other essential items to curb inflation.

The Third Phase   In the third phase, Robespierre's death at the hands of those who fear his extremism ushers in the period known as the **Directory** (1795-1799), a short-lived government dominated by corrupt leaders who ignore the economic problems facing the country and continue to wage war.

NAPOLEON IN POWER

In the final phase, in a November 1799 **coup d'état**, a young general, **Napoleon Bonaparte** (1769-1821) heads the troops that overthrow the Directory and establishes a new form of republic, the Consulate. Napoleon centralizes authority by setting up the machinery of government headed by a Council of State with himself as chief administrator. He rules as first consul, and then as emperor in 1804. He appoints prefects who administer local government along with the mayors, his appointees as well, and consolidates his power even further with tight censorship of press and news. How shall his rule be evaluated?

Napoleon's Domestic Policies   To his credit, Napoleon undid to some extent the great tactical blunder of the Revolution—the establishment of a national church, with priests chosen by voters and the clergy required to take a loyalty oath to the new civil constitution. French Catholics had turned against the Revolution. The pope himself had condemned it.

Napoleon and Pope Pius VII signed the **Concordat** (1801), which made Catholicism the "preferred religion" of France. Napoleon nominated the bishops, who were consecrated by the pope. The French leader recognized the social power of religion as a unifying force for his country.

He also understood the importance of allegiance to the state and created a Legion of Honor to reward middle-class abilities. "It is with trinkets that mankind is governed," he allegedly said. And by setting up lycées, elite secondary schools, and instituting primary schools, all of which were controlled by the University of France, another of his creations, Napoleon was able to direct the curriculum to ensure loyal citizens.

And for his loyal citizens he maintained the principles of legal equality in the **Code Napoléon**, the codes of law that he drew up. The principles were brief and clear in the areas of civil, criminal, commercial, and family law, among others.

DOCUMENT-BASED PARAGRAPH EXERCISE

Read the excerpt below and describe in a written paragraph the nature of conjugal relationships prescribed in the Code Napoléon. Consider whether Napoleon was fulfilling or aborting any ideals of the French Revolution.

EXCERPT FROM CODE NAPOLÉON

CHAPTER VI.

Of the Rights and Respective Duties of Husband and Wife

212. Husband and wife mutually owe to each other fidelity, aid, and assistance

213. The husband owes protection to his wife, the wife obedience to her husband.

214. The wife is obliged to live with her husband, and to follow him wherever he thinks proper to dwell. . . .

215. The wife can do no act in law without the authority of her husband, even where she shall be a public trader. . . .

Napoleon's Foreign Policy

In the realm of foreign policy, Napoleon conducted a series of campaigns against shifting coalitions of foreign powers. However, he was able to secure alliance with Russia by the **Treaty of Tilsit** (1807). His downfall came with his determination to defeat England at any cost. His **Continental System** (a blockade against foreign trade with England) failed. He failed, too, in conquering Spain in the **Peninsular War** (1808–1813) and in successfully invading Russia after it withdrew from the Continental System. Napoleon's army was subsequently defeated at Waterloo, and as a result the Napoleonic Empire crumbled.

MULTIPLE-CHOICE QUESTIONS

1. Which of the following factors precipitated the convening of the Estates-General in 1789?
   a. the storming of the Bastille
   b. the government's massive debt
   c. peasant rejection of increased manorial dues
   d. royal abolition of guild controls
   e. religious warfare between Catholics and Huguenots

2. Which of the following would serve as proof that members of the bourgeoisie were the direct beneficiaries of the French Revolutions?
   a. Declaration of the Rights of Man and Citizen
   b. law of the maximum
   c. Declaration of the night of August 4, 1789
   d. establishment of the Committee of Public Safety
   e. Civil Constitution of the Clergy

3. "They demanded economic reforms and their popular uprising was successful. After several violent incidents at Versailles, the King agreed to assure a regular supply of bread to Paris . . . and also agreed to return to live in Paris under popular surveillance." The event referred to is
   a. the Tennis Court oath
   b. Bastille Day
   c. the October women's march
   d. the night of August 4, 1789
   e. passage of the law of the maximum

4. By refusing to register royal decrees of the French king, this body could, in effect, veto the king's law and serve as a legislature. The body referred to in this statement is the
   a. National Assembly
   b. Estates-General
   c. Parlement of Paris
   d. Committee of Public Safety
   e. Third Estate

5. Which of the following groups in France were most opposed to the Civil Constitution of the Clergy?
   a. deists
   b. liberal aristocrats
   c. bourgeoisie
   d. peasants
   e. Jacobins

6. In May 1789, the chief aim of the representatives of the Third Estate was to
   a. secure political power commensurate with their economic power
   b. establish a constitutional republic
   c. abolish feudalism and seigneurial dues
   d. expand France's borders into eastern Europe
   e. set up a voting system based on universal male suffrage

7. Which of the following facts could be used to charge that Napoleon was *not* a true son of the French Revolution?
   a. Napoleon allowed the peasants to keep all the land gained during the Revolution.
   b. Government officials were chosen on the basis of merit.
   c. Under the Code Napoléon, a body of law concerning contracts, leases, and debts was developed.
   d. Napoleon encouraged the return of some of the emigrés and restored their titles.
   e. Napoleon established a state education system.

8. Hearing church bells, Napoleon was supposed to have said, "What an impression that makes upon the ears of the credulous!" Coupled with the Concordat of 1801, one might conclude that Napoleon recognized
   a. the social importance of religion
   b. the pope as the highest authority in France
   c. the need to tolerate Protestants and Jews
   d. that the church had to be compensated for confiscated lands
   e. that the government was required to pay a tenth of its income to the church

9. The purpose of Napoleon's Continental System was to
   a. prevent trade between England and other European countries
   b. share power with Russia on the Continent
   c. achieve a balance of trade between French imports and exports
   d. weaken the Prussian army through a series of military defeats
   e. create a common market with a single currency

10. The downfall of Napoleon I can be attributed to
    a. his establishment of the French Empire
    b. his granting of amnesty to a hundred thousand emigrés
    c. his support of a national spy and surveillance system
    d. his June 1812 invasion of Russia
    e. his agreement to the Treaty of Tilsit

PRACTICE ESSAY QUESTIONS

Use the questions below to practice essay writing. For each question write an essay that includes an introductory thesis, a body of supporting and/or illustrative data, and a conclusion.

1. "The essential cause of the French Revolution was a 'wounded sense of dignity' on the part of the members of the bourgeoisie." Defend or refute this statement with specific examples to support your position.
2. Is Robespierre best described as a zealous tyrant or a passionate democrat? In answering this question, trace the highlights in his career from 1789 to 1794.
3. To what extent did Napoleon fulfill the ideals of the French Revolution, and to what extent did he abort them?
4. Is there justification for the term *French Revolution*? How and in what ways was the period 1789-1815 a watershed in Western European history?
5. To what extent did women benefit from the French Revolution?

ESSAY WRITING TIPS: EXAMINING DOCUMENTS FOR TENSION AND TONE, FOR SIMILARITIES AND OPPOSING VIEWPOINTS, AND FOR MAKING INFERENCES

Below is a document-based question with the accompanying selected and edited documents. Following is a model essay. After reading the DBQ and the documents, read the essay closely for the ways in which it points out

1. tension, or disagreements in authors' viewpoints
2. the tone of the documents
3. groupings among documents that have similar or dissimilar positions and for the ways the essay makes inferences and/or analyzes reasons for positions taken in the documents

As you read the essay, mark it up, underlining and noting the special characteristics that you are looking for. Compare your notes with the evaluation that follows the essay.

DOCUMENT-BASED ESSAY QUESTION

On the basis of the accompanying documents, describe the role and status of women in pre- and postrevolutionary France. To what extent did women benefit from the French Revolution during the period 1789-1794?

1. "I am not out to draw attention to myself, but I swear that I do want to shatter our conventions and guarantee women the justice that men refuse to them as if on a whim."

Mme de Montenelos, editor of Journal des Dames, *1774*

2. "We ask for Enlightenment and jobs, not to usurp men's authority, but to rise in their esteem and to have the means of living safe from misfortune."

Petition of the women of Tiers to the king, January 1789

3. "Women, at least as things now stand, children, foreigners, in short those who contribute nothing to the public establishment, should have no direct influence on the government."

Abbé Sieyes, July 1789

4. "Why should people prone to pregnancy and passing indispositions be barred from the exercise of rights no one would dream of denying those who have gout or catch cold easily?"

Condorcet, 1790

5. "If our strength had equalled our courage, we would, like you, have hastened to take up weapons and would have shared with you the glory of having won our freedom. But it took stronger arms than ours to defeat the enemies of the Constitution; our weakness has prevented us from taking part in this Revolution. We content ourselves with admiring your efforts."

Free speech by women of Epinal, July 1790

6. "All women are born free and remain equal to men in rights. . . . The aim of all political associations is the preservation of the natural and inalienable rights of women and men. . . . The nation is the union of women and men. . . . Law is the expression of the general will; all female and male citizens have the right to participate, or through their representatives, in its formation."

Olympe de Gouges, Rights of Woman, *September 1790*
(Olympe de Gouges, a playwright, was executed by the Jacobin government in 1793. She was a supporter of the Girondin cause. The semiofficial Feuille du Salut Public *wrote: "It seems that the law has punished this conspirator for having forgotten the virtues that suit her sex.")*

7. "All the lessons taught in public schools will aim particularly to train girls for the virtues of domestic life and to teach them the skills useful in raising a family."

Talleyrand, "Projet de décret," September 1791

8. "Citizens, legislators, you have given men a Constitution; now they enjoy all the rights of free beings; but women are very far from sharing these glories. Women count for nothing in the political system. We ask for primary assemblies and, as the Constitution is based on the Rights of Man, we now demand the full exercise of these rights for ourselves."

Address to the National Convention from women from the Beaurepaire section, summer 1793

9. "There is another aspect of women's associations that seems dangerous. If we take into account the fact that the political education of men is still at its very beginnings, that all the principles are not yet developed, and that we

still stammer over the word ''liberty,'' then how much less enlightened are women, whose moral education has been practically non-existent. . . . women, by their constitution, are open to an exaltation (delusive euphoria) which could be ominous in public life. The interests of the state would soon be sacrificed to all the kinds of disruptions and disorder that hysteria can produce.''

Report to the National Convention by André Amar, Committee of General Security, October 1793

10. ''Women! Do you want to be Republicans? . . . Be simple in your dress, hardworking in your homes, never go to the popular assemblies wanting to speak there. But let your occasional presence there encourage your children. Then *la Patrie* will bless you, for you will have done for it what it has a right to expect from you.''

Feuille du Salut Public (semiofficial publication), November 1793

11. ''I am often annoyed to see women arguing over privileges that do not suit them; even the title of ''author'' seems ridiculous for a woman to me. However gifted they may be in these fields, they ought not to display their talents to the public.''

Mme Roland (wife of the Girondin minister of the interior; she was executed in the fall of 1793 by the Jacobin government)

12. ''Woe indeed to those women who, scorning the glorious destiny to which they are called, express, in order to free themselves of their duties, the absurd ambition to take over men's responsibilities.''

Mme Tallien, April 1794

Essay

The role and status of women were subjects for discourse during the early phases of the French Revolution. Views on proper activities and position in society were polarized, and support for and against changing roles cut across gender lines. If women benefited at all, it would be in a raised consciousness that heightened their insistence on change.

Economic forces impelled some women to challenge prescribed family roles that Talleyrand praised (document 7). A petition by women of the Third Estate to the king even before the calling of the Estates-General in May 1789 drove the economic point home that they wished "to have the means of living safe from misfortune" (document 2). They couched their request in moderate terms—careful to point out that they were not taking over from men, not "usurp[ing] men's authority." Such soft tones were echoed in a speech by women of Epinal in 1790 (document 5). Content to stand on the sidelines, these women praised the revolutionaries and confessed their own physical weakness. Whether they saw a relationship between physical and mental inadequacies is unclear. One might suspect they did.

On the other hand, there were voices that must have appeared strident to persons like Abbé Sieyes and André Amar. These men were adamant in their view that women had no rightful place in the political arena (documents 3, 9). Their stunted moral development and erratic physical makeup by necessity excluded women from political activity. In likely agreement with Talleyrand, these men believed women were best fitted for domestic roles.

Not so, some rising voices claimed. Educated women—an editor and a playwright, as well as ordinary women—stood firm. Shaped by Enlightenment views of natural rights, they called for equal participation of women in the political process, directly and indirectly through their representatives (documents 1, 6 and 8). They even found an ally among the famous philosophes. Condorcet agreed that the natural cycles of women's bodily changes in no way disbarred them from public participation in government (document 4).

But as some men crossed the gender lines on this issue, so too did some women. Upper-class women like Mme Roland and Mme Tallien were distressed to see women entering the political battle and the public arena (documents 11, 12). They agreed with the party line that women maintain low profiles and stick to household duties in general (document 10). It is likely that these women had economic security and lacked professional ambitions. Perhaps it was hard for them to see the economic situations and intellectual dreams of those like Mme de Montenelos and Olympe de Gouges.

In any event, it appears that there was no breakthrough in conventional roles and status for women from 1789 through Robespierre's takeover. But women may have benefited nevertheless. The dialogue and debate most likely drew attention to the issue of women's rights and roles in society. Without legal and economic change, however, it is possible to argue that the benefits were nonexistent, in any practical sense.

Evaluation

The essay is worthy of study. It illustrates the ways in which documents may be examined for tension (women disagreeing with women; men disagreeing with men) and for tone (consider, in particular, the pique and annoyance of Mme Roland and Mme Tallien).

It also illustrates the ways in which documents can be woven together—i.e., relationships can be established among the documents by Talleyrand, Amar, and Abbé Sieyes. It is important to look for similarities in documents as well as opposing viewpoints in other sources, and then to group them.

Last, a student—like the historian—can make inferences and can analyze. Why was it that Mme Roland and Mme Tallien had such little sympathy for the women's cause? Did their own economic status shield them from the problems and concerns of other women? And why was Condorcet a supporter? Had he applied gender stereotypes to the test of analytical reason and found them wanting?

The historian, like the detective, tries to fit the pieces of the puzzle together. There is much we can never know for sure. Yet by examining the evidence and clarifying our suppositions, we are more likely to come closer to what may be true.

IDENTIFICATIONS

Ancien régime (Old Regime)—France prior to the French Revolution.

Banalités—Fees that peasants were obligated to pay landlords for the use of the village mill, bakeshop, and winepress.

Bastille—The political prison and armory stormed on July 14, 1789, by Parisian city workers alarmed by the king's concentration of troops at Versailles.

Cahier de doléances–List of grievances that each Estate drew up in preparation for the summoning of the Estates-General in 1789.

Code Napoléon–The codification and condensation of laws assuring legal equality and uniformity in France.

Committee of Public Safety–The leaders under Robespierre who organized the defenses of France, conducted foreign policy, and centralized authority during the period 1792-1795.

Concordat (1801)–Napoleon's arrangement with Pope Pius VII to heal religious division in France with a united Catholic church under bishops appointed by the government.

Continental System–Napoleon's efforts to block foreign trade with England by forbidding importation of British goods into Europe.

Corvées–Roadwork; an obligation of peasants to landowners.

Coup d'état–Overthrow of those in power.

Declaration of the Rights of Man and Citizen (August 27, 1789)–Document that embodied the liberal revolutionary ideals and general principles of the philosophes' writings.

Directory (1795-1799)–The five-man executive committee that ruled France in its own interests as a republic after Robespierre's execution and prior to Napoleon's coming to power.

Estates-General–The French national assembly summoned in 1789 to remedy the financial crisis and correct abuses of the ancien régime.

Great Fear–The panic and insecurity that struck French peasants in the summer of 1789 and led to their widespread destruction of manor houses and archives.

Jacobins–The dominant group in the National Convention in 1793 who replaced the Girondins. It was headed by Robespierre.

Law of the maximum–The fixing of prices on bread and other essentials under Robespierre's rule.

Levée en masse–The creation, under the Jacobins, of a citizen army with support from young and old, heralding the emergence of modern warfare.

Napoleon Bonaparte (1769-1821)–Consul and later emperor of France (1799-1815), who established several of the reforms (Code Napoléon) of the French Revolution during his dictatorial rule.

Night of August 4, 1789–Date of the declaration by liberal noblemen of the National Assembly at a secret meeting to abolish the feudal regime in France.

Parlement–Law court staffed by nobles that could register or refuse to register a king's edict.

Peninsular War (1808-1813)–Napoleon's long-drawn-out war with Spain.

Robespierre (1758-1794)–Jacobin leader during the Reign of Terror (1793-1794).

Sans-culottes–A reference to Parisian workers who wore loose-fitting trousers rather than the tight-fitting breeches worn by aristocratic men.

Taille–A direct tax from which most French nobles were exempt.

Tennis Court oath–Declaration mainly by members of the Third Estate not to disband until they had drafted a constitution for France (June 20, 1789).

Treaty of Tilsit (1807)–Agreement between Napoleon and Czar Alexander I in which Russia became an ally of France and Napoleon took over the lands of Prussia west of the Elbe as well as the Polish provinces.

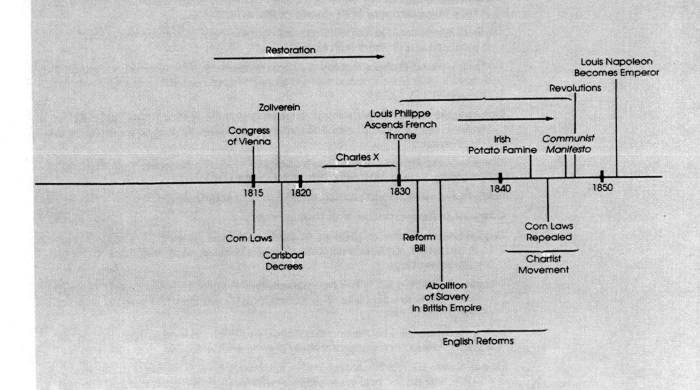

REACTION AND CONTINUING REVOLUTIONS, 1815-1850

CHAPTER 7

THE REVOLUTIONS OF 1848

February	Revolt in Paris against Louis Philippe's "bourgeois monarchy"; Louis Philippe abdicates; proclamation of a provisional republic
February–June	Establishment and rapid growth of government-sponsored workshops in France
March 3	Hungarians under Kossuth demand autonomy from Austrian Empire
March 13	Uprising of students and workers in Vienna; Metternich flees to London
March 19–21	Frederick William IV of Prussia is forced to salute the bodies of slain revolutionaries in Berlin and agrees to a liberal constitution and merger into a new German state
March 20	Ferdinand I of Austria abolishes serfdom and promises reforms
March 26	Workers in Berlin issue a series of socialist demands
April 22	French voters favor moderate republicans over radicals, 5–1
May 15	Parisian socialist workers invade the Constitutional Assembly and unsuccessfully proclaim a new revolutionary state

May 18	Frankfurt Assembly begins writing a new German constitution
June 17	Austrian army crushes working-class revolt in Prague
June 22-26	French government abolishes the national workshops, provoking an uprising, June Days: republican army defeats rebellious Parisian working class
October	Austrian army besieges and retakes Vienna from students and working-class radicals
December	Conservatives force Ferdinand I of Austria to abdicate in favor of young Francis Joseph
	Frederick William IV disbands Prussian Constituent Assembly and grants Prussia a conservative constitution
	Louis Napoleon wins a landslide victory in French presidential elections
March 1849	Frankfurt Assembly elects Frederick William IV of Prussia emperor of the new German state; Frederick William refuses and reasserts royal authority in Prussia
June-August 1849	Hapsburg and Russian forces defeat the Hungarian independence movement

THE CONGRESS OF VIENNA

The Congress of Vienna (1814-1815) tried to reestablish the balance of power in Europe after the French Revolution and the Napoleonic Wars. The architect of the Congress, **Prince Klemens von Metternich** (1773-1859) of Austria, a member of the landed nobility, wished to preserve the Europe of pre-1789. Like the political theorist **Edmund Burke** (1729-1797), he envisioned society as an organic growth of enduring traditions and institutions. Government was a partnership between those who are living, those who are dead, and those who are yet to be born. An orderly society rested upon the pillars of monarchy, aristocracy, church and a bureaucracy staffed by civil servants of the Junker class. Metternich was a foe of liberalism and nationalism, both of which threatened the aristocracy and order in the Austrian Empire. In particular, nationalism would wreak havoc in the empire, which was a patchwork quilt of diverse ethnic groupings.

Terms of the Treaty of Pans

At the congress, the **Quadruple Alliance** of great powers (Austria, Britain, Prussia, Russia) allied to restore the status quo ante and construct a balance of power. The treaty was a lenient one. Louis XVIII, a Bourbon, was restored to the French throne as king of a constitutional monarchy. And if no one power could dominate the others politically or militarily, the victors nevertheless wanted some rewards. Austria took territories in Italy, Venetia, and Lombardy, but lost others in Belgium and southern Germany. Russia obtained a small Polish kingdom, and Prussia received some of Saxony and territory in the Rhineland on France's eastern border. England received Malta, Ceylon, and the Cape of Good Hope.

Even after Napoleon's unsuccessful attempt at a second takeover of France, the second Peace of Paris was moderate, with some loss of territory and indemnity payments required of France. The aim of the congress was to protect the privileges of the European elite—the monarchs, noble landowners, and bureaucrats—against the middle and working classes and, under the principles of the **Holy Alliance**, to rule on the basis of Christian principles. The middle class was calling for representative government; the socialists for greater economic equality. Any ideas that threatened the status quo were to be vigorously suppressed.

Nationalist and revolutionary opponents emerged: in the German states, the **Burschenschaften**; in Russia, the **Decembrists**; in Italy, the **Carbonari**. Most notable, the **Carlsbad Decrees** of 1819, prompted by the assassination of a reactionary dramatist by a member of the Burschenschaften (a youth group), were a series of laws that crushed the Burschenschaften and set up rigid censorship and press control. The aim was to create a system for rooting out subversives in schools and universities. Metternich, who designed the laws, opposed the liberal reformers who dreamed of a united Germany in place of the weak confederation of thirty-nine states.

DOCUMENT-BASED READING AND STATEMENT-CORRECTION EXERCISE

Below is an excerpt from Metternich's writings, followed by a series of statements. Read the document and place a check next to those statements that can be inferred from his views. If the statement cannot be inferred, rewrite it so that it can be read as implicit in the document.

THE POLITICAL PHILOSOPHY OF METTERNICH

The Governments, having lost their balance, are frightened, intimidated, and thrown into confusion by the cries of the intermediary class of society, which, placed between the Kings and their subjects, breaks the sceptre of the monarch, and usurps the cry of the people—that class so often disowned by the people and nevertheless too much listened to. . . .

We see this intermediary class . . . applying itself to the task of persuading Kings that their rights are confined to sitting upon a throne, while those of the people are to govern, and to attack all that centuries have bequeathed as holy and worthy of man's respect—denying, in fact, the value of the past, and declaring themselves masters of the future. . . .

. . . The first and greatest concern for the immense majority of every nation is the stability of the laws, and their uninterrupted action—never their change. Therefore, let the Governments govern, let them maintain the groundwork of their institutions, both ancient and modern; for if it is at all times dangerous to touch them, it certainly would not now, in the general confusion, be wise to do so. . . .

. . . Let them not encourage by their attitude or actions the suspicion of being favourable or indifferent to error; let them not allow it to be believed that experience has lost all its rights to make way for experiments which at the least are dangerous. . . .

In short, let the great monarchs strengthen their union, and prove to the world that if it exists it is beneficent, and ensures the political peace of Europe: that it is powerful only for the maintenance of tranquillity at a time when so many attacks are directed against it; that the principles which they profess are paternal and protective, menacing only the disturbers of public tranquillity.

1. Middle-class intellectuals threaten the state. (EXAMPLE)
2. The church, the monarchy, and the government bureaucracy are institutions that have temporary value in society.
3. In times of trouble, don't tamper with the system.
4. Hierarchies are necessary for the smooth operation of society.
5. Ordinary people are ill equipped to govern.
6. Elitism generally destroys political stability.
7. Every new generation is bound to the values of past generations.
8. Political change must be based on carefully considered reflection.
9. Children should be reared as obedient, willing subjects of the state.
10. Constitutional monarchy is the most favorable form of government.

NATIONALIST AND LIBERAL UPHEAVALS

In spite of reactionary governments, liberal ideologies continued to surface. Greeks revolted against Turkish rule and won independence by 1829. In France, spontaneous protests by those wanting a republic rather than the constitutional monarchy resulted in the "bourgeois monarchy" of the citizen king Louis Philippe in 1830. While members of the bourgeoisie were pleased, the working class was disenchanted. They failed to get the right to vote.

By 1830 there were tiny fractures in Metternich's concert of Europe. In addition to Greek independence and the "bourgeois monarchy" of Louis Philippe, Belgium received its independence. Seeds of reform throughout Europe planted by the Napoleonic era were beginning to sprout.

ENGLAND: SOCIAL CLASS CONFLICTS

A similar split between working and middle classes occurred in England. At first the two groups were allied in their efforts to wrest power from the landowning aristocracy. Radicals like **Jeremy Bentham** (1748-1832) and **John Stuart Mill** (1806-1873) were opposed to the exclusive power held by the great noble families elected to Parliament by depopulated boroughs (the so-called **rotten boroughs**). Bentham, the father of utilitarianism, or the belief in the greatest good for the greatest number, and Mill wanted manhood suffrage, secret voting, equal electoral districts, and payment of members of Parliament.

The **Reform Bill of 1832** did away with the rotten boroughs. The wealthy and well-to-do middle class in the cities and counties received the vote. Ministers were responsible to the House of Commons rather than to the king. Hereafter the monarch would reign and the House of Commons would govern.

Political and Social Reforms

Working-class supporters for reform felt cheated. The 1832 Reform Bill, which was not a democratic measure, enabled only one man in seven to vote. Nevertheless, in the 1830s, some new legislation served the working class in England: the **Factory Act**, public works programs, police organization, and money grants to schools. The **Poor Law of 1834**, however, restricted the number of the poverty-stricken who were eligible for aid. Disappointed, however, with the reforms, a working-class movement, known as Chartism, formed, that sought to win universal male suffrage—but that goal was not attained until the passage of two franchise bills, in 1867 and 1884. In the mean-

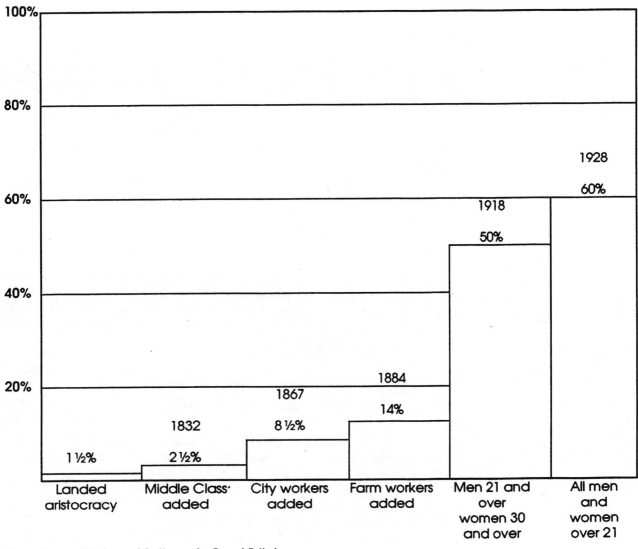

Steps Toward Universal Suffrage in Great Britain

while, however, the **Test Act** was repealed, the **Catholic Emancipation Bill** was passed, **slavery** was abolished in the British Empire, and the **Corn Laws** were repealed.

REVOLUTIONS OF 1848

But if England was avoiding revolution by providing doses of democracy, the same is not true for countries on the Continent. In the year 1848, the forces for liberalism and, in Germany and Italy, the forces for nationalism as well as liberalism resisted the conservative regimes that thwarted change.

DOCUMENT-BASED ESSAY QUESTION

The year of revolution—1848—began in France. Using the documents below, write an essay identifying the French social groups seeking charges. Describe their revolutionary aims.

FROM A CAMPAIGN SPEECH BY AUGUSTE LEDRU-ROLLIN, JULY 1841

The sovereignty of the people . . . what has become of this sovereignty? It has disappeared from the realm of facts. Today the people are a herd guided by a few privileged beings who are called electors, and then still by a few privileged people who are given the title of deputies. And if these people who are not represented, rises in order to claim their rights, they are thrown into prison. Electoral reform is the first step to take. This reform must be so radical, so that every citizen may be an elector; so that the deputy will belong to the nation, and not to wealth.

FROM *WORKERS' ORGANIZATION*, BY LOUIS BLANC, 1847

But does not the poor man have a right to better himself? Rights, considered in an abstract manner, are the mirage which since 1789 has deluded the people. We want a government which intervenes in industry because in a situation where loans are made only to the rich, there is need of a social banker who will lend to the poor.

FROM SPEECH TO THE CHAMBER OF DEPUTIES BY ALEXIS DE TOCQUEVILLE, JANUARY 1848

Look at what is happening among the working classes who at present I admit are tranquil. Do you not see that there are spreading bit by bit in their midst opinions and ideas which are not aimed at overturning this or that law, ministry, or government, but society itself. Do you not see that bit by bit it is being said among them that everything located above them is incapable and unworthy of governing them; that the distribution of property made until now in the world is unjust; that property rests on bases which are not equitable?

Repression and Revolution in France

On February 22, 1848, the French government opposed and forbade a political banquet of republican leaders. Rioting in Paris brought down the "bourgeois monarchy" of King Louis Philippe and his prime minister **François Guizot** (1787-1874). In the confusion, **Louis Napoleon Bonaparte** (1808-1873) was elected president of the short-lived Second Republic (1848-1851), which he overthrew to establish the Second Empire (1852) and assume the title of Napoleon III.

The Spread of Revolution

Representative government, constitutional rights, and *liberty* were the inflammatory words provoking soldiers' shots and then the erection of barricades in Vienna, Berlin, Milan, and Venice. In Prussia, **Frederick William IV** (1840-1861) promised constitutional reforms. Economic reforms as a result of the **Zollverein**, or tariff union, had been improving life since 1818. A National Assembly convened in Frankfurt to hammer out the laws for a united Germany. In Hungary a constitutional regime was also set up and a free press and national guard were allowed. Other areas under Austrian control demanded autonomy: Czechs, Croats, Romanians, and the Italians in Milan and Venice.

Results of 1848   Yet 1848 was the year that failed to turn in the direction of liberal and constitutional reform. Why? In brief, the consolidation among the opposition was temporary. Middle-class and working-class allies against the aristocratic elite had conflicting aims. The solid bourgeoisie and the landowning peasantry rebelled against the working-class demands for complete political *and* economic democracy. Socialist demands (to be discussed in the next chapter) split the fragile alliance of the revolutionaries. Their weakness enabled the reactionaries to work together to suppress the upheavals. For example, Russian forces came to the aid of the Austrian emperor Francis Joseph to destroy the radicals in Vienna and the revolutionaries in Hungary. Still, Metternich was ousted from power. The defeated forces had learned a few lessons, however, even while losing their idealism. The forces of nationalism, socialism, and liberalism would continue to be key issues in the national and class struggles throughout the century.

MULTIPLE-CHOICE QUESTIONS

1. The main theme of European politics after the fall of Napoleon in 1815 was
    a. the struggle between dynastic legitimacy and the forces of nationalism and liberalism
    b. the establishment of a common market with common currency and an international bank
    c. the conflict between socialists who wanted total abolition of private property and those whose key aim was universal suffrage
    d. welfare provisions for the poor and recognition of the labor unions of urban artisans
    e. the undermining of the balance of power politics in favor of German hegemony

2. Metternich was a strong believer in
    a. freedom of the press
    b. university censorship
    c. separation of church and state
    d. national autonomy
    e. government by meritocracy

3. Which of the following was the key aim of the British Corn Laws in the early 1800s?
    a. to export grain at cheaper prices to continental Europe
    b. to weaken the power of the middle class in finance and banking
    c. to improve the production and quality of British grain
    d. to protect the interests of British grain producers
    e. to set up a common market in grain and foodstuff production in Western Europe

4. The destruction of revolutionary movements in central Europe in 1848 was largely the result of
    a. the alliance between workers and aristocrats
    b. English military assistance on the Continent
    c. the withdrawal of middle-class support when Germany was unified
    d. the divisions among national groups, each willing to deny rights of the others
    e. widespread recognition that only legitimate dynasties could ensure justice and order

5. The phenomenon of "rotten boroughs" in England in the nineteenth century can best be attributed to
    a. environmental waste and pollution
    b. plague and disease
    c. shifts in population as industrial cities grew
    d. religious segregation of Anglicans and Dissenters
    e. the collapse of the Chartist movement

6. The struggle for mastery in Germany in the first half of the nineteenth century occurred between which two countries?
    a. Hungary and Austria
    b. Russia and Denmark
    c. Poland and Saxony
    d. Prussia and Bohemia
    e. Prussia and Austria

7. In the cartoon below, who is the individual whose "candle" is being snuffed out by a symbol of revolutionary force in 1848?

Cartoon by John Leech,
March 1848

    a. Louis Blanc
    b. Charles X
    c. the poet Lamartine
    d. the citizen king Louis Philippe
    e. Louis Napoleon Bonaparte

8. Which of the following was not a demand of the Chartists in England?
   a. universal adult suffrage
   b. equal electoral districts
   c. annual Parliaments
   d. vote by ballot
   e. abolition of the property qualification for members of Parliament

9. To pass the Reform Bill of 1832 in England required which of the following?
   a. the king's threat to create new seats in the House of Lords
   b. pitched battles in London on the eve of passage
   c. a legislative act to ensure that women be denied the vote even with extension of the franchise
   d. the union of the Whigs and Tories into a single party
   e. amendments to the bill that restricted parliamentary terms of office

10. "The crown is no crown. The crown which a Hohenzollern could accept . . . is not created by an Assembly born of a revolutionary seed. . . . It must be a crown set with the seal of the Almighty." The author of this quotation, Frederick William, rejected all the following EXCEPT for
    a. the position of emperor in a German constitutional monarchy
    b. a liberal document promulgated by the Frankfurt Assembly in 1849
    c. the principle of rule based on divine-right monarchy
    d. the forces of political change spawned by the French Revolution
    e. a head-on collision with Austria over German leadership

PRACTICE ESSAY QUESTIONS

Use the questions below to practice essay writing. For each question write an essay that includes an introductory thesis, a body of supporting and/or illustrative data, and a conclusion.

1. How "liberal" were the liberal reforms in Great Britain in the first half of the nineteenth century?
2. To what extent was 1848 a triumph for liberalism? To what extent was it a defeat?
3. How pragmatic were the peacemakers of Europe in 1815, and how idealistic were they?
4. "The problem with France between 1815 and 1848 was that its rulers ignored the French Revolution while its citizenry did not." Assess the validity of this statement.
5. What factors contributed to the failure to achieve German unification in 1848? Which factor was the most important?

ESSAY-WRITING TIPS: DEFENDING A THESIS

Often students believe that there is one right answer to a history question. In fact, there may be several, depending on how terms are defined and how much weight is given to different factors. In writing an essay, you should be able to see the other side of the position that you are taking and to concede that it exists. When you make such a "concession statement," you are acknowledging an opponent's viewpoint, even if you have decided that it has little merit.

The two essays below address the question: "How liberal were the liberal reforms in Great Britain in the first half of the nineteenth century?" The essays have opposing viewpoints that they attempt to defend. The purpose of this "tip" is to show how materials can be cited and arranged to defend a thesis. After you read the essays, write a paragraph in which you consider: Is one essay better than the other? What makes a better essay?

Essay A

Early nineteenth-century Britain (1815–1848) mirrored to a large degree the political conservatism of continental Europe. In spite of the social and economic dislocations spawned by industrialization, the British upper classes maintained a tight hold on political and economic privilege. This is not to say that the landed aristocracy held power exclusively, for they were forced to grant some concessions in the Reform Bill of 1832 and in the 1848 repeal of the Corn Laws, symbol of their landholding power. But power—political, social, and economic—was still narrowly held by the aristocracy and the newly emerging industrial class of factory owners.

As for the urban workers, they received neither the vote nor representation in Parliament. Some factory legislation temporarily improved the working conditions of women and children. These were scant benefits, however, for a working class that had allied with the middle class for extension of the vote and repeal of the Corn Laws.

In the tradition of "civilized people," the working class had sought enfranchisement through peaceful and constitutional means. Working-class leaders organized the Chartist movement, which sought to petition Parliament for electoral reforms and extension of the franchise. In spite of the fact that the workers amassed millions of signatures, those in power ignored their requests.

In short, early nineteenth-century *liberal reform* is at best a euphemism for maintenance of power among the old and the newly rich and powerful in the developing industrial England of the nineteenth century.

Essay B

How "liberal" were the liberal reforms in Great Britain in the first half of the nineteenth century? They were decidedly liberal. The underpinnings of the landholding aristocracy's political control and economic privilege weakened significantly with the Reform Bill of 1832 and the repeal of the Corn Laws in 1848, symbol of aristocratic power. *Liberal*, of course, is being defined in its early eighteenth-century classical sense, as providing political representation to the wealthy and propertied commoners (bourgeoisie) and economic freedom from government restraints on free trade. *Liberal* is not being defined in the late-nineteenth- and twentieth-century sense of the term, with its assumption that the government must legislate for the economic underdog. However, even in the first half of the nineteenth century, some laws were passed to improve working hours and conditions for women and children factory laborers—a harbinger of democratic liberal reform. In essence, however, this essay argues that a newly emerging social class, the industrial bourgeoisie, pressured successfully for political change—greater political representation in Parliament—and economic change—elimination of barriers that artificially maintained the high cost of grain. Improvement in the lives of urban and agricultural workers was not part of the classical liberal agenda, and it would be ahistorical to fault those wise reforms in the early nineteenth century for not meeting the needs and goals of the "unwashed masses."

IDENTIFICATIONS

Jeremy Bentham (1748-1832)–British theorist and philosopher who proposed utilitarianism, the principle that governments should operate on the basis of utility, or the greatest good for the greatest number.

Edmund Burke (1729-1797)–Member of British Parliament and author of *Reflections on the Revolution in France* (1790), which criticized the underlying principles of the French Revolution and argued conservative thought.

Burschenschaften–Politically active students around 1815 in the German states proposing unification and democratic principles.

Carbonari–Italian secret societies calling for a unified Italy and republicanism after 1815.

Carlsbad Decrees (1819)–Repressive laws in the German states limiting freedom of speech and dissemination of liberal ideas in the universities.

Decembrists–Russian revolutionaries calling for constitutional reform in the early nineteenth century.

Frederick William IV (1840-1861)–King of Prussia who promised and later reneged on his promises for constitutional reforms in 1848.

François Guizot (1787-1874)–Chief minister under Louis Philippe. Guizot's repression led to the revolution of 1848.

Holy Alliance–An alliance envisioned by Alexander I of Russia by which those in power were asked to rule in accord with Christian principles.

Louis Napoleon Bonaparte (1808-1873)–Nephew of Napoleon I; he came to power as president of the Second French Republic in 1848.

Prince Klemens von Metternich (1773-1859)–Austrian member of the nobility and chief architect of conservative policy at the Congress of Vienna.

John Stuart Mill (1806-1873)–British philosopher who published *On Liberty* (1859), advocating individual rights against government intrusion, and *The Subjection of Women* (1869), on the cause of women's rights.

Poor Law of 1834–Legislation that restricted the number of poverty-stricken eligible for aid.

Quadruple Alliance–Organization, made up of Austria, Britain, Prussia, and Russia, to preserve the peace settlement of 1815; France joined in 1818.

Rotten boroughs–Depopulated areas of England that nevertheless sent representatives to Parliament.

Zollverein–Economic customs union of German states established in 1818 by Prussia and including almost all German-speaking states except Austria by 1844.

Major English Reforms, 1815-1848

Repeal of Test Act (1828)–Allowed Protestants who were not members of the Church of England to hold public office.

Catholic Emancipation Bill (1829)–Enabled Catholics to hold public office for the first time.

Reform Bill of 1832–Gave vote to all men who paid ten pounds in rent a year; eliminated the rotten boroughs.

Slavery–Abolished in the British Empire, 1833.

Factory Act–Limited children's and adolescents' workweek in textile factories, 1833.

Corn Laws–Repealed in 1846. They had imposed a tariff on imported grain and were a symbolic protection of aristocratic landholdings.

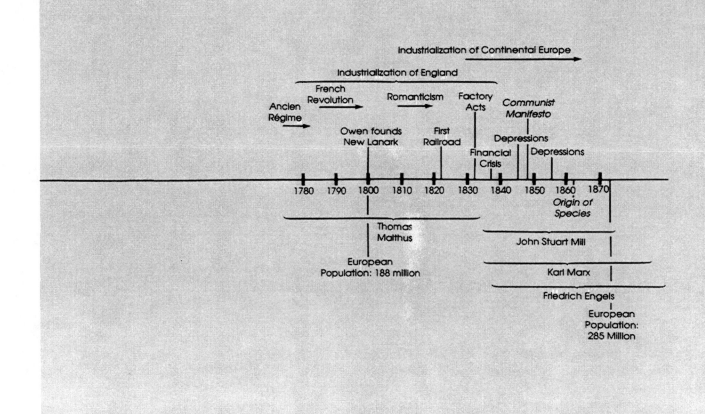

INDUSTRIALIZATION AND
THE "ISMS"

CHAPTER 8

SOCIETY IN TRANSITION

Nationalism and liberalism were two of the social forces unleashed by events in the eighteenth century. Other forces surfaced as well: socialism, Romanticism, and feminism (although this term is generally not used in texts). Elements of these forces emerged, in part, in response to the circulating ideals of the French Revolution. But the Industrial Revolution in Great Britain and in Western Europe also fostered these changes.

Industrialization, best defined as the rise of factories and the use of machinery in the production of goods, occurred first in England in the late 1700s. Most workers and their employers had to adjust to the organization and technology of factory industry. The traditional approach to the Industrial Revolution has been one of looking at inventions, factory commission reports, wages, prices, and death rates. Another perspective, from the angle of social history, examines work behavior and attitudes and tries to discover changes between preindustrial patterns of work and early industrialization.

The chart below compares the work behavior and work attitudes of artisans and factory workers in the nineteenth century. Artisans were skilled craftsmen and craftswomen. They were descendants of the medieval guild master who had possessed a definite economic skill that had been learned during a period of apprenticeship. Artisans included printers, tailors, bootmakers, bakers, coachmakers, watchmakers, butchers, carpenters, masons, weavers, and goldsmiths. They worked with simple tools and generally carried on the entire operation by themselves in a domestic setting, with family members operating as a productive economic unit, joined by apprentices and journeymen. The social class lines among work members were blurred as a result of the **domestic system**.

GENERAL COMPARISONS

Artisan	Factory Worker

Work Behavior (ways in which individuals perform work)

Artisan	Factory Worker
1. Family or intimate setting	1. Impersonal setting, large number of workers
2. Simple tools, personally owned	2. Sophisticated machinery, fast-paced
3. Recreation and work combined	3. Sole attention to work required
4. Completes entire work operation	4. Works on one part of the entire production (assembly line work)
5. Irregular rhythms of work—intense work followed by slower work periods; dictated by seasons, sunrise and sunset	5. Regular rhythms of work, punctuated by whistles and bells; long hours

Work Attitudes (variations existed and can best be inferred)

Artisan	Factory Worker
1. General pride and satisfaction in skill, product, and respect that artisan's status commanded in society	1. *Satisfaction* resulting from (a) higher pay, (b) regular employment, (c) ability to purchase meat and butter; mainly true of unskilled workers from the countryside with a rural-bred resignation to work.
2. Distress as occupational illnesses deformed artisans and health deteriorated (lead poisoning, chest diseases)	2. *Dissatisfaction* and shock and resistance, especially among those from small town craft backgrounds. The majority looked upon their work as exhausting, noisy, boring, dangerous to their health. They expressed their dissatisfaction through strikes over hours of work and vacation times, lowered production levels, frequently changed jobs, drunkenness, high rates of absenteeism, and membership in socialist parties.
3. Familial atmosphere contributed to sense of ease and pleasure in work	

The factory worker was generally an unskilled, propertyless individual of farm or craft background whose unit of employment comprised at least twenty workers; more often, upward into the hundreds. The factory workers performed their tasks on fast-paced machinery that required division of labor or an assembly line to increase production and productivity. Relationships between factory workers and their managers and owners were largely impersonal. The Industrial Revolution, then, spawned a class division of labor and also a sexual division of labor. The cult of domesticity assigned bourgeois women to the home, apart from the workplace, where lower-class women continued to sell their labor.

THE MIDDLE-CLASS ETHOS

Samuel Smiles, a popular author whose books sold widely in England through the middle decades of the nineteenth century, preached the path of economic success. Based on the excerpt below, what did Smiles believe was the key to economic success?

> The instances of men, in this and other countries, who, by dint of persevering application and energy, have raised themselves from the humblest ranks of industry to eminent positions of usefulness and influence in society, are indeed so numerous that they have long ceased to be regarded as exceptional. . . .
>
> Fortune has often been blamed for her blindness; but fortune is not so blind as men are. Those who look into practical life will find that fortune is usually on the side of the industrious, as the winds and waves are on the side of the best navigators. . . . Hence, it happens that the men who have most moved the world, have not been so much men of genius, strictly so called, as men of intense mediocre abilities, and untiring perseverance; not so often the gifted, of naturally bright and shining qualities, as those who have applied themselves diligently to their work, in whatsoever line that might lie.

PROPONENTS OF LAISSEZ-FAIRE

Smiles's prescriptions did not work for all. Nineteenth-century industrialization spawned the urban poor. Theorists **Thomas Malthus** (1776–1834) and **David Ricardo** (1772–1823) justified, however, the economic tenet of **classical liberalism**—that is, laissez-faire. Both men believed that poverty could not be ameliorated. According to Malthus, the population increases geometrically and the food supply arithmetically. Only sexual continence could remedy the problem.

Ricardo agreed. His "iron law of wages" held that an increase in the wages of the poor would only produce more mouths (babies), resulting once again in deplorable living conditions. Late-nineteenth-century social Darwinism, with its concept of "survival of the fittest," coined by **Herbert Spencer** (1820–1903), was additional ammunition for government neglect.

OPPONENTS OF LAISSEZ-FAIRE

But classical liberalism had its opponents. The utilitarians, Jeremy Bentham (1748-1832) and, later, John Stuart Mill, attacked the laissez-faire aspect of classical liberalism. Bentham argued that government should "create the greatest good for the greatest number" and play an activist role in redressing the social ills spawned by industrialization. Mill's liberalism, known as democratic or humanitarian liberalism, included the goals of universal suffrage, women's rights, universal free education, and government legislation to improve the living and working conditions of the masses. Neither Bentham nor Mill threatened private property and the private means of production. On this point, they differed with the two breeds of nineteenth-century socialists: the utopians and the Marxists.

Utopian Socialism

Utopian socialists included **Charles Fourier** (1772-1837), Henri de Saint-Simon (1760-1825), Louis Blanc (1811-1882), **Flora Tristan** (1803-1844), and Robert Owen (1771-1858). They believed that enlightened men applying reason to the ills of industrialized societies could eradicate social inequalities. They championed economic cooperation rather than competition as an underlying social value.

Marxism

Marxists–the followers of **Karl Marx** (1818-1883) influenced by the **Hegelian dialectic**–subscribed to economic laws governing historical change and development, known as **dialectical materialism**. The final stage in the series of class struggles, that between proletariat and bourgeoisie, would erupt, according to Marx, destroy bourgeois society, and result in the historically determined utopia–i.e., "an association in which the free development of each is the condition for the free development of all." The means of production would be held in common; private property would be abolished; social class distinctions would fade, uniting all in common brotherhood and sisterhood.

Marx's inflammatory message "Workers unite, you have nothing to lose but your chains" was written in the *Communist Manifesto*, by Marx and **Friedrich Engels** (1820-1895). The work was commissioned in 1848 by the German Workers Party. Called a time bomb with a delayed fuse, the manifesto would become the basis for the revolution in Russia in November 1917.

SOCIALISM AND FEMINISM

Concern for the plight of the poor, in particular the female poor, redounds in the writings of Flora Tristan, a Frenchwoman whose personal misfortunes sensitized her to the sufferings of others.

DOCUMENT-BASED QUESTION PRACTICE

Read the excerpt below from Tristan's work *L'Union Ouvrière* (1843) and summarize in writing (1) the nature of the social change that she prescribes for society, and (2) the source from which she expects change to come.

(FROM *L'UNION OUVRIÈRE* BY FLORA TRISTAN

I demand rights for women because I am convinced that all the misfortunes in the world come from the neglect and contempt in which women's natural and inalienable rights have so far been held. I demand rights for women because that is the only way they will get an education, and because on their education depends the education of men in general, and men of the lower classes in particular. I demand rights for women because that is the only way to obtain their rehabilitation in the Church, under the law, and in society, and because this preliminary rehabilitation is necessary to arrive at the rehabilitation of the workers themselves. All working class woes can be summed up in two words: poverty and ignorance; ignorance and poverty. I see only one way to get out of this labyrinth: start by educating women, because women have the responsibility for educating male and female children.

Workers, the way things stand now, you know what is going on in your home. You, man—the master—with rights over your wife, do you live contentedly with her? Tell me, are you happy? No, no, it is easy to see that, despite your rights, you are neither content nor happy. Between master and slave, there is nothing but the weariness caused by the weight of the chain that binds them together. There cannot be any happiness when the lack of liberty is felt.

Men always complain about the ill temper, the sly and secretly mean character that women reveal in almost all their relationships. Oh! I would indeed have a very poor opinion of women if, in the state of abjection in which the law and mores have maintained them, they yielded under the weight of their bonds without uttering a word. Thank God, it is not so; their protests have been continuous since the beginning of time. But, since the Declaration of the Rights of Man—a solemn act which proclaimed the neglect and contempt the new men felt for them—women's protests have taken on a tone of energy and violence which proves that the exasperation of the slave has reached a climax.

Workers, you have a good sense and one can reason with you. . . . Imagine for a moment that women are, by right, the equals of men. Well, what would happen?

ROMANTICISM

Another powerful "ism" emerged in the late nineteenth century in the writings of **J. G. Herder** (1744–1803) in Germany, and then flowered during the century. Its representatives were Goethe and the Grimm brothers in Germany; Chateaubriand, Victor Hugo, Alexandre Dumas, and some claim Jean-Jacques Rousseau as its leading light in France; and Wordsworth, Blake, Byron, Shelley, and Edmund Burke in England.

Definition   *Romanticism* is an umbrella term. It is notoriously difficult to define. Yet, for a start, it's an "ism" that refers to an aesthetic revolt that is also allied with a political philosophy. Aesthetically, it is a revolt against classical standards in art and poetry. It exalts experience in all its richness and complexity. It stresses the will, emotions, and feeling. It is also an attack against the perceived brutalization of the landscape brought about by the Industrial Revolution.

Nature is viewed as a living, organic whole, beautiful and mysterious. Romantics looked back to the Middle Ages for the genesis of national character in myths and fairy tales; they championed the individual and unique personality. Although the movement was international, its strongest roots lay in Germany.

German Romanticism

In the writings of Herder, the concept of *Volk*, or common people, emerged. Herder sought to promote a cultural nationalism that recognized the individual worth of each national entity, based on the *Volksgeist*, or spirit of a people. Later, however, this Romantic and cultural nationalism turned virulent as writers like **J. G. Fichte** (1762-1814) exalted the German spirit as more noble and purer than that of other peoples. Hitler (to be discussed later) would justify genocide in the name of protecting the purity of the "German race."

VISUAL-BASED PRACTICE ESSAY: ROMANTICISM—ANALYZING ART AS A CHALLENGE TO TRADITIONAL VALUES

Study the two paintings shown below and describe in writing how each painting (1) breaks with the neoclassical style, and (2) asserts values opposed to the political and intellectual conventions of nineteenth-century bourgeoisie.

Liberty Leading the People, *by Eugène Delacroix*

The Shipwreck, *by J. M. W. Turner*

The Clore Collection, Tate Gallery, London/Art Resource, NY.

Romanticism in Music

In music too there was a revolution. The softly sweet and organized cadences of Hayden and Mozart gave way to the thunderous passion of Beethoven. Orchestras had to be heroic in size to accommodate the theatrical visions of Berlioz and Mendelssohn.

As the Enlightenment had appealed to reason, Romanticism appealed to the human heart. Its use, however, would be heinous in the virulent nationalism of Hitler in the twentieth century. The concept of *Volksgeist*, spirit of the people, would be infused with meaning that Herder had never intended.

MULTIPLE-CHOICE QUESTIONS

1. Which of the following was a goal of early nineteenth-century liberals?
    a. universal manhood suffrage
    b. careers open to men of talent
    c. government regulation of factories and wages
    d. an established state church
    e. tariffs on goods imported from colonies

2. Which of the following was a belief shared by utopian and scientific socialists?
   a. The labor of the middle class determines the value of a product.
   b. Class struggle is the necessary means to achieve social change.
   c. Private property should be abolished.
   d. History is determined by economic laws.
   e. Within the family and society, patriarchy should shape power relations between the sexes.

3. Population when unchecked increases in a geometric ratio. Subsistence only increases in an arithmetic ratio. A slight acquaintance with the numbers will show the immensity of the first power in comparison with the second. These statements were used for which of the following purposes?
   a. to promote laissez-faire
   b. to encourage class revolution
   c. to explain working-class poverty
   d. to extend the franchise
   e. to encourage overseas investments

4. One impulse from a vernal wood
   May teach you more of man
   Of moral evil and of good
   Than all the sages can.

   The views stated in this poem are an example of which of the following "isms"?
   a. nationalism
   b. liberalism
   c. socialism
   d. Romanticism
   e. naturalism

5. According to laissez-faire economic philosophy, society benefited when
   a. the government administered price controls in urban housing
   b. unions organized and were recognized as legitimate bargaining units
   c. the coordination of markets was achieved by impersonal forces
   d. a sexual division of labor required women to tend home and family
   e. government subsidies promoted improvement in the national infrastructure

6. One feature of England that gave it an advantage over France in industrializing earlier was
   a. accessible deposits of raw materials
   b. a national banking system
   c. an expanding population
   d. a stable government in the hands of the upper classes
   e. the absence of internal customs

7. "The scanty wages given to many forms of labor, as well as the high price of rent and provisions, make it almost impossible for a man alone to support the family. Hence, most of the wives of the unskilled workpeople

have to forego their maternal duties, and devote themselves to some kind of drudgery to add to the petty household income. If then the mother be away from home the greater part of her time, and the children be left to gambol in the gutter with others as neglected, what reward can society look for from this moral anarchy and destitution? Here is the real explanation of juvenile delinquency."

H. Mayhew and J. Binny, *The Criminal Prisons of London*, 1862

This view on the cause of juvenile delinquency would most likely be supported by a
a. social Darwinist
b. Marxist
c. utilitarian
d. Romantic
e. anarchist

8. The stimulus for the "takeoff" into sustained economic growth in England was provided by
a. the textile industry
b. the banking industry
c. iron and steel development
d. shipbuilding
e. pottery and glass manufacturing

9. He made a fortune by the age of twenty-eight from spinning mills in Manchester, and then bought a mill in Scotland that he tried to make into a model socialist community. He set up the same experiment in Indiana, for he believed that social classes could be harmoniously reconciled. This individual is
a. Charles Fourier
b. Claude de Saint-Simon
c. Robert Owen
d. Louis Blanc
e. Francis Lowell

10. He awakened the conscience of the British to the conditions of the slums and the poor; in the English novel he had the ideal instrument for spreading his message of outrage and sympathy. This individual is
a. Henry Fielding
b. William Makepeace Thackeray
c. Walter Scott
d. Benjamin Disraeli
e. Charles Dickens

PRACTICE ESSAY QUESTIONS

Use the questions below to practice essay writing. For each question write an essay that includes an introductory thesis, a body of supporting and/or illustrative data, and a conclusion.

1. Describe the economic position and the political outlook of the middle class and the working class in the mid-nineteenth century. In what ways were they alike and in what ways were they different?
2. What was the social and economic impact of the Industrial Revolution in England on working women and on middle-class women?
3. How did classical liberals justify the nonintervention of government in the economy? What factors and events modified liberal views?
4. To what extent was Karl Marx indebted to the Enlightenment? To what extent was he indebted to Romanticism?
5. Did socialism succeed or fail in achieving its goals in the nineteenth century?

ESSAY WRITING TIPS: INTEGRATING QUOTATIONS INTO THE BODY OF AN ESSAY

In writing a document-based question, students often find desirable quotations that they wish to incorporate into their essays. Quotations, however, cannot stand alone. They must connect in a meaningful way to the general ideas you are expressing. Their meaning and significance must be explained to the reader in context.

Below are several key sentences from Karl Marx's *Communist Manifesto*.

a. "The history of all hitherto existing society is the history of class struggles."
b. "Our epoch, the epoch of the bourgeoisie, possesses, however, this distinctive feature: it has simplified the class antagonisms."
c. "Owing to the extensive use of machinery and to division of labour, the work of the proletarians has lost all individual character. . . . He becomes an appendage of the machine, and it is only the most simple, most monotonous, and most easily acquired knack, that is required of him."
d. "You are horrified at our intending to do away with private property. But in your existing society, private property is already done away with for nine-tenths of the population."
e. "Let the ruling classes tremble at a Communist revolution. The proletarians have nothing to lose but their chains. They have a world to win."

Yet these sentences as they stand are too long to incorporate in a short and/or timed essay. In most instances they need to be shortened to a brief part or phrase so that they can be manageably incorporated into the text as part of the narrative flow. Below are examples of selections from the longer sentences above. Use all of them to write an essay that answers the question: On what basis did Karl Marx predict the demise of capitalism?

Quotations

a. "The history of all hitherto existing society is the history of class struggles. . . .
b. ". . . the epoch of the bourgeoisie has simplified the class antagonism."
c. ". . . an appendage of the machine . . ."
d. ". . . private property is already done away with for nine-tenths of the population."
e. "The proletarians have nothing to lose but their chains. They have a world to win."

INTEGRATING QUOTATIONS INTO THE BODY OF A TEXT: A SAMPLE ESSAY

The Political Theories of Karl Marx

Karl Marx was a nineteenth-century political theorist who claimed that he had uncovered the "natural laws" that governed historical development and change. His so-called scientific brand of socialism differed from the utopian socialists' in his emphasis on class conflict as the motor force of historical change.

According to Marx, "*the history of all hitherto existing society is the history of class struggles. . . .*" Marx saw in past eras, and in the nineteenth century, similar patterns of social class exploitation. The actors may have changed–patrician and plebeian; feudal lord and serf; aristocracy and bourgeoisie–but the scenario remained the same. In each past era, the oppressed rose up and overthrew their oppressors. Marx felt that "*. . . the [nineteenth-century] epoch of the bourgeoisie [had] simplified the class antagonisms.*" Various gradations in the social class structure were reduced to two opposing economic classes–the bourgeoisie and the proletariat. Members of the proletariat, or workers, were society's victims.

Marx saw the workers as exploited and dehumanized in their factory settings. They had lost their human qualities and had become simply "*. . . an appendage of the machine. . . .*" Only as cooperative members in a socialist economy could the workers regain the quality of humanness, according to Marx.

The socialist state that Marx envisaged would abolish private property. To critics who pointed out the criminal nature of property seizure, Marx pointed out that "*. . . private property is already done away with for nine-tenths of the population.*" He was referring to the ownership of property by the bourgeois minority of the population and the dispossession of property by the proletarian majority. In his assessment of the workers' barren state, Marx's rhetoric must have inflamed passions when he wrote "*the proletarians have nothing to lose but their chains. They have a world to win.*"

As an outraged moral theorist, Karl Marx operated within the tradition of the Enlightenment. He applied reason and observation to uncover the "natural laws" and workings of European society. What Marx could not foresee, however, were the government reforms and benefits for workers in the late nineteenth century. These reforms averted the inevitable revolution that Marx had predicted, but, perhaps, his dire predictions contributed to and hastened the necessary reforms.

IDENTIFICATIONS

Classical liberalism–Middle-class (bourgeois) doctrine indebted to the writings of the philosophes, the French Revolution, and the popularization of the Scientific Revolution. Its *political goals* were self-government (concept of the general will); a written constitution; natural rights (speech, religion, press, property, mobility); limited suffrage; its *economic goals* were laissez-faire (free trade)–i.e., no government interference in the workings of the economy.

Dialectical materialism–The idea, according to Karl Marx, that change and development in history results from the conflict between social classes. Economic forces impel human beings to behave in socially determined ways.

Domestic system–The manufacture of goods in the household setting, a production system that gave way to the factory system.

Friedrich Engels (1820-1895)–Collaborator with Karl Marx. Engels was a textile factory owner and supplied Marx with the hard data for his economic writings, most notably *Das Kapital* (1867).

J. G. Fichte (1762-1814)–German writer who believed that the German spirit was nobler and purer than that of other peoples.

Charles Fourier (1772-1837)–A leading utopian socialist who envisaged small communal societies in which men and women cooperated in agriculture and industry, abolishing private property and monogamous marriage as well.

Hegelian dialectic–The idea, according to G. W. F. Hegel (1770-1831), a German philosopher, that social change results from the conflict of opposite ideas. The thesis is confronted by the antithesis, resulting in a synthesis, which then becomes a new thesis. The process is evolutionary. Marx turned Hegel "upside down" and made class conflict, not ideas, the force driving history forward.

J. G. Herder (1774-1803)–Forerunner of the German Romantic movement who believed that each people shared a national character, or *Volksgeist*.

Thomas Malthus (1776-1834)–English parson whose *Essay on Population* (1798) argued that population would always increase faster than the food supply.

Karl Marx (1818-1883)–German philosopher and founder of Marxism, the theory that class conflict is the motor force driving historical change and development.

David Ricardo (1772-1823)–English economist who formulated the "iron law of wages," according to which wages would always remain at the subsistence level for the workers because of population growth.

Herbert Spencer (1820-1903)–English philosopher who argued that in the difficult economic struggle for existence, only the "fittest" would survive.

Flora Tristan (1803-1844)–Socialist and feminist who called for working women's social and political rights.

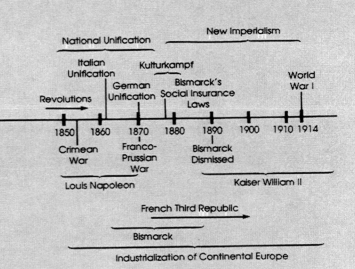

THE AGE OF
NATIONALISM: 1850–1900

CHAPTER 9

UNIFICATION OF ITALY

1821	Austria suppresses a rebellion by the Carbonari
1831-1832	Austria suppresses another insurrection by the Carbonari
1832	Mazzini forms the Young Italy
March 1848	Austrians are forced to withdraw from Milan and Venice
November 1848	Pope forced to flee Rome
1848-1849	Austria reasserts its authority in Milan and Venice; Louis Napoleon crushes revolutionaries in Rome
1858	Napoleon III agrees to help Sardinia against Austria
1859	Austro-Sardinian War; Sardinia obtains Lombardy from Austria; Parma, Modena, Tuscany, and Romagna vote to join with Sardinia
1860	Garibaldi invades the Kingdom of Two Sicilies
March 17, 1861	Victor Emmanuel of Sardinia is proclaimed king of Italy
1866	Italy's alliance with Prussia against Austria results in annexation of Venetia by Italy
1870	Rome is incorporated into the Italian state and unity is achieved

UNIFICATION OF GERMANY

1815	Formation of the German Confederation
1823	Establishment of the Zollverein under Prussian leadership
1848	Failure of the liberals to unify Germany
1862	Bismarck becomes chancellor of Prussia
1864	Austria and Prussia defeat Denmark in a war over Schleswig-Holstein
1866	Seven Weeks' War between Austria and Prussia; Prussia emerges as the dominant power in Germany
1866	Formation of North German Confederation under Prussian control
1870–1871	Franco-Prussian War
January 18, 1871	William I becomes German kaiser

NATIONALISM

Nationalism is a force that has shaped much of nineteenth-century history. It continues, even in our day, to play a decisive role in world events. There are many ingredients of nationalism, including a certain defined unit of territory; a recognition that members of the geographical entity are compatriots sharing a common language, culture, and history; a common pride in the nation's achievements and a common sorrow in its tragedies; and a hope that the nation will become and remain great in some way.

UNIFICATION OF ITALY

Such was the force that drove a number of reformers to unify Italy and Germany in the second half of the nineteenth century. In the case of Italy, Napoleon's reforms had helped create national feelings among the conglomeration of separate city-states, each with its own government and internal structure that made up this "geographical expression." Middle-class Italians hoped that, if foreign powers were expelled, liberal reforms would continue and would promote economic growth. The liberals faced opponents: impoverished rural masses indifferent to unification; the church, reluctant to lose any control of the papal lands; and an aristocracy fearful of liberal ideals and the dilution of its power that reform would bring.

Secret societies, such as the Carbonari, had formed in the 1820s, but were repressed. New leaders, however, emerged. Among them was **Giuseppe Mazzini** (1805–1872), a cultural nationalist who dreamed of a world of independent states based on the principles of republicanism and democracy.

If Mazzini was the poetic soul of Italian unification and founder of **Young Italy**, **Count Cavour** (1810–1861) of Sardinia, more commonly known as Piedmont, ruled by the **House of Savoy**, was its brain. He was the chief architect of Italian unification, or **Risorgimento**. In trying to wrest independence from Austrian control in the north, Cavour found support from Napoleon

III, even though temporary. Cavour won Lombardy in his fight against the Austrians, and other Italian states voted to join with Piedmont.

Cavour was seeking control only of northern Italy. It was **Giuseppe Garibaldi's** (1807-1882) involvement that unified the entire peninsula. Garibaldi, the "sword" of unification, led his army of **Red Shirts** against Bourbon forces in Sicily and southern Italy. On the pretext of protecting the papal states, Cavour sent the armies of Piedmont to occupy them. The defender of the papal states, Napoleon III, however, was diverted from his cause as he faced war with Prussia.

Resulting Problems

Plebiscites were held—all favorable to national unification. The result was the unification of the peninsula with Victor Emmanuel king ruling under the Piedmontese constitution, which proved to be an illiberal doctrine. The

THE UNIFICATION OF ITALY 1859-70

franchise was limited to 2 percent of the population. The government was highly centralized and unable or unwilling to address the endemic social and economic problems that Italy faced. Key among them was the disparity of the industrial north and the agrarian south. The south often felt victimized in its dealings with the north and remained economically backward well into the twentieth century, when capital investments would be made to modernize the region.

As for the papal states, they were reduced in size. The pope condemned the unification and secluded himself in the Vatican.

VISUAL-BASED PRACTICE: ANALYZING A POLITICAL CARTOON

The political cartoon by Tenniel was published in the British magazine *Punch*, October 1, 1870. Study it carefully and answer in writing the questions below.

1. Who are the key figures in the cartoon and what does the object each of them is holding represent?

ITALY IN ROME.

Papa Pius (to King of Italy). "I MUST NEEDS SURRENDER THE *SWORD*, MY SON BUT *I KEEP THE KEYS!*"

2. What is being said about the contest for power?
3. In the cartoonist's view of the relationship between the two men, who is the victor?

UNIFICATION OF GERMANY

The history of German unification is due in single measure to the work of **Otto von Bismarck** (1815-1898), a Prussian aristocrat, or Junker. By uniting the military aristocracy of Prussia with the German middle class, Bismarck was able to weld two disparate social groups into an organic whole.

In a series of three wars beginning in the 1860s and the last being the Franco-Prussian War of 1870-1871–initiated by Bismarck's clever editing of the **Ems telegram**–the Prussian army scored stunning victories against Schleswig-Holstein, Austria, and then France. German liberals had sought unification as well as constitutionalism. Bismarck provided the unification and also a democratic facade that satisfied liberal yearnings, so much so that the liberals even passed the **indemnity bill** (1867), legitimating Bismarck's earlier unconstitutional collection of taxes. Although the imperial constitution called for a **Bundesrat** (Federal Council) and a **Reichstag** (lower house), real power lay with Chancellor Bismarck, who was responsible to Kaiser William I. The lower house was elected by manhood suffrage, yet it proved to be little more than a debating society.

Domestic Policies

Bismarck proved to be the consummate leader, a practitioner of **Realpolitik**. He imposed tariffs on imported grain and steel, thus satisfying the large Junker landholding class and the liberal manufacturing bourgeoisie. He introduced bills on social insurance and pensions, thus placating rank-and-file members of the working class and diverting their attention to bread-and-butter issues.

His wars and the **Treaty of Frankfurt** had added the French provinces of **Alsace** and **Lorraine**, territories rich in coal and iron. Austria, Prussia's chief rival in central Europe, was excluded from a united Germany and could no longer compete against the growing power of a rapidly industrializing Germany.

In the early 1860s, when Kaiser William I had faced parliamentary defeats at the hands of the liberals over the issue of increased taxes to modernize the army, Bismarck had been summoned at the twelfth hour to save the day. Bismarck simply chose to collect taxes without parliamentary approval. The great issues of the day, he stated, were resolved not by parliamentary debates but by blood and iron. His authoritarian policies worked. Germany was unified, but its illiberal constitution weakened an opportunity for a bona fide democratic regime to develop. According to A. J. P. Taylor, the British historian, "The capitalists accepted Junker rule because it gave them prosperity and unification; the working classes accepted Junker rule because it gave them social security and the vote. The only loss was freedom."

Bismarck's policies were not always totally successful, however. His **Kulturkampf**, or struggle against the power of the Catholic church, and his repressive laws against socialists did not diminish the powers of their supporters and leaders like **Ferdinand Lassalle** (1825-1864). He was forced to abandon the Kulturkampf. As for the socialists, Bismarck defused their revolutionary spirit with his extensive social legislation–insurance by the state against accidents, sickness, and old age.

Foreign Policy after Unification   The economic union of Germany had begun in 1818 with the creation of the Zollverein. The political union of Germany was completed in 1871 with the defeat of France and the humiliating **Siege of Paris** in the Franco-Prussian war. The patriotic fervor of that war persuaded the southern states to join the North German Confederation. Bismarck, the "Iron Chancellor," declared himself sated, interested only in preserving in peace the new balance of power. For the next twenty years he did keep the peace, but at great social and political cost to the ambitions of the old German liberals who found themselves frozen in the archaic social hierarchy of Prussia.

DOCUMENT-BASED ESSAY QUESTION

Using the documents below, summarize in writing the role that Bismarck played in shaping the political consciousness of youth during his reign as chancellor of Germany.

(A) laudable deepening and clarification of national consciousness is taking place in our academic youth. The fantastic and hazy ideas regarding political and national questions which in earlier times dominated our universities are apparently giving way to a clear and positive attitude. According to my opinion, a healthy national and monarchical spirit is spreading among them. The politicizing professors, who belong to that epoch against which the movement in question is reacting, are likely to do their utmost to repress the national and conservative tendencies of our student body and to further the (liberal left).

Bismarck, 1881

Students shall politicize as little as they shall teach or practice (a profession). While it suits them well to burn for the fatherland . . . they should nevertheless eschew the parties of the day.

Physiologist Emil DuBois-Reymond, professor at Berlin University, 1882

In my opinion it is completely incompatible with academic morality or order and the purpose of attending a university for students to engage in active and practical participation in politics and especially to agitate in political assemblies as speakers or members of the presidium.

German minister of education Bosse, 1894

There is a saying that tomorrow belongs to the young; I want to add: In Germany, he who commands the allegiance of academic youth possesses the future. Therefore, we adults look confidently ahead. We know that German students will forever follow the banner that Prince Bismarck has raised. They will defend the unity, power, honor, and greatness of our fatherland.

Hamburg mayor Mönckeberg to an audience of German students gathered to honor Bismarck on his eightieth birthday, 1 April 1895

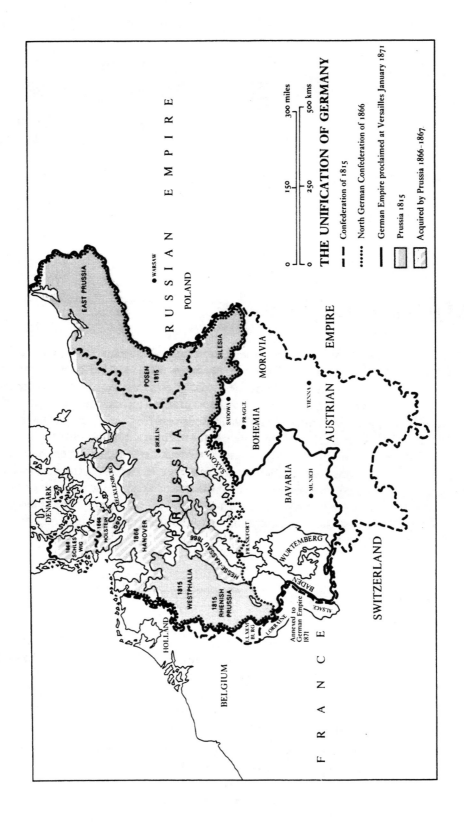

THE UNIFICATION OF GERMANY

- – – Confederation of 1815
- · · · · North German Confederation of 1866
- —— German Empire proclaimed at Versailles January 1871
- ▨ Prussia 1815
- ☐ Acquired by Prussia 1866–1867

RUSSIAN EMPIRE

POLAND

●WARSAW

EAST PRUSSIA

SILESIA

POSEN
1815

BERLIN●

PRUSSIA

MORAVIA

SADOWA●
●PRAGUE

BOHEMIA

SAXONY

AUSTRIAN EMPIRE

●VIENNA

BAVARIA

●MUNICH

DENMARK

HOLSTEN
1866

SCHLES
WIG
1866

MECKLENBURG

1815
HANOVER

HESSE-NASSAU
1866

FRANKFORT

WURTEMBERG

1815
WESTPHALIA

1815
RHENISH
PRUSSIA

LUXEM-
BURG

BADEN

ALSACE

LORRAINE

Annexed to
German Empire
1871

HOLLAND

BELGIUM

FRANCE

SWITZERLAND

DISTRIBUTION OF UNIVERSITY STUDENT ORGANIZATIONS IN 1914

Type	Number	Percent
Dueling	288	31.9
"Fraternities"	114	12.6
Political	53	5.9
Reform	60	6.6
Religious	102	11.3
Scholarly	124	13.7
Social	21	2.3
Sport	75	8.3
Women	40	4.4
Other	26	2.9
TOTAL	903	100

FRANCE UNDER NAPOLEON III

As for France, its defeat in the Franco-Prussian War ended the rule of Louis Napoleon. As Emperor **Napoleon III** (1852-1870) he had rebuilt Paris, increased the role of the Catholic church in primary and secondary education as defense against radicalism, and granted unions the right to form and to strike. Although the French Parliament was elected by universal male suffrage, like the German Reichstag it was little more than a debating society. And yet by 1870, Napoleon III had granted a new constitution that showed France evolving in a more democratic direction. However, in 1870, the Second Empire, which had lasted for eighteen years, was discarded. The greatest loss, though, was not the empire but Alsace and most of Lorraine, the border regions lost to Germany, along with payment of an astronomical war indemnity of five billion gold francs.

MULTIPLE-CHOICE QUESTIONS

1. Which of the following resulted from Bismarck's unification of Germany?
   a. Austria was ousted from a position of leadership in Germany.
   b. The Zollverein failed to spur economic growth.
   c. France achieved hegemony in Western Europe.
   d. The Socialist Party declined in number and influence.
   e. The opposition between liberals and Junkers strengthened.

2. Which of the following reasons contributed most to the German workers' loss of revolutionary fervor?
   a. the death of Karl Marx, in 1883
   b. the tariff on imported steel
   c. social insurance laws and the pension act
   d. Bismarck's halt of the Kulturkampf
   e. Germany's victory in the Franco-Prussian War

3. Germany's industrial "takeoff" in the nineteenth century can be credited to development in which of the following industries?
   a. fishing
   b. submarines
   c. canning and food production
   d. machinery and mining
   e. silk manufacturing

4. All of the following contributed to the growth of the Second Empire of Napoleon III EXCEPT
   a. the completion of the French railroad network
   b. a governmental program of public works
   c. the negotiation of treaties of tariff reduction with foreign partners
   d. the law granting the right of "limited liability"
   e. French participation in the Crimean War

5. "He was a nationalist of a new breed who had no respect for Mazzini's ideals. A strong monarchist, he rejected republicanism. It was economic and material progress rather than Romantic ideals that required a large unified state on the peninsula. This quotation is a reference to
   a. Garibaldi
   b. Louis Napoleon
   c. Bismarck
   d. Count Cavour
   e. Victor Emmanuel II

6. Even after 1870, the unredeemed territories of Trent and Trieste sparked the hostility of patriotic Italians against
   a. England
   b. France
   c. Austria
   d. Germany
   e. Hungary

7. A major problem facing Italy after its unification was
   a. papal interference in political elections
   b. the uneven economic development of the north and south
   c. the Sicilian claim for autonomy
   d. the loss of Venetia to Germany
   e. the inability to formulate a constitution

8. After 1870, Bismarck's chief international aim was to
   a. acquire colonies
   b. maintain the peace
   c. ally with France
   d. annex Austria
   e. achieve naval supremacy over Great Britain

PRACTICE ESSAY QUESTIONS

Use the questions below to practice essay writing. For each question write an essay that includes an introductory thesis, a body of supporting and/or illustrative data, and a conclusion.

1. To what extent was 1870 a watershed in German history? Provide examples to support or refute the notion of 1870 as a watershed.
2. "The unification of Italy was unrealized in every sense except the political." Assess the validity of this statement.
3. How and in what manner did Bismarck's unification of Germany weaken the political and economic agendas of the liberals and the socialists?
4. Justify the labeling of Mazzini as the "soul," Cavour as the "brains," and Garibaldi as the "sword" of Italian unification.

ESSAY-WRITING TIPS: METAPHORS IN HISTORICAL WRITING

Question 1 above asks whether or not 1870 was a watershed in German history. In the context of the question, a watershed is a crucial and dividing line. One may live through a "watershed" and never recognize it as such, because historical assessments that are made long after the date determine whether or not a *crucial* event in fact took place.

It can be argued that Bismarck's completion of his goal to unify Germany in 1870 signifies the attainment of a dream envisioned by liberals and nationalists. But the basis for this recognition of 1870 as a watershed is political—the political unification of Germany.

In 1834, the Zollverein was established and enlarged. The economic union of Germany was achieved, an economic union that paved the way for political unity. Is not 1834 therefore the watershed?

Then again, in September 1866, after Bismarck's defeat of Austria and the creation of the North German Confederation, Bismarck asked for and received an "indemnity," or a certificate from the Prussian Parliament ascertaining that all the funds he had illegally collected since 1861 from obedient German taxpaying citizens had been legally collected and spent. The German liberal deputies were so dazzled by Bismarck's military successes that they passed the indemnity bill and gave him a handsome cash gift to boot. Is 1866, therefore, the watershed in German history?

The concept of a watershed is a useful one. It highlights the notion of a dramatic change in historical patterns of a nation. On the other hand, there are enduring continuities in history. The above-mentioned dates may have had little or no effect on patterns of childrearing, family life, work, leisure activities, crime and punishment, and the myriad events that make up ordinary life. To declare a watershed is to take a stand that requires a compelling argument to convince the reader of the special significance of the time or date in question. Such is the task of the historian exercising the powers of her or his analysis.

Below are a series of "events" in nineteenth-century European history. In each case, write a paragraph explaining whether or not the event could be assessed as a historical watershed.

1. 1804—Napoleon declares himself emperor of France.
2. 1833—Abolition Act: Slavery abolished in the British Empire.
3. 1837—Mme de Mauchamp presents petition to the French Chamber of Deputies to have article 210, "The Wife owes obedience to her husband," removed from the Civil Code.
4. 1859—Charles Darwin's *Origin of Species* gives evidence for and explanation of evolution.

5. 1865–Industry manufactures washing machines.
6. 1870–Franco Prussian War begins.
7. 1882–Married Women's Property Act in England gives wives right of ownership independent of their husbands.
8. 1880–Canned fruits and meats first appear in stores.
9. 1894–Bismarck is dismissed from office.

IDENTIFICATIONS

Otto von Bismarck (1815-1898)–Prussian chancellor who engineered a series of wars to unify Germany under his authoritarian rule.

Bundesrat–The upper house, or Federal Council, of the German Diet (legislature).

Count Cavour (1810-1861)–Italian statesman from Sardinia who used diplomacy to help achieve unification of Italy.

Ems telegram–The carefully edited dispatch by Bismarck to the French ambassador that appeared to be insulting and thus requiring retaliation by France for the seeming affront to French honor.

Giuseppe Garibaldi (1807-1882)–Soldier of fortune who amassed his "Red Shirt" army to bring Naples and Sicily into a unified Italy.

House of Savoy–The Italian dynasty ruling the independent state of Piedmont-Sardinia. Its head was King Victor Emmanuel II.

Indemnity bill (1867)–The bill passed by the German Reichstag that legitimated Bismarck's unconstitutional collection of taxes to modernize the army in 1863.

Kulturkampf–Bismarck's anticlerical campaign to expel Jesuits from Germany and break off relations with the Vatican. Eventually, after little success, Bismarck halted these policies.

Ferdinand Lassalle (1825-1864)–Leader of the revisionist socialists, who hoped to achieve socialism through the ballot rather than the bullet. They agreed to work within the framework of the existing government.

Giuseppe Mazzini (1805-1872)–Idealistic patriot devoted to the principle of united and republican Italy in a world of free states.

Napoleon III (1852-1870)–The former Louis Napoleon, who became president of the Second Republic of France in 1848 and engineered a coup d'état, ultimately making himself head of the Second Empire.

Nationalism–The shared belief among peoples of a common heritage, culture, and customs, and speaking a similar language (there may be dialect differences).

Realpolitik–The "politics of reality," i.e., the use of practical means to achieve ends. Bismarck was a practitioner.

"Red Shirts"–Volunteers in Garibaldi's army.

Reichstag–The lower house of the German Diet, or legislature.

Risorgimento–Italian drive and desire for unity.

Siege of Paris–The four-month Prussian assault on the French capital after Napoleon III's surrender in 1870.

Treaty of Frankfurt–The end of the Franco-Prussian War, which ceded the territories of Alsace and most of Lorraine to Germany.

Young Italy–An association under the leadership of Mazzini that urged the unification of the country.

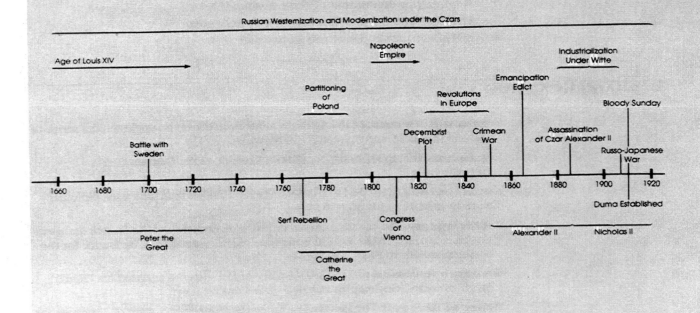

RUSSIA: FROM PETER THE GREAT TO NICHOLAS II IN THE EARLY 1900S

CHAPTER 10

RUSSIA

It is necessary to shift our attention to the developments that took place since the seventeenth century in the stretch of territory from the Arctic to the Black Sea and from the Baltic to the Pacific. The territory is Russia. Its importance in European history for our purposes dates from the reign of Peter the Great (1682-1725), of the Romanov dynasty. His major policy was to westernize Russian society.

PETER THE GREAT

Peter directed Russian attention westward. He waged war with Sweden for Baltic control. He built a palace and an entire city in St. Petersburg on territory conquered from the Swedes. From the Persians he gained control of territory on the Caspian Sea.

Although Peter did not seek political liberty for his people, he wanted to raise the low standards of Russian civilization and alter the customs that distinguished the Russians from the European gentility. He made the nobles, or **boyars**, adopt Western dress and manners. He forced them and the city workers to cut off their beards and shorten their long coats. The czar even encouraged marriages based on personal choice rather than parental decision.

As an absolute monarch, Peter created a more modern army and state. Service in the army or in the bureaucracy was compulsory for the nobility, who were given privilege and wealth in exchange for conscription into public service. The nobles also controlled serfs and peasants who supported the entire superstructure with their labor and taxes. Peasants had to serve in the regular standing army for life, or else work in factories and mines if they were not tilling the vast landholdings of the nobility. Their lives resembled those of draft animals.

Under Peter the three essentials of European state power—a strong army, a strong navy, and an efficient civil service—were built. And in matters of religion, according to the **Church Statute of 1721**, both laypersons and clergy had to swear allegiance to the czar. Russia emerged as a dominant power in European affairs.

CATHERINE THE GREAT

Peter's successor, **Catherine the Great** (1762-1796), was an "enlightened despot" who was influenced by the French philosophes. She tried domestic reform, including the codification of laws, restriction of torture, improvements in education, and limited religious toleration. However, an uprising of serfs under **Pugachev** (1726–1775) in 1773 over serfdom, taxes, and army service convinced her to give the nobles absolute control over their serfs once again. The nobles remained a privileged elite caste who paid no taxes. Under Catherine, Poland was partitioned. Prussia, Austria, and Russia each gained a slice. By the end of the 1700s, Poland had disappeared from the European map.

ALEXANDER II

In the 1800s, Russia was a preindustrial country, using backward agricultural techniques. Serfs or "souls" could be sold. Secret societies in the Russian officer corps, such as the Decembrists, called for reform and led the **Decembrist revolt** in 1825. Politically, however, Russia was ruled by an autocratic series of monarchs, the most liberal of whom was **Alexander II** (1855–1881). He decided that if reform did not come from above, then surely it would come from below. Russia's defeat in the **Crimean War** exposed internal weaknesses and raised the possibility of social upheaval. In 1861, Alexander issued the **Emancipation Edict**. On paper it improved the lot of the peasants, who made up 75 percent of the population. In actuality their conditions of life were not much improved. Living on the **mir**, or village commune, they were responsible for long-term debts to the state. They could not leave the commune without permission, and even then they were liable for taxes owed to the government.

DOCUMENT-BASED QUESTION

Read the document below and write a paragraph explaining the nature of the serf's confusion in regard to the Emancipation Edict.

FROM D. MACKENZIE WALLACE, *RUSSIA*, 1877

(After the emancipation of the Russian serfs) the peasants found that they were still to pay dues even for the Communal land which they regarded as unquestionably their own! . . . But the thing was incredible. Either the proprietors must be concealing or misinterpreting the law, or this was merely a preparatory measure, which would be followed by the real Emancipation. . . . The peasants naturally imagined that, as soon as the Czar said they were free, they were no longer obliged to work for their old masters—that all obligatory labor ceased as soon as the Manifesto was read. In vain the proprietors endeavored to convince them that, in regard to labor, the old relations must continue, as the law enjoined, until a new arrangement had been made. To all explanations and exhortations the peasants turned a deaf ear . . . not unfrequently the birch had to be applied. Indeed, I am inclined to believe, from the numerous descriptions of this time which I have received from eyewitnesses, that rarely, if ever, had the serfs seen and experienced so much flogging as during these first three months after their liberation. . . .

Economic Reforms under Count Witte

Alexander tried other reforms. He attempted to set up an institution of representative social government known as the **zemstvo** to reform the legal system. He also encouraged economic growth. Railroad construction expanded; grain was being exported. But in 1881 Alexander II was assassinated by **Sofia Perovskaia**. His son **Alexander III** (1881-1894) was a political reactionary. Yet under his finance minister **Sergei Witte** (1849-1915) industrialization proceeded at great pace. The Trans-Siberian Railway was constructed. The steel and coal industry in the Ukraine was built with foreign investment, and tariffs were imposed to build up Russian industry. Russia was also put on the gold standard. In short, under the leadership of Witte, Russia industrialized more rapidly than in any period between the reign of Peter the Great and Stalin in the 1930s and 1940s. By 1900, Russia was producing more pig iron than France and was the world's largest steel producer.

But the accelerated industrialization was also producing an urban proletariat whose discontents would be fueled by intellectual descendants of Karl Marx. They would call for an end to capitalism.

NICHOLAS II

Under the final czar of the Romanov dynasty, **Nicholas II** (1894-1917) modernization continued. Western technology was raising agricultural yields. Production was market-oriented. **Peter Stolypin** (1862-1911), a statesman, tried to create a class of independent farmers, or **kulaks**, who would support the czarist regime rather than overthrow it. Education improved for the young. Russia was producing luminaries in art and science: Tolstoy, Chekhov, Stravinsky, Tchaikovsky, Pavlov, and Mendeleyev.

In short, Nicholas II might have ridden successfully across the crest of modernization were it not for his quarrel with Japan in 1904-1905 that exposed the cracks in the Russian military as had the earlier Crimean War. The social and economic dislocations brought on by the Russo-Japanese War sparked the revolution of 1905. It foreshadowed the collapse of Nicholas's regime in 1917. In a country that was modernizing economically, socially, and culturally,

Russia's political backwardness stands in sharp contrast. Pressures for democracy and representative government wrested concessions from Nicholas II. After the demonstration of workers and their families led by **Father Gapon** to petition the czar that ended in the fateful "Bloody Sunday," Nicholas issued his October Manifesto and set up the **Duma**. But as the Duma operated, it failed to secure bona fide representation for the people. Nicholas appointed ministers who did not need to command a majority in the Duma. He revised electoral laws so only the propertied classes held power. And finally, he dismissed the Duma. The czar relied on the support of extreme right-wing groups. He used anti-Semitism as a political weapon and shocked world opinion and the liberal forces at home. His political policies helped pave the way for the revolutions of 1917.

DOCUMENT-BASED ESSAY QUESTION

On the basis of the following two documents, summarize in writing the nature of Czar Nicholas II's relationship to two strata of the common people described below. From your descriptions, what inferences can you make regarding his perceptiveness and compassion?

FROM G. KENNAN, *SIBERIA AND THE EXILE SYSTEM*, 1819

In the course of a talk one afternoon about America, Mr. Pavlovski, turning the conversation abruptly, said to me, "Mr. Kennan, have you ever paid any attention to the movement of young people to Siberia? . . . Some (of them) are young men and women of high attainments—men with a university training and women of remarkable character . . . who, under other circumstances, might render valuable services to their country.

(On this subject of political exiles), Mr. Pavlovski said that they had all been banished without judicial trial, upon mere executive orders, signed by the Minister of the Interior and approved by the czar. . . .

"What is the nature of the crimes for which these young people were banished?" I inquired. "Were they conspirators? Did they take part in plots to assassinate the czar?"

"Oh, no," said Mr. Pavlovski with a smile; "they were only untrustworthy. Some of them belonged to forbidden societies, some imported or were in possession of forbidden books, some had friendly relations with other more dangerous offenders, and some were connected with disorders in the higher schools and universities. . . . The real conspirators and revolutionists— the men and women who have actually been engaged in criminal activity—are sent to more remote parts of Siberia and into penal servitude."

FROM HENRY NORMAN, "RUSSIA OF TODAY," *SCRIBNER'S MAGAZINE*, OCTOBER 1900

The czar, as the source of promotion and the fountain of honors, dwells still alone upon the heights. . . . From ruler to ruled is a natural transition, and especially so in Russia, where there is no middle class in which the two qualities coalesce. Indeed this is the most striking aspect of Russian society: at the top, the imperial family, surrounded by the nobility; at the bottom, the "common people." The development of industrialism, with its rapidly made fortunes, is changing this condition so far as the large towns are concerned, but it still remains true of the country as a whole. . . . All the shops which offer wares to the people do so, not in words, but with pictures. . . . Why is this? Simply because a majority of potential customers cannot read! . . . Poverty and illiteracy naturally go hand in hand. . . . Russia is still first and foremost an agricultural country. . . . But it is in her most fertile districts that the worst famines occur, for famine—a little one every year, a big one every seven years—has now become a regular occurrence.

MULTIPLE-CHOICE QUESTIONS

1. Which of the following goals did Peter the Great fail to achieve?
   a. opening Russia to Western influences
   b. eliminating opposition to his authority
   c. finding a warm-water port
   d. gaining access to the Mediterranean
   e. surpassing European countries in the production of iron

2. During her reign, Catherine the Great did which of the following?
   a. abolished serfdom
   b. avoided foreign wars
   c. drew up legislative reforms based on Enlightenment principles
   d. increased the compulsory state service of the nobility
   e. opposed the partition of Poland

3. The leaders in the Russian political reform movements in the late nineteenth century were drawn from which of the following groups?
   a. Orthodox Christians opposed to repressive religious policies
   b. the peasantry eager to introduce socialism
   c. generals who wanted to double the army's soldiers
   d. intellectuals who sought representative government
   e. industrial entrepreneurs anxious to modernize the Russian infrastructure

4. The Decembrists can best be described as
   a. a selected unit of the Russian military officer corps
   b. members of the Populist Party
   c. leaders of an underground union of steelworkers
   d. peasants oppressed by increasing manorial obligations
   e. the Russian affiliate of the Italian Carbonari

5. Which of the following contributed to the oppression of the serfs after 1861?
   a. revocation of the Emancipation Edict
   b. establishment of zemstvo assemblies
   c. implementation of trial by jury
   d. redemption payments required for occupying the mir
   e. establishment of schools for primary education

6. They called on the Russian people to destroy the institution of family, church, property, and the state. They espoused violence in the overthrow of government but had minimal plans for what would follow. The revolutionary group referred to is the
   a. nihilists
   b. anarchists
   c. Social Democrats
   d. Populists
   e. Fascists

7. Count Sergei Witte tried to encourage the economic development of Russia by
   a. increasing protective tariffs
   b. discouraging foreign investment
   c. taking Russia off the gold standard
   d. balancing the government's budget
   e. importing trained workers from Western Europe

8. Which of the following was *not* a major goal of the revolutionaries in 1905?
   a. an eight-hour day
   b. a minimum daily wage
   c. representative government
   d. abolition of the monarchy
   e. reform of the government bureaucracy

PRACTICE ESSAY QUESTIONS

Use the questions below to practice essay writing. For each question write an essay that includes an introductory thesis, a body of supporting and/or illustrative data, and a conclusion.

1. "Peter the Great, in spite of his efforts, failed to westernize Russia." Assess the validity of this statement.
2. "Catherine the Great's policies of enlightened reform were stymied more by internal pressures than external threats." Support or refute this statement.
3. To what extent did the Russian peasantry remain the enduring problem preventing modernization in nineteenth-century Russia?
4. Nicholas II almost succeeded in closing the gap between Russia and the West. What circumstances and policies contributed to the closure? What policies and circumstances prevented it?
5. "The currents that bring economic, cultural, and scientific modernization also bring demands for political modernization." Evaluate this statement with respect to the reign of Nicholas II.

ESSAY-WRITING TIPS: FOLLOWING DIRECTIVES

Essays ask students to perform various tasks. The directive words *analyze*, *assess*, *compare*, *contrast*, *describe*, *discuss*, *evaluate*, and *explain* have different charges.
   In brief, consider the following:

1. Analyze why Nicholas II failed to politically modernize Russia.
2. "Nicholas was an incompetent ruler, fearful of losing his autocratic power." Assess the validity of this statement through an examination of his policies.
3. Compare the policies of Nicholas II and his predecessor, Alexander II (1855 -1881). Who was the more successful modernizer?
4. Contrast the status of the serfs under the rules of Catherine the Great and Alexander II.
5. Describe the ways in which Russian artists of the nineteenth century detailed the inner life and struggles of individuals within the context of everyday life.
6. Discuss whether or not Peter "the Great" deserves the title.
7. "The Emancipation Edict was a success." Evaluate the validity of this statement with respect to the Russian peasants' response.
8. Explain how Sergei Witte and Peter Stolypin advanced the cause of modernization in Russia.

Each of these directive words requires a particular approach to answering the question. Here are concise summary meanings:

analyze–break down into component parts
assess–judge the value or truth of
compare–note similarities and differences
contrast–focus on the differences only
describe–give a full account of
discuss–write about in full detail
evaluate–consider both sides (the pros and the cons)
explain–make clear or plain in detail

IDENTIFICATIONS

Alexander II (1855-1881)–Reforming czar who emancipated the serfs and introduced some measure of representative local government.

Alexander III (1881-1894)–Politically reactionary czar who promoted economic modernization of Russia.

Boyar–Russian noble.

Catherine the Great (1762-1796)–An "enlightened despot" of Russia whose policies of reform were aborted under pressure of rebellion by serfs.

Church Statute of 1721–A Holy Synod that replaced the office of patriarch. All of its members (lay and religious) had to swear allegiance to the czar.

Crimean War (1853-1856)–Conflict ostensibly waged to protect Orthodox Christians in the Ottoman Empire, in actuality to gain a foothold in the Black Sea. Turks, Britain, and France forced Russia to sue for peace. The Treaty of Paris (1856) forfeited Russia's right to maintain a war fleet in the Black Sea. Russia also lost the principalities of Wallachia and Moldavia.

Decembrist revolt–The 1825 plot by liberals (upper-class intelligentsia) to set up a constitutional monarchy or a republic. The plot failed, but the ideal remained.

Duma–Russian national legislature.

Emancipation Edict (1861)–The imperial law that abolished serfdom in Russia and, on paper, freed the peasants. In actuality they were collectively responsible for redemption payments to the government for a number of years.

Father Gapon–Leader of the factory workers who assembled before the czar's palace to petition him on January 1905 (Bloody Sunday).

Kulak–An independent and propertied Russian farmer.

Mir–Village commune where the emancipated serfs lived and worked collectively in order to meet redemption payments to the government.

Nicholas II (1894-1917)–The last czar of the Romanov dynasty, whose government collapsed under the pressure of World War I.

Sofia Perovskaia–The first woman to be executed for a political crime in Russia. She was a member of a militant movement that assassinated Czar Alexander II in 1881.

Pugachev (1726-1775)–Head of the bloody peasant revolt in 1773 that convinced Catherine the Great to throw her support to the nobles and cease internal reforms.

Peter Stolypin (1862-1911)–Russian minister under Nicholas II who encouraged the growth of private farmers and improved education for enterprising peasants.

Sergei Witte (1849-1915)–Finance minister under whom Russia industrialized and began a program of economic modernization.

Zemstvo–A type of local government with powers to tax and make laws; essentially, a training ground for democracy, dominated by the property-owning class when established in 1864.

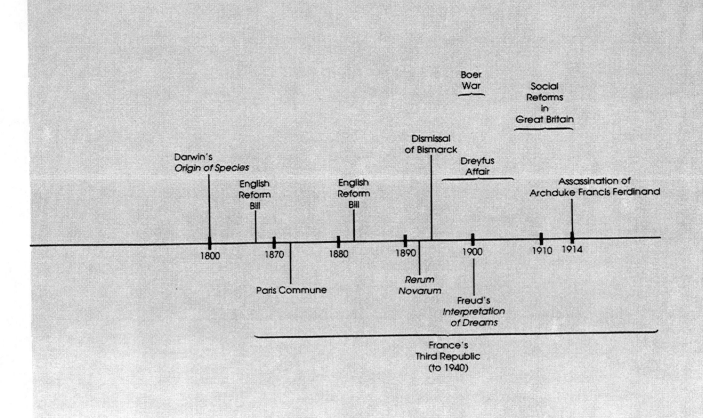

THE WESTERN WORLD, 1871-1914

CHAPTER 11

The period 1871-1914 was an amalgam of conflicting political, social, and intellectual forces en route to World War I. The predominant mood may have been one of general optimism, but occasional voices questioned the fundamental premises of traditional beliefs and focused on the irrational side of humans.

FRANCE

In France the Third Republic was proclaimed, following the Franco-Prussian War and the defeat of the radical **Paris Commune**. Moderate anticlerical republicans were in charge. Although they recognized unions, they devised few projects of social welfare. In fact, the energies of the new republic were often spent defending the new regime.

Domestic Crises   The republican government had to deal with a series of crises. First, General Boulanger attempted a coup d'état in 1889—with the military, the clerical forces, and the monarchists behind him. Second, the Panama Canal scandal revealed corruption among deputies and senators who badly mismanaged investments in the canal. The third and possibly most unsettling crisis was the Dreyfus affair. **Alfred Dreyfus** (1859-1935), a captain in the army and a Jew, was unjustly victimized by an anti-Semitic conspiracy of top-level officials who sought to save the reputation of the army and bureaucracy rather than mete out justice. The case lasted from 1894 to 1906. Treason had been committed, but not by Dreyfus. Nevertheless, inflamed public opinion demanded that the person guilty of giving military intelligence to Germany be found and convicted. Dreyfus, convicted of treason, was sent to prison. The real culprit, a Major Esterhazy, was discovered, put on trial, and acquitted even though the evidence against him was indisputable.

The affair split France into Dreyfusards and anti-Dreyfusards. The political Right supported the army and the government; the political center and Left, Dreyfus. In 1906, after the public turmoil instigated by Emile Zola (1840-1902), the novelist, Dreyfus was vindicated and given the Legion of Honor, as well as promoted to major in the army.

Another matter of general concern in France prior to the war was the growing power of working-class movements. Trade unions, or **syndicats**, were legalized in 1884. Most members preferred the general strike (**syndicalism**) rather than political activity. Yet there were socialist leaders like **Jean Jaurès** (1859-1914) who championed working within the Parliament to gain benefits for the working class. A socialist and pacifist, Jaurès was assassinated by a superpatriot. With Jaurès's death, France lost a voice of reason among the shrill clamors for war.

GERMANY

In Germany, Marxist **revisionists** like **Eduard Bernstein** (1850-1932) recognized that capitalism was not collapsing. Social intransigence, he felt, would hardly benefit the workers. Bernstein urged the **SDP** (Social Democratic Party) to cooperate with the bourgeoisie in the Reichstag to bring gradual reforms for the laboring classes. The SDP did, in fact, cooperate; yet its rhetoric remained militant.

After Bismarck's Dismissal

In 1894, William II dismissed Bismarck (known as the dropping of the pilot). There were four chancellors after him. William's insistence on armed strength enlisted support from Junkers and industrialists who opted for empire, high tariffs, and persecution of socialists, Jews, and foreigners. Enlarging the German army, William encouraged the passage of a naval bill in 1898 providing funds to construct a fleet that rivaled Great Britain's. As the war approached, Germany remained authoritarian and aristocratic. Ministers were responsible to the Crown and not to the members of the Reichstag. And in spite of the social welfare programs begun under Bismarck, the SDP continued to grow.

ENGLAND

In England, the Tory (or Conservative) Party won electoral victories with their emphasis on empire. The Dutch Boers (or farmers) occupied the Transvaal and Orange Free State in South Africa. In 1877, the British annexed Transvaal, where the discovery of gold and diamonds led to British settlement, the building of railroads, and finally war with the Boers in 1890. The **Conservative Party**, engineering the expansion, consolidated its political strength. To strengthen their power, party members introduced reforms at home. The party restructured local government, allowed the middle class to enter civil service, and passed the Education Act of 1902, which organized the primary, secondary, and technical school education needed to increase the number of qualified people necessary for a modern society. **Benjamin Disraeli** (1804-1881), a leader of the Conservative Party, who stated, "The palace is not safe when the cottage is not happy," wanted his party to be advocates for the common people in his rivalry with **William Gladstone** (1809-1898), the Liberal Party leader.

Social Legislation

But a new party was drawing the common people's support. In the early 1900s, the Labor Party formed. It drew its members from the trade unions and from the **Fabian Society**, the English socialists who believed that capitalism had to be whittled away gradually through electoral victories. Labor's growth in Parliament was due in large measure to the Taff-Vale Act (1902), which ruled that a company was entitled to damages from union funds for losses suffered during a strike by its employees. Labor members of Parliament introduced their own bill, which exempted unions from all claims for damages. The **Liberal Party**, in power, accepted the bill as its own and won the election in 1906. Thereupon, the Liberals, pressured by labor, put through Parliament a great deal of social legislation in the next decade, including sickness, old-age, and unemployment insurance, and a progressive income tax. The ire of the landed aristocracy flared, and the House of Lords threatened to veto the bills. The **Parliament Act of 1911**, however, deprived the House of Lords of all veto power in money matters. The Labor Party, nevertheless, continued its rise. After the First World War, the Conservatives and the Labor Party would be the major political parties in Great Britain.

Women's Suffrage

The period before the war also witnessed the militant attack on the social order by suffragists seeking the vote. Notable among them was **Emmeline Pankhurst** (1858-1928), founder of the Women's Social and Political Union. In Great Britain the suffragettes destroyed property, went on hunger strikes, slashed paintings in museums, bombed, and committed arson; one woman committed suicide by throwing herself under the king's horses in the British Derby.

DOCUMENT-BASED ESSAY QUESTION

Certainly the notion of "separation of spheres" had been an integral element in the Victorian sensibility. Consider the two sets of documents below. Write a paragraph using Group A to describe the gender roles prescribed in Victorian Britain and another paragraph using Group B to analyze the arguments that challenged these roles.

GROUP A: THE PROPER ROLE OF THE SEXES

From Margaretta Greg's *Diary*, 1853

. . . a lady, to be such, must be a mere lady, and nothing else. She must not work for profit, or engage in any occupation that money can command, lest she invade the rights of the working classes, who live by their labour. . . .

From J. Ruskin, *Sesame and Lilies*, 1865

The man . . . must encounter all peril and trial; to him, therefore, must be the failure, the offence, the inevitable error; often he must be wounded, or subdued; often misled, and *always* hardened. But he guards the woman from all this; within his house, as ruled by her, unless she herself has sought it, need enter no danger, no temptation, no cause of error or offence. This is the true nature of the home—it is the place of peace; the shelter, not only from all injury, but from all terror, doubt, and division.

From S. A. Sewell, *Woman and the Times We Live In*, 1869

It is a man's place to rule, and a woman's to yield. He must be held up as the head of the house, and it is her duty to bend so unmurmuringly to his wishes, that the rest of the household will follow her example, and treat him with the due respect his sex demands.

GROUP B: CHALLENGES TO CONVENTIONAL SEX ROLES

From Florence Nightingale, *Cassandra*, 1852

Women are never supposed to have any occupation of sufficient importance not to be interrupted . . . and women themselves accepted this. . . . They have accustomed themselves to consider intellectual occupation as mere selfish amusement, which it is their "duty" to give up for every trifler more selfish than they. . . .

From "The Maternal Instinct," *Saturday Review*, 1895

The only woman at the present time who is willing to be regarded as a mere breeding machine is she who lacks the wit to adopt any other role.

From John Stuart Mill, a Speech in Parliament, 1867

Women and men are, for the first time in history, really each others' companions. . . . the two sexes now pass their lives together, the women of a man's family are his habitual society; the wife is his chief associate, his most confidential friend, and often his most trusted advisor.

The Aftermath   We have already noted in an earlier chapter that England was able to avert revolution in the nineteenth century by providing "doses of reform." The series of reform bills, in 1832, 1867, and 1884, had enfranchised various sectors of the male population. Women, however, in spite of pressures exerted to give them the vote, were unsuccessful. They suffered ridicule, imprisonment, and physical humiliation, as under the **"Cat and Mouse Act,"** passed in 1913. Nineteenth-century feminists like **Caroline Norton** (1808–1877) had worked for many years to challenge British laws that gave all property, income, and child custody rights to husbands. It was not until 1883 that the Married Women's Property Act gave women the same property rights as unmarried women. And women knew that without the franchise they could hardly exert political power. When women did gain the vote, it was not until 1919—and then for women over the age of thirty—and largely because of their contribution to the war effort rather than from the earlier logic of their demands. In 1928, women at age of twenty-one did receive the vote.

DOCUMENT-BASED ESSAY QUESTION

Using the documents below, write an essay explaining how views of gender shaped opposition to women's right to vote.

Again the underlying assumption in the national franchise is that the voter, who has to decide on the well-being and even the existence of his country, can argue out his views for his country's good on equal terms with his fellow, and in the last resort can knock him down if he chance to be the better man. No such assumption could be possible were women to have the vote.

The Times, *15 June 1908*

June 14, 1884.]   PUNCH, OR THE LONDON CHARIVARI.

"THE ANGEL IN 'THE HOUSE;'" OR, THE RESULT OF FEMALE SUFFRAGE.
(A Troubled Dream of the Future.)

Punch, *14 June 1884*

The fear I have is, lest we should invite her (woman) unwittingly to trespass upon the delicacy, the purity, the refinement, the elevation of her own nature, which are the present sources of its power.

Female Suffrage, a letter from the Rt. Hon. W. E. Gladstone, Member of Parliament, to Samuel Smith, M.P., 1892

In controlling a vast Empire like our own, an Empire built by the mental and physical capacity of men, and maintained, as it always must be maintained, by the physical and mental capacity of masterly natures—I ask: "Is there a place for women?"

Mr. J. A. Grant, Member of Parliament for West Cumberland, in a speech in the House of Commons, 5 May 1913

EUROPEAN THOUGHT: DARWIN AND FREUD

Intellectual currents undermined traditional patterns of thought. Consider the impact of Darwin's theory of evolution. **Charles Darwin** (1809-1882) himself was not a social philosopher but a scientist who presented an orderly scheme of evolution. He had explained *how* changes happened, not *why* they happened. Many inferences, however, were drawn from his theories. In the famous Huxley-Wilberforce debate, the Reverend Samuel Wilberforce resisted, "I would rather not claim a monkey for ancestor." To which Thomas Huxley retorted, "I'd rather be descended from an honest ape than from one who though endowed with brains refused to use them."

Darwin's study of flora and fauna was applied to the evolution of humans. The conclusion was drawn by a number of writers that the human race was driven forward by an economic struggle that determined "the survival of the fittest."

Even more shocking to the sensibilities of the Victorians were the ideas of **Sigmund Freud** (1856-1939). He explored the continuity between primitive and civilized humankind. Freud claimed that he wanted to make humans comprehensible, not contemptible. Nevertheless, his theories of infantile sexuality, his model of the human personality as the battleground of conflict between the id, the ego, and the superego, and his view of God as a creation by humans to allay their anxieties brought him widespread notoriety. Freud was a pioneer in the discipline of modern psychology, but his writings, like the famous *The Interpretation of Dreams* (1900), went beyond his clinical work. In 1929, following World War I, he published *Civilization and Its Discontents*.

DOCUMENT-BASED QUESTION

In the excerpt below, *Freud* pinpoints the relationship between human nature and civilization. In a paragraph, explain what he argues is the task of civilization, given the essential nature of humans, and discuss how the title of his book relates to his thesis.

FROM *CIVILIZATION AND ITS DISCONTENTS* (1929), BY SIGMUND FREUD

The element of truth behind all this, which people are so ready to disavow, is that men are not gentle creatures who want to be loved, and who at the most can defend themselves if they are attacked; they are, on the contrary, creatures among whose instinctual endowments is to be reckoned a powerful share of aggressiveness. As a result, their neighbour is for them not only a potential helper or sexual object, but also someone who tempts them to satisfy their aggressiveness on him, to exploit his capacity for work without compensation, to use him sexually without his consent, to seize his possessions, to humiliate him, to cause him pain, to torture and to kill him. . . .

The existence of this inclination to aggression, which we can detect in ourselves and justly assume to be present in others, is the factor which disturbs our relations with our neighbour and which forces civilization into such a high expenditure (of energy). In consequence of this primary mutual hostility of human beings, civilized society is perpetually threatened with disintegration. The interest of work in common would not hold it together; instinctual passions are stronger than reasonable interests. Civilization has to use its utmost efforts in order to set limits to man's aggressive instincts and to hold the manifestations of them in check. . . .

The fateful question for the human species seems to me to be whether and to what extent their cultural development will succeed in mastering the disturbance of their communal life by the human instinct of aggression and self-destruction. . . . Men have gained control over the forces of nature to such an extent that with their help they would have no difficulty in exterminating one another to the last man. They know this, and hence comes a large part of their current unrest, their unhappiness and their mood of anxiety.

Impact of Freud's Theories

In essence, Freud was exploring the limits of rationality. He was using the scientific method and analytic reason to understand the irrational. His impact on writers and artists was widespread. Stream-of-consciousness writing in the novels of James Joyce, depictions of the unconscious in the surrealist paintings of Dali, de Chirico, Magritte, and the expressionist works of Eduard Munch and Ludwig Kirchner owe their creative inspiration to the explorations of Freud.

FIN DE SIÈCLE

For the ordinary citizens, however, the works of Freud and his contemporary **Friedrich Nietzsche** (1844-1900), who pronounced the death of all philosophic absolutes in his dictum "God is dead," were remote from their daily lives. In the heavily industrialized Western and central European nations, ordinary people were gaining such benefits as adult male suffrage and free compulsory education. The legalization of trade unions provided a countervailing weight in dealing with employers. And as colonies were acquired in Africa and the Far East, citizens developed jingoistic pride and often benefited from economic expansion.

In a society increasingly secular, the Roman Catholic Church counterattacked. In the 1864 **Syllabus of Errors**, Pope Pius IX (1846-1878) denounced belief in reason and science and attacked liberalism and modern civilization. Six years later, the **Vatican Council** pronounced the doctrine of papal infallibility on matters of faith and morals. Yet the succeeding pope, Leo XIII (1878-1903), sought to accommodate to the modern age. In the encyclical *Rerum Novarum* (1891), he upheld the right of private property but assailed the injustices of capitalism and urged that Catholics form political parties and unions to reform the economic injustices.

Still, urban life was improving as governments took responsibility for health, water, lighting, and sewer disposal. Public transportation facilitated urban travel, and urban centers witnessed building and rebuilding in areas of decay. The general mood was one of optimism. As earlier noted, unions were concentrating on bread-and-butter issues—higher wages, improved working conditions—in short, collective bargaining. Before the First World War, socialism had become "nationalized," as the movement lost its radical nature. The rhetoric may have remained radical, but the actions were moderate. Few could envision or predict the physical and emotional destruction that World War I would bring to the European community and the Atlantic civilization.

MULTIPLE-CHOICE QUESTIONS

1. Material and industrial growth, international peace, optimistic faith in science, rational thinking, and progress, and the extension of the suffrage in representative governments characterized which of the following periods in modern European history?
   a. 1660-1689
   b. 1774-1793
   c. 1815-1848
   d. 1870-1910
   e. 1919-1945

2. The "new Industrial Revolution" occurring after 1870 was characterized chiefly by the
   a. use of steam power
   b. expansion of metallurgical industries
   c. development of textiles and the growth of the industry
   d. advent of the railroad
   e. invention of the internal combustion engine

3. They took their name from the ancient Roman general who urged gradual methods in accomplishing his goals. As critics of capitalism, they believed that social reform could be realized without bitter class conflict. The group referred to is the
   a. syndicalists
   b. Fabians
   c. Marxists
   d. nihilists
   e. Chartists

4. He perceived democracy and Christianity as promoting a "slave morality" in which the weak emasculated the strong. In particular, he called for an *Übermensch*, or Superman, who would rise above the inhibitions of bourgeois society he detested. The individual referred to is
   a. Friedrich Nietzsche
   b. Auguste Comte
   c. Georges Sorel
   d. Ludwig Wittgenstein
   e. Henri Bergson

*From a New York Newspaper Showing Zola Engaged in a Battle for Truth
in the Dreyfus Affair.*

5. Which of the following groups would have most likely supported this
   cartoon in turn-of-the century France?
   a. monarchists
   b. nationalists
   c. clerics
   d. militarists
   e. socialists

6. Which of the following statements would Freud have subscribed to?
   a. Human nature is basically rational.
   b. Dreams are products of our subconscious.
   c. Ethical behavior is inborn.
   d. Sexuality is an adult phenomenon.
   e. Civilization encourages the release of libidinal drives.

7. The years 1832, 1867, and 1884 are important in British politics for
   a. improvements in women's political rights
   b. the extension of male suffrage
   c. the formation of trade unions in craft industries
   d. reforms in the British penal code
   e. the exacerbation of hostilities in Ireland

8. These artists believed that they should present life in objective detail. They
   wrote descriptions of industrial and Parisian life with precise detail. They
   acted as social critics bringing issues of political and social values that
   troubled society into the realm of aesthetics. One such artist was
   a. Franz Kafka
   b. Emile Zola
   c. Jane Austen
   d. Herbert Spencer
   e. Anthony Trollope

9. A central feature of the *Rerum Novarum* (1891) was its
   a. unqualified support of industrial capitalism
   b. denunciation of private property
   c. encouragement of the formation of Christian socialist parties
   d. reconciliation with Protestantism
   e. creation of the Vatican State in Italy

10. A major impact of industrial expansion in Britain in the late nineteenth century was
    a. the increasing impoverishment of the working classes
    b. a decrease in the number of women working as domestics
    c. a decline in labor-saving technology for the home
    d. an increase in mortality rates
    e. long-range unemployment and declining gross national product

PRACTICE ESSAY QUESTIONS

Use the questions below to practice essay writing. For each question write an essay that includes an introductory thesis, a body of supporting and/or illustrative data, and a conclusion.

1. How did the Dreyfus Affair reveal the political divisions in France that threatened the republican regime?
2. "Although a series of reform bills extended the suffrage in the nineteenth century, Great Britain failed to become democratic." Assess the validity of this statement.
3. Describe how Darwin, Nietzsche, and Freud challenged the conventional wisdom of the nineteenth century. Which man had the greatest impact?
4. "Liberalism evolved from a classical to a democratic form in the period 1871-1914 in Western Europe." Defend or refute this statement, using specific evidence to support your position.
5. Why did women fail to receive the vote in Great Britain prior to World War I?

ESSAY-WRITING TIPS: AVOIDING ETHNOCENTRISM

Consider the following two paragraphs that conclude essay 5, "Why did women fail to receive the vote in Great Britain prior to World War I?" One of these exhibits ethnocentrism. The other takes a culturally relativist position. Read the paragraphs and compare them. Write a paragraph explaining which of them is ethnocentric and why.

Paragraph A   Women, in conclusion, failed to receive the vote because parliamentary leaders were ignorant. They had no right to deny women what was their due. Even today, we see women fighting for political and economic rights. It is wrong now and it was wrong then to restrict opportunities to only the male sex. The right to vote is a basic right that must be given to both sexes. That the political leaders of Victorian England were foolish and stubborn explains their refusal to give women the vote.

Paragraph B   Women, in conclusion, failed to receive the vote for reasons relating to perceptions of gender roles. Male and female spheres were viewed differently, each with its attendant rights and responsibilities, as well as dominant concerns and intrinsic powers. From today's perspective, it is difficult to understand the fear and outright opposition to giving women the vote that provoked such violence on the part of the opposition. Yet history teaches us that ideas are powerful forces, difficult to change and move in spite of compelling arguments.

Commentary   Paragraph A exhibits ethnocentrism–i.e., judging other cultures (or periods in history) by the standards and values of today. The historian does not ask: Was X wrong? but rather Why did X behave in that particular manner? Of course, it is not always easy to divest oneself of the values and views that are part of the cultural cloak we find comfortable and familiar. Nevertheless, the historian's task is to try to understand the past, not judge it for its failure to live up to today's expectations.

IDENTIFICATIONS

Eduard Bernstein (1850-1932)–Revisionist German Social Democrat who favored socialist revolution by the ballot rather than the bullet–i.e, by cooperating with the bourgeois members of Parliament and securing electoral victories for his party (the SDP).

"Cat and Mouse Act" (1913)–Law that released suffragettes on hunger strikes from jail and then rearrested and jailed them again.

Conservative Party–Formerly the Tory Party, headed by Disraeli in the nineteenth century.

Charles Darwin (1809-1882)–British scientist whose *Origin of Species* (1859) proposed the theory of evolution based on his biological research.

Benjamin Disraeli (1804-1881)–Leader of the British Tory Party who engineered the Reform Bill of 1867, which extended the franchise to the working class.

Alfred Dreyfus (1859-1935)–French Jewish army captain unfairly convicted of espionage in a case that lasted from 1894 to 1906.

Fabian Society–Group of English socialists, including George Bernard Shaw, who advocated electoral victories rather than violent revolution to bring about social change.

Sigmund Freud (1856-1939)–Viennese psychoanalyst whose theory of human personality based on sexual drives shocked Victorian sensibilities.

William Gladstone (1809-1898)–British Liberal Party leader and prime minister, a chief rival of Disraeli. Gladstone's ministry included reforms in public education, civil service exams, and secret balloting.

Jean Jaurès (1859-1914)–French revisionist socialist who was assassinated for his pacifist ideals at the start of World War I.

Liberal Party–Formerly the Whig Party, headed by Gladstone in the nineteenth century.

Friedrich Nietzsche (1844-1900)–German philosopher and forerunner of the modern existentialist movement; he stressed the role of the *Übermensch*, or "Superman," who would rise above the common herd of mediocrity.

Caroline Norton (1808-1877)–British feminist whose legal persistence resulted in the Married Women's Property Act (1883), which gave married women the same property rights as unmarried women.

Emmeline Pankhurst (1858-1928)–British suffragette and founder of the Women's Social and Political Union.

Parliament Act of 1911–Legislation that deprived the House of Lords of veto power in all money matters.

Paris Commune–The revolutionary municipal council, led by radicals, that engaged in a civil war (March-May 1871) with the National Assembly of the newly established Third Republic, set up after the defeat of Napoleon III in the Franco-Prussian War.

Rerum Novarum (1891)–Papal encyclical of Leo XIII (1878-1903) that upheld the right of private property but criticized the inequities of capitalism. It recommended that Catholics form political parties and trade unions to redress the poverty and insecurity fostered under capitalism.

Revisionists–Marxists who believed that workers empowered to vote could obtain their ends through democratic means without revolution and the dictatorship of the proletariat, known as revisionism.

SDP–The Social Democratic Party in Germany, based on Marx's ideology.

Syllabus of Errors (1864)–Doctrine of Pope Pius IX (1846-1878) that denounced belief in reason and science and attacked "progress, liberalism, and modern civilization."

Syndicalism–The French trade-unionist belief that workers would become the governmental power through a general strike that would paralyze society.

Syndicats–French trade unions.

Vatican Council of 1870–Gathering of Catholic church leaders that proclaimed the doctrine of papal infallibility.

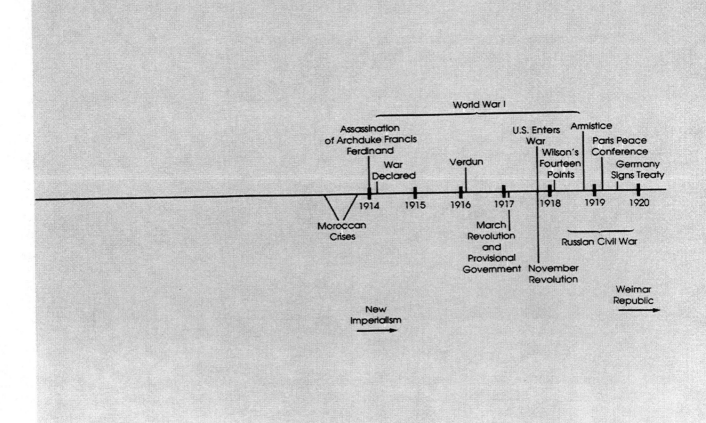

IMPERIALISM AND THE
COMING OF WORLD WAR I

CHAPTER 12

IMPERIALISM

Imperialism in the late nineteenth century involved expansion and partition. The very word has a charged meaning today—one of conquest, control, and exploitation. Various factors have been cited to explain the suddenness and speed with which Africa and Asia were carved up by the great industrial states of Europe, among them economic, political, diplomatic, racial, religious, and nationalist.

DOCUMENT-BASED ESSAY QUESTION

Below are two excerpts that deal with French colonialism. The first appeared in *The Bulletin of the Society of Colonial and Maritime Studies,* published in the 1870s. The second excerpt, written by Anatole France, a French author and critic, appeared in the German newspaper *Neue Freie Presse* in 1904. Read and compare in writing the two sources in terms of (1) the reason each author cites for imperialism, (2) the attitudes toward imperialism cited in the document, and (3) the author's views toward the colonizers and the colonized people. (Note the directive *compare*; see p. 117.)

FROM *THE BULLETIN*

No one in France . . . doubts the benefits of colonization and the advantages which it offers both to the country which undertakes it and to that which receives it. Everyone agrees that colonies offer markets for raw materials, the means of production, the products lacking to the mother-country; that they open markets to all the commerce and all the industries of an old country, by the wants, by the new needs of the people with whom they are in relation. . . .

FROM A NEWSPAPER ARTICLE BY ANATOLE FRANCE

We Frenchmen, a thrifty people, who are careful not to have more children than we can support, careful not to adventure into far lands . . . why do we need colonies? What can we do with them? France has paid in lives and money so that the Congo, Cochinchina, Annam, Tonkin, Guinea, and Madagascar may buy cotton from Manchester, munitions from Birmingham, liquor from Danzig, and wine from Hamburg. For the last seventy years France has attacked, persecuted and chased the Arabs in order that Italians and Spaniards might live in Algeria!

But while the French people get nothing from the territories in Africa and Asia, their governments find it most profitable. It is a way of gaining favor with the military and naval leaders who get promotions, pensions and decorations. . . . with shipowners, army contractors, and shady politicians. It is a way of flattering the ignorant mob, which thinks that owning an overseas empire will make the Germans and the English turn green with envy. . . .

The world's resources can be fully developed only by the cooperation of all races, white, yellow, and black.

Some historians have suggested that France sought colonies to redress the humiliating loss of Alsace and Lorraine in 1870. And still others claim that France was seeking conquest to train African soldiers to make up for the declining birthrate in France. Whatever the motives, their complex intertwinings contributed to the buildup of tensions among the great powers that led to war. But other factors contributed to the First World War as well, as described in the next section.

FACTORS CONTRIBUTING TO WORLD WAR I

The following factors were chiefly responsible:

1. Nationalism and the "ethnographic" untidiness of Austria-Hungary. The empire included Bohemians, Romanians, Croats, Serbs, Slovaks, and Poles, along with the Germans and Hungarians who ruled the **Dual Monarchy** of Austria-Hungary. The Slavs, who shared language and culture, sought assistance from the independent Slavic state of Serbia in an attempt to break away from Hapsburg rule. Serbia, in turn, looked for Russian assistance to expand its borders to include people of Serbo-Croatian heritage.
2. **Pan-Slavism** in the Balkans. A series of crises contributed to unrest in the Ottoman Empire. Young Turks rebelling against a reactionary sultan gave Austria the opportunity to annex the territories of Bosnia and Herzegovina in 1908. Serbia was opposed but could not obtain the military support of

Russia at this time. A later conflict erupted among the Balkan powers of Serbia, Bulgaria, Greece, and Romania that resulted in the independence of Albania and thwarted ambitions among the other countries in this volatile area, known as the "powder keg" of Europe.

3. The alliance system: the **Three Emperors' League**, the **Triple Alliance**, the **Entente Cordiale**, and the **Triple Entente**. As chancellor, Bismarck had formed alliances with Austria and Russia to isolate France and subdue its spirit of ***revanche*** (revenge) for its losses in 1870.

   With Bismarck's dismissal in 1890, Kaiser William II, now in command, let the Reinsurance Treaty with Russia elapse. Closer relations formed between Russia and France sparked by French investments in Russia's economic expansion. France and Britain also formed friendly relations in opposition to German expansion (the Entente Cordiale). With promises of liberal reform, Russia was invited to join the Entente. In effect, Germany and its major ally, Austria-Hungary, faced **encirclement**.

4. Germany's shipbuilding program, leading to a naval arms race between Germany and Great Britain. Germany's expansion of big-gun battleships (dreadnoughts) and William II's dream of **Weltpolitik** exacerbated tensions by forcing Great Britain to spend on battleships rather than social programs.

5. Militaristic **social Darwinism**. The writings of the German historian Heinrich Treitschke exalted the inevitability and desirability of war. Social Darwinism promoted the concept of the "survival of the fittest," taken to mean that war would cleanse humankind of the unfit in a cataclysmic

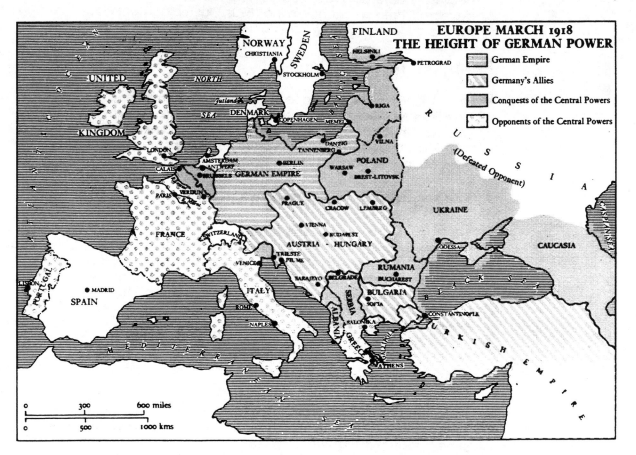

struggle. Such ideas, while not universally held, did attract an enthusiastic following among military chiefs, some artists, and students eager for adventure. Yet forces do not bring about war as such. Human actors impelled by ideas and events play the major dramatic roles.

DOCUMENT-BASED ESSAY QUESTION

The comments below are an inventive re-creation of what might have been said if the European leaders had met after World War I. The imaginary comments are drawn from historical accounts and analyses. Review them and write an essay deciding who and what particular forces were responsible for the war.

BISMARCK

It is certainly true that I formed a series of alliances with Austria-Hungary and Russia (the Three Emperors' League) and the Triple Alliance with Austria-Hungary and Italy, and that I cemented relations with Russia in the Reinsurance Treaty—but this was before I was removed from office in 1890. Surely, I was not responsible.

FRENCH REPRESENTATIVE

He lies! He tried to set up a system that isolated my nation. As for me, in necessary defense, I reached a friendly understanding with Russia, which developed into an alliance in the 1890s. Our Triple Entente lasted as long as the Triple Alliance. Surely, I am not responsible.

RUSSIAN REPRESENTATIVE

Don't blame me. Our alliance with France had much merit. Loans and arms from France sweetened our relationship. France needed a friend, and so did we. France became our big brother. Furthermore, Austria-Hungary created the problems by getting involved in issues that were the business of Slavs, and Slavs alone. We Russians are surely not responsible.

AUSTRO-HUNGARIAN REPRESENTATIVE

Did I hear my name mentioned? Something about Slavic issues? Whatever you decide, it is quite certain that I am guiltless. To begin, Bosnia was under Austro-Hungarian rule. Serbia, an adjacent state, riddled with Serbian nationals, tried to promote Slavic fanaticism in Bosnia. Bosnia was rightfully under our rule. Russia, no doubt, was instigating the Serbs. When our Archduke Francis Ferdinand rode into **Sarajevo**, Serbian terrorists belonging to the **Black Hand** awaited him. He and his wife were assassinated. We demanded justice. That does not make us guilty. We were not responsible.

SERBIAN REPRESENTATIVE

It wasn't justice they demanded but our sovereignty. After the archduke was shot, the Austro-Hungarian government demanded an apology (which we gave), required that we ban Austro-Hungarian propaganda (which we did), and demanded that Austro-Hungarian representatives enter our nation and freely conduct the investigation of those responsible. Would you compromise your nationhood in that way? That last demand was outrageous. Of course, we refused. And then Austria-Hungary declared war on us. We were not guilty for the act of a single terrorist. Neither are we guilty for World War I.

AUSTRO-HUNGARIAN REPRESENTATIVE

It is true. We did declare war on Serbia, but Germany gave its approval. Kaiser William II was behind us all the way. Does that make us guilty?

WILLIAM II

What's this? Have I heard my name mentioned? No doubt you are referring to the so-called **blank check**, the unconditional support we gave to our ally, Austria-Hungary. Another act of irresponsibility on the part of William II, you are thinking. True, I had some problems with the French because of the **Moroccan crisis** at **Agadir** and did get slapped on the wrist at the **Algeciras** conference in 1906, when French interests were recognized by the other major powers. As for the ''blank check,'' *did* I do that? Well, possibly. After all, if Germany didn't support our friend Austria-Hungary, who would? The French were planning to support the Russians. Britain proposed a conference, and France and Russia agreed. But I said let the Serbs and Austro-Hungarians settle their own mess. Look, if Russia had not mobilized, nothing would have happened. Blank checks are not armies on the border. Don't look at me. I'm not responsible.

RUSSIAN MILITARY STAFF LEADER

Wait a minute. Let's get things straight. Austria-Hungary declared war on Serbia, our Slavic friend, and was prepared to occupy Serbian territory. Were we supposed to just stand around? I wanted a partial mobilization to shake up the Germans a bit, but, unfortunately, our military leaders had no plans for a partial mobilization—only a general, or full, mobilization. So that's what we had to do. Germany demanded that we demobilize in twelve hours. Our best friend, France, also mobilized, but had kept troops six miles from the frontier. We wanted no incidents, I assure you. Yet what did the Germans do? *They* mobilized and declared war on us, Russia. We military men of Russia are not to blame.

GERMAN MILITARY STAFF LEADER

Did we really have a choice when Russia and France called up their troops? Did anyone measure the six-mile distance from the border? By necessity, I tell you, we had to declare war on Russia and France. We were encircled, as if we were in a pincer. And then we had to invade Belgium according to the **Schlieffen Plan** to get to our enemy France. We had no choice, I repeat. If only the British had made clear what they intended, the whole spectacle might have been avoided. Certainly we are not to blame.

BRITISH REPRESENTATIVE

One minute. We did not want war, that should be clear. It was long known by all the European nations that we would come to the defense of Belgium if her neutrality was violated. The neutrality of Belgium had been guaranteed by an international treaty in 1839. We had tried to save the peace. We had sought mediation between Austria and Serbia and even between Austria and Russia—to no avail. Remember also that we are a parliamentary government and our cabinet was divided over the issue of the war. When Germany invaded Belgium in its effort to quickly defeat France, we had no recourse but *then* to declare our intentions. We declared war on Germany. The issue seems to be one of big brothers supporting irresponsible little brothers. Where then does the guilt lie? Certainly not with us.

THE AFTERMATH OF WORLD WAR I

Certainly miscalculations played a part in the outbreak. Nations like Austria, Germany, and Russia hoped to preserve and increase their power with victory. Military leaders believed that the war would be short and swift—a matter of a few weeks. With a first-strike, decisive knock-out punch, the enemy would summarily collapse.

Yet the war, lasting for four long years, destroyed the great powers. The concern with a first strike enabled the generals to take over for the diplomats. As a result, negotiations quickly collapsed.

The Peace Settlements

The peace settlement was finally arrived at through a series of treaties, the most famous signed at Versailles on June 28, 1919. The United States, which had entered the war following the German sinking of the **Lusitania** and the delivery of the **Zimmermann telegram**, played a key role. The U.S. president, **Woodrow Wilson** (1856–1924), hoped that liberal and democratic principles would be upheld in his **Fourteen Points**. He similarly dreamed of a workable **League of Nations**, which would enforce international agreements among the major signatories.

Among the Fourteen Points the key ones were

- open covenants of peace, openly arrived at
- adequate guarantees given and taken that national armaments would be reduced to the lowest point consistent with domestic safety
- stipulations that all French territory should be freed and the invaded portions restored, and that the wrong done to France by Prussia in 1871 in the matter of Alsace-Lorraine should be righted
- a free, open-minded, and absolutely impartial adjustment of all colonial claims, based on the principle that, in questions of sovereignty, the interests of the populations concerned must have equal weight with the governments whose title is to be determined
- a readjustment of the frontiers of Italy along clearly recognizable lines of nationality
- evacuation and restoration of Belgium, without any attempt to limit the sovereignty which she enjoys
- absolute freedom of navigation on the seas

President Wilson's chief aims were those of **self-determination** for ethnic populations, **free trade** resulting from the removal of trade barriers, the reduction of armaments, open diplomacy, and the improvement of the welfare of colonial populations. The United States was a major power at the peace

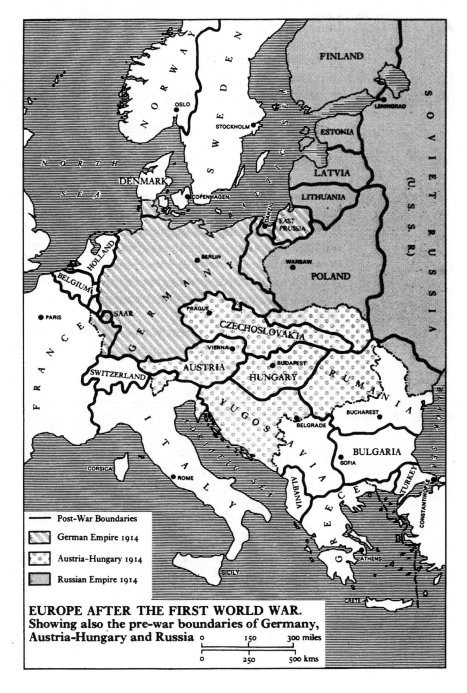

EUROPE AFTER THE FIRST WORLD WAR.
Showing also the pre-war boundaries of Germany,
Austria-Hungary and Russia

Post-War Boundaries

German Empire 1914

Austria-Hungary 1914

Russian Empire 1914

conference, but there were other major voices as well, those of Great Britain
and France. Germany was not allowed to take part, and Russia was locked in
civil war (see Chapter 13). The leaders of Great Britain and France (Lloyd
George and Clemenceau, respectively) insisted on a dictated peace to Germany. Germany was blamed for World War I. **Article 231** of the Treaty of
Versailles read: "The Allied and Associate Governments affirm and Germany
accepts the responsibility of Germany and her allies for causing all the loss and
damage to which the Allied and Associated Governments and their nationals
have been subjected as a consequence of the war."

Germany's Defeat In addition to being required to accept responsibility for the war, Germany lost colonies to France, Britain, and Japan as League of Nations mandates, as well as land on the Continent ceded to the new Polish state (the Polish Corridor). In addition, the treaty enabled the allies to control the Rhineland for fifteen years; after that a plebiscite would decide its fate. The coal mines of the Saar basin were transferred to France. So too were Alsace and Lorraine. Finally, Germany had to pay heavy **indemnities** and its army and navy were limited in size.

The peace treaty was humiliating for Germany. Article 231, the so-called war guilt clause, along with the efforts to reduce Germany to a third-rate status, hurt the newly established Weimar Republic in Germany as it and the other European countries attempted recovery from the war. As for the League of Nations, isolationist attitudes prevented the United States from joining. Without U.S. involvement, the League could handle only the business that the Great Powers deemed worthy. It failed to develop the machinery to prevent war. Its weapon of boycotting an aggressor nation proved futile, since the determination of the aggressor in a conflict was unclear, particularly if one's vital interests were not involved.

The notion that the Great War, or World War I, was the war to end all wars proved to be a chimera. Discontents paved the way for totalitarianism in the following decades.

MULTIPLE-CHOICE QUESTIONS

1. Trench warfare became common during which of the following wars?
   a. Crimean War
   b. Franco-Prussian War
   c. Boer War
   d. Russo-Japanese War
   e. World War I

2. The Austrian annexation of Bosnia in 1908 threatened the nationalist aspirations of which of the following countries?
   a. Turkey
   b. Romania
   c. Serbia
   d. France
   e. Herzegovina

3. Which of Wilson's goals was fully achieved?
   a. Armaments were reduced to levels consistent with national safety.
   b. The League of Nations became an instrument for preventing war.
   c. France regained the provinces of Alsace and Lorraine.
   d. Italy's borders were readjusted to include all Italian nationals.
   e. No punitive demands were imposed on the loser nations.

4. A theory that held the power of nationalism, along with the glorification of violence and militarism, was largely responsible for World War I would most likely blame which of the following countries for the war?
   a. Germany
   b. France and Russia

    c. Serbia
    d. Austria-Hungary
    e. Italy

5. Great Britain entered the war when
    a. Russia mobilized
    b. Belgium was invaded
    c. Germany issued its "blank check"
    d. Austria-Hungary declared war on Serbia
    e. Serbia refused to accept the Austro-Hungarian ultimatum

6. In spite of the general enthusiasm for the war, this political leader foretold gloom. He stated, with the onset of the war, that "the lamps are going out all over Europe [and] we shall never see them lit again in our lifetime." The author of this statement was
    a. William II, emperor of Germany
    b. Edward Grey, the British foreign secretary
    c. Georges Clemenceau, prime minister of France
    d. Winston Churchill, member of the British Parliament
    e. Woodrow Wilson, president of the United States

7. It embraced a patchwork quilt of competing nationalities in 1914. There was no way it could sanction nationalism as a legitimate force to be acknowledged. The country referred to is
    a. Italy
    b. Russia
    c. Turkey
    d. Austria-Hungary
    e. Poland

8. Women's roles changed as increasing numbers of women entered the labor force during World War I. Their entrance was the result largely of
    a. their acquiring the right to vote
    b. higher mortality rates
    c. declining birthrates
    d. an excess of demand for labor
    e. changing sexual attitudes

9. The dismissal of Bismarck by Kaiser William II paved the way for an alliance between which of the following countries during the First World War?
    a. France and Russia
    b. Germany and Italy
    c. Germany and Austria-Hungary
    d. Great Britain and Belgium
    e. Serbia and Russia

10. European writers, such as Erich Remarque in *All Quiet on the Western Front*, portrayed warfare in World War I in terms of
    a. patriotic nationalism
    b. a loss of innocence
    c. a cleansing of human pollutants
    d. a struggle between bourgeoisie and proletariat
    e. anarchic individualism

PRACTICE ESSAY QUESTIONS

Use the questions below to practice essay writing. For each question write an essay that includes an introductory thesis, a body of supporting and/or illustrative data, and a conclusion.

1. If no one wanted a major war, why did the First World War occur?
2. "The First World War marks a watershed in modern European history." How can this statement be justified?
3. Discuss the strengths and weaknesses of the Treaty of Versailles. In which ways did it succeed in resolving the issues dividing the major European powers? In which ways did it fail?
4. "World War I was a dominant factor in revolutionizing women's place in Western society." Assess the validity of this statement.
5. "In an era of nation-states, Austria-Hungary was an anomaly—a condition that made the First World War inevitable." Defend or refute this statement.

ESSAY-WRITING TIPS: THE USE OF STATISTICAL DOCUMENTS

A document-based question may include a statistical document. In a DBQ on World War I, the following chart might be included in a question relating to the impact of the war.

MILITARY FATALITIES IN WORLD WAR I

Germany	2,000,000
Russia	1,700,000
France	1,500,000
Austria-Hungary	1,250,000
British Empire	1,000,000
Italy	500,000
Ottoman Empire	500,000
United States	100,000

Review the information and then read the two paragraphs below. Both were written to incorporate the quantitative data in a question on the impact of the war. Write a brief paragraph that judges which paragraph better handles the information.

Paragraph A

Among the armed forces, casualties ran high. Germany lost 2 million; Russia, 1.7 million; France, 1.5 million; Austria-Hungary, 1.25 million; the British Empire, 1 million; Italy and the Ottoman Empire, one-half million each; and the United States, 100,000. All in all, 8,550,000 lives were lost in the war.

Paragraph B

The First World War had a major impact on European and U.S. populations. Combat deaths in most European countries were in the millions. And if one adds in the number of wounded, maimed, and disabled among the military and adds to it the deaths and injuries in the civilian population, the casualty numbers become astronomical. These deaths and injuries not only destroyed human life and talent but also signified the loss of producers and consumers who would have contributed to industrial growth and expansion as well as to the creation of future generations. The loss in human lives was staggering—a testament to the ill-sighted judgment of those who thought the war would be swift and decisive, with minimal casualties.

Commentary

In using statistical documents, it is unnecessary to quote them verbatim. It is important to look for the *sense* of a document in terms of the way it can answer the question. Certainly, one might compare the military fatalities of Germany and the United States, for example, if the question asked about the severity of human damage among the Great Powers' populations. But if the question is a broad one, then the document should be used in a general sense.

There is a great deal that these figures do not tell us. Paragraph B mentions the number of wounded and disabled, as well as the loss among the civilian population. We know nothing, for example, about the social classes from which the military casualties came. Were young men from the elite schools in each nation wiped out? France had an older population and a low birthrate at the turn of the century. What was the demographic impact on France when an entire generation was lost in the war? And are the numbers in the chart conservative estimates? Figures are useful, and they should be used in formulating answers—but with reservation and a degree of caution about what they reveal and also fail to reveal.

IDENTIFICATIONS

Article 231–Provision of the Versailles Treaty that blamed Germany for World War I.

Black Hand–The Serbian secret society alleged to be responsible for assassinating Archduke Francis Ferdinand.

Blank check–Reference to the full support provided by William II to Austria-Hungary in its conflict with Serbia.

Dreadnought–A battleship with increased speed and power over conventional warships, developed by both Germany and Great Britain to increase their naval arsenals.

Dual Monarchy–An 1867 compromise between the Germans of Austria-Bohemia and the Magyars of Germany to resolve the nationalities problem by creating the empire of Austria and the kingdom of Hungary, with a common ministry for finance, foreign affairs, and war.

Encirclement–Before both world wars, the policy of other European countries that, Germany claimed, prevented German expansion, denying it the right to acquire "living room" (*Lebensraum*).

Entente Cordiale–The 1904 "gentleman's agreement" between France and Britain establishing a close understanding.

Fourteen Points–Wilson's peace plans calling for freedom of the seas, arms reduction, and the right of self-determination for ethnic groups.

Free trade–An economic theory or policy of the absence of restrictions or tariffs on goods imported into a country. There is no "protection" in the form of tariffs against foreign competition.

Imperialism–The acquisition and administration of colonial areas, usually in the interests of the administering country.

Indemnities–Financial demands placed on loser nations.

League of Nations–A proposal included in Wilson's Fourteen Points to establish an international organization to settle disputes and avoid future wars.

Lusitania–British merchant liner carrying ammunition and passengers that was sunk by a German U-boat in 1915. The loss of 139 American lives on board was a factor bringing the United States into World War I.

Moroccan crises
1. **Algeciras**–The site of the 1906 conference in Spain at which German involvement in Morocco was rebuffed by Britain and France acting in unison.
2. **Agadir**–The site of the landing of the German gunboat in Morocco in 1911. William II tried to force the French to make concessions to Germany in Africa. Like the first crisis, this one drew Britain and France closer together.

Pan-Slavism–The movement to unite Slavs in the Balkans.

Revanche–The French desire for revenge against Germany for the loss of Alsace and Lorraine in the Franco-Prussian War (1870).

Sarajevo–The Balkan town in the Austro-Hungarian province of Bosnia where Gavrilo Princip assassinated Archduke Francis Ferdinand, heir to the throne.

Schlieffen Plan–Top-secret German strategy to fight a two-front war against Russia and France. The idea was to invade neutral Belgium for a quick victory against France, and then direct German forces against a more slowly mobilizing Russia.

Self-determination–The ability of an ethnic group to decide how it wishes to be governed, as an independent nation or as part of another country.

Social Darwinism–The belief that only the fittest survive in human political and economic struggle.

Three Emperors' League–The 1873 alliance between Germany, Austria, and Russia.

Triple Alliance–The 1882 alliance between Germany, Austria, and Italy.

Triple Entente–After 1907, the alliance between England, France, and Russia.

Weltpolitik ("world politics")–The policy of making Germany a major global power through an expanding navy and the acquisition of colonies–the dream of William II.

Woodrow Wilson (1856-1924)–President of the United States and key figure in the peace conferences following World War I; he intended to make the world "safe for democracy."

Zimmermann telegram–A secret German message to Mexico supporting the Mexican government in regaining Arizona and Texas if the Mexicans declared war on the United States–a factor propelling the United States into World War I in April 1917.

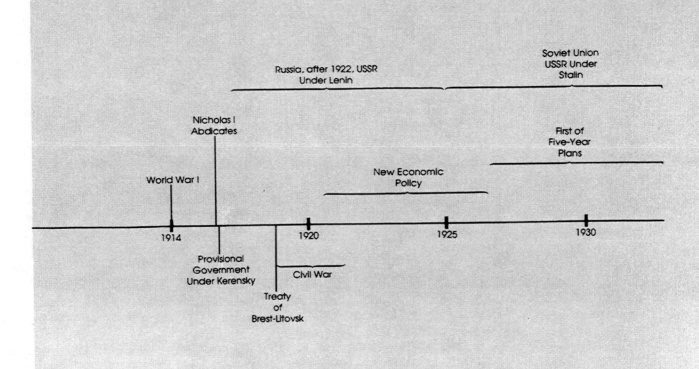

THE RUSSIAN
REVOLUTIONS OF 1917

CHAPTER 13

THE RUSSIAN REVOLUTION

1914	Russia enthusiastically enters the First World War
1915	Two million Russian casualties
	Progressive Bloc calls for a new government responsible to the Duma, not the czar
	Czar Nicholas adjourns the Duma and departs for the front; control of the government falls to Alexandra and Rasputin
December 1916	Murder of Rasputin
March 8, 1917	Bread riots in Petrograd (St. Petersburg)
March 12, 1917	Duma declares a provisional government
March 15, 1917	Czar Nicholas abdicates without protest
April 3, 1917	Lenin returns from exile and denounces the provisional government
May 1917	Kerensky forms a moderate socialist government and continues the war
	Petrograd Soviet issues Army Order no. 1, granting military power to committees of common soldiers

Summer 1917	Agrarian upheavals: peasants seize estates, peasant soldiers desert the army to join in
October 1917	Bolsheviks gain a majority in the Petrograd Soviet
November 6, 1917	Bolsheviks seize power; Lenin heads the new "provisional workers' and peasants' government"
November 1917	Lenin ratifies peasant seizure of land and worker control of factories; all banks nationalized
January 1918	Lenin permanently disbands the Constituent Assembly
February 1918	Lenin convinces the Bolshevik Central Committee to accept a humiliating peace with Germany in order to pursue the revolution
March 1918	Treaty of Brest-Litovsk: Russia loses one-third of its population
	Trotsky as war commissar begins to rebuild the Russian army
	Government moves from Petrograd to Moscow
1918–1920	Great civil war
Summer 1918	Eighteen competing regional governments; White armies oppose the Bolshevik revolution
1919	White armies on the offensive but divided politically; they receive little benefit from Allied intervention
1920	Lenin and Red armies victorious, retaking Belorussia and the Ukraine

The First World War was the forcing hothouse for the Russian Revolution; actually, there were two revolutions—one in March and the second in November 1917. Both were related to the dislocations and difficulties engendered by the war, a war Russia was ill equipped to enter.

THE MARCH REVOLUTION

Russia did not have the resources to fight a modern war. The country lacked munitions and food to sustain an army forced to stand on the defense. Nicholas II was failing at the front, and the Czarina Alexandra, advised by **Rasputin**, lost favor at home. The March revolution was a spontaneous one. Striking workers, men and women, paralyzed St. Petersburg. Soviets (councils of workers and soldiers) joined a Duma committee mobilizing to oppose czarist forces. Nicholas II (1894-1917), the last of the Romanov czars, abdicated in this bloodless revolution. A provisional government, headed by Prince Lvov (1861-1925), was set up. Promising to call a Constituent Assembly, it promulgated civil liberties, the eight-hour day for workers, a constitution for Finland, and independence for Russian Poland, among other reforms. Yet the government was handicapped from its very beginning.

The Provisional Government

In effect, there were two centers of power in St. Petersburg: (1) the **provisional government**, comprising the liberal bourgeoisie (the **Constitutional Democrats**, or Cadets) and moderate or revisionist socialists like

Alexander Kerensky (1881-1970), who were willing to cooperate with the bourgeoisie; and (2) the **Petrograd Soviet** (St. Petersburg Soviet) of urban workers, soldiers, and radical intellectuals, where Lenin and Trotsky would eventually gain power and which from the very start had weakened army discipline by issuing **Army Order no. 1**.

Attacks from the Left and Right

The war issue continued to divide the political parties. The Cadets wanted to continue the war and support their allies. Right-wing Marxists (**Mensheviks**) and left-wing Marxists (**Bolsheviks**) were opposed to the war. A third party, the **Social Revolutionaries** (heirs of the nineteenth-century Populist movement that called for dictatorship of the peasantry) favored continuing the war as well. The party was headed by Kerensky, who, eventually becoming head of the provisional government, had succeeded in aborting coups by the Bolsheviks and by General Kornilov, a right-winger. Ironically, armed Bolshevik troops assisted in the Kornilov defeat–assistance that redeemed them. Following this event, **Leon Trotsky** (1879-1940) convinced the Petrograd Soviet to form a special military-revolutionary committee with him as its leader (October 1917). Since the provisional government had no effective army, this meant that military power had passed into Bolshevik control.

LENIN AND THE NOVEMBER REVOLUTION

The leader of the Bolsheviks was **V. I. Lenin** (1870-1924), an orthodox Marxist who refused to cooperate with the bourgeoisie in the provisional government. He proclaimed, "All power to the Soviets." Under his direction and formulation, Marxism became Marxism-Leninism, a modification of Marxist ideas within the Russian setting. As early as 1902, in the essay **"What Is to Be Done?"** Lenin argued that the revolution had to be led and engineered by a small conspiratorial elite of revolutionaries. According to Lenin, waiting for the so-called proletarian revolution in agricultural Russia would be futile. Urban workers would only develop a "trade-union consciousness" and lose their vigor and determination for social reform.

Three years later, in **"Two Tactics for Social Democracy"** (1905), Lenin theorized that the two revolutions–bourgeoisie and proletariat–could be telescoped. It was not necessary to wait for a country to become highly industrialized with a large proletariat, as Marx had stated. A socialist revolution could take place in a preindustrialized, agrarian nation. In fact, Lenin's November revolution followed swiftly on the heels of the March 1917 "bourgeois revolution," which had led to Nicholas II's abdication.

When Nicholas II abdicated, Lenin was in exile in Switzerland. The Germans sent him in a sealed train back to Russia with the understanding that he would pull Russia out of the war. When Lenin arrived in April 1917, representing the Bolshevik party, he promised **"Peace, land, and bread."** He was able to put together workers' armed forces, known as the **Red Guards**. His supporters won key positions on factory committees and in the district soviets. On November 6, one of the Red Guard detachments and the regular army seized the main government buildings. There was little bloodshed, and Lenin announced a new government called the **Council of People's Commissars**. With Lenin as chairman, the council immediately announced the state's expropriation of all land and its distribution to those who worked on it. Lenin's government also ratified workers' control of factories by workers' committees.

Russia Pulls Out of the War

In the **Treaty of Brest-Litovsk** (March 1918), Lenin conceded that Russia had lost the war with Germany. The treaty sliced away one third of the Russian population to Germany. Poles, Lithuanians, Finns, and other non-Russians living in the western territories were absorbed into Germany, along with land, factories, and rich resources.

Civil War in Russia

A call for a new Constituent Assembly produced a Social Revolutionary majority. Lenin thereupon disbanded the new government and established his one-party government, with himself at the helm. Civil war ensued, with opponents of the Bolsheviks, known as Whites, fighting against the armies of the Bolsheviks, known as Reds. The Reds won, in large measure due to Trotsky's leadership and the disunited fighting force of the Whites. To supply the Reds, the Bolsheviks introduced **war communism**, the concept of total war to the civilian conflict. The Bolsheviks nationalized banks and industries; they seized grain and introduced rationing; and they reestablished the **Cheka,** or secret police, to exterminate alleged foes.

Lenin renamed the Bolsheviks. As *Communists* they would encourage worldwide revolution based on the principles of socialism and one-party government. They would direct the creation of a universal society based on human liberty and freedom, with class and gender divisions abolished. In 1920, the German Marxist **Clara Zetkin** (1857-1933) interviewed Lenin.

DOCUMENT-BASED ESSAY QUESTION

An excerpt from the exchange between Zetkin and Lenin is reprinted below. Read the document and explain in an essay what it reveals regarding Lenin's view of women's problems in relation to his goal of international revolution. Compare the points or issues on which Zetkin and Lenin agree. On what points or issues do they disagree?

THE EMANCIPATION OF WOMEN, FROM THE WRITINGS OF V. I. LENIN

Comrade Lenin repeatedly discussed with me the problem of women's rights. He obviously attached great importance to the women's movement, which to him was an essential component of the mass movement that in certain circumstances might become decisive. Needless to say he saw full social equality of women as a principle which no Communist could dispute. . . .

''We must by all means set up a powerful international women's movement on a clear-cut theoretical basis,'' he began after greeting me . . . ''we need the greatest clarity of principle . . . (yet) I have been told that at the evenings arranged for reading and discussion with working women, sex and marriage problems come first. They are said to be the main objects of interest in your political instruction and educational work. I could not believe my ears when I heard that. The first state of proletarian dictatorship is battling with the counter-revolutionaries of the whole world. The situation in Germany itself calls for the greatest unity of all proletarian revolutionary forces, so that they can repel the counter-revolution which is pushing on. But active Communist women are busy discussing sex problems and the forms of marriage. . . .''

I interposed that where private property and the bourgeois social order prevail, questions of sex and marriage gave rise to manifold problems, conflicts and suffering for women of all social classes and strata. As far as women are concerned, the war and its consequences exacerbated the existing conflicts and suffering to the utmost precisely in the sphere of sexual relations. . . . The makings of new relations between people were appearing. . . . Knowledge of the modifications of the forms of marriage and family that took place in the course of history, and of their dependence on economics, would serve to rid the minds of working women of their preconceived idea of the eternity of bourgeois society. The critically historical attitude to this had to lead to an unrelenting analysis of bourgeois society. . . .

Lenin nodded with a smile. "There you are! You defend your comrades and your Party like a lawyer. What you say is of course true. But that can at best excuse, not justify, the mistake made in Germany. It remains a mistake. Can you assure me in all sincerity that during those reading and discussion evenings, questions of sex and marriage are dealt with from the point of view of mature, vital historical materialism? . . . is this the time to keep working women busy for months at a stretch with such questions as how to love or be loved, how to woo or be wooed? . . . true emancipation of women is not possible except through communism."

Economic Recovery

After the civil war, Lenin, facing economic collapse, introduced his **New Economic Policy** (NEP), designed to restore and improve the Russian economy. The policy introduced some aspects of private ownership among the peasants. They could sell surpluses in free markets and buy from private traders and manufacturers. And he substituted a grain tax on their output, rather than requisition their grain outright.

Historians have called Lenin a supreme pragmatist. The peasants were a force that could have overturned his government. He compromised his Marxist ideals in order to survive. NEP was a partial restoration of capitalism. Heavy industry, banks, and railroads still remained nationalized, however.

STALIN'S TAKEOVER

When Lenin became ill and died in 1924, a struggle ensued between Joseph Stalin (1879-1953) and Leon Trotsky for power. Stalin won out, because of the support of his allies within the Communist Party bureaucracy in Moscow. Trotsky had spent his energies on exporting communism globally, whereas Stalin saw the need to develop it in the Soviet Union first, then export it after achieving a solidly entrenched basis at home. Much later, it is alleged, Stalin arranged for the assassination of Trotsky, who was living in exile in Mexico City.

Domestic Policies

Stalin's domestic goal was to modernize Russia through a series of Five-Year Plans, beginning in 1928, which set targets for industrial and agricultural production. A component of the plans was the collectivization of farms. This meant war on the independent peasant farmer, or kulak, since collectivization required the consolidation of individual peasant farms into large, state-controlled enterprises.

Through the spectacular purge trials of the mid-1930s, in which old Bolshevik leaders confessed to plots against Stalin and the Communist Party, Stalin was able to create a state under which government officials were totally subordinate to him. Stalin's twenty-five years of terror enabled him to build an industrial giant and military superpower in the name of Marxist-Leninist communism.

MULTIPLE-CHOICE QUESTIONS

1. The March Revolution in 1917 in Russia was the result of
    a. Lenin's takeover of the Petrograd Soviet
    b. economic and social dislocations caused by the First World War
    c. the relationship between Rasputin and the Czarina Alexandra
    d. peasant rebellion against landlords and high taxes
    e. a declaration by the Duma to establish a constitutional monarchy

2. Which of the following describes the government set up immediately following the abdication of Nicholas II?
    a. a dictatorship
    b. a constitutional monarchy
    c. a liberal-democratic regime
    d. a federal republic
    e. a peasant-dominated multiparty system

3. The one group in Russia that called for peace and a social revolution rather than a stronger war effort was the
    a. Social Revolutionaries
    b. Constitutional Democrats
    c. Populists
    d. Bolsheviks
    e. Petrograd Soviet

4. Which of the following helps to explain Lenin's agreement to sign the Treaty of Brest-Litovsk with Germany in March 1918?
    a. He expected that the Russian Revolution was only the first stage in a world revolution, to occur next in Germany and the Baltic regions.
    b. He wanted Germany to win the war and defeat France.
    c. He was uninterested in those territories where non-Slavs resided.
    d. He believed that the Germans were likely to lose the war and the treaty would thus be ineffective.
    e. He received personal funds from the German government to sign the treaty.

5. Lenin's New Economic Policy (NEP) in 1921 can best be described as
    a. an attempt to make the Soviet Union a military superpower
    b. an expedient retreat from war communism
    c. a tactical maneuver to win the civil war
    d. an apostasy from Marxist beliefs
    e. a strategy to establish capitalism in the Soviet Union

6. "We are fifty or a hundred years behind the advanced countries. . . . We must make good this lag in ten years. Either we do it or they crush us." This statement is best attributed to
   a. Lenin
   b. Trotsky
   c. Czar Nicholas II
   d. Alexander Kerensky
   e. Stalin

7. Which group probably benefited financially the most from Lenin's NEP?
   a. factory workers
   b. steel industrialists
   c. local party officials
   d. kulaks
   e. former aristocrats

8. The major purpose of Stalin's purges in the 1930s was to
   a. destroy the independent farmers
   b. consolidate control over the party apparatus
   c. censor radical intellectuals
   d. earn the approval of Western industrialists
   e. reinstate Lenin as a cult hero

STUDY QUESTIONS

1. "The revolutions of 1917 were instrumental in steering Russia on a Western course." Assess the validity of this statement with reference to both the March and November revolutions in Russia.
2. "If Marxism was a time bomb with a delayed fuse, Lenin was the individual who lit the fuse." To what extent do you agree with this statement?
3. "Lenin was neither exclusively an idealist nor a pragmatist. Rather, he was a practitioner of both theories, depending on the circumstances confronting him." Support this statement with specific references to the policies and actions of Lenin.
4. How and in what ways did Stalin's Five-Year Plans benefit the Soviet Union? How and in what ways did they harm it?
5. Compare the Russian Revolution of 1917 with the French Revolution of 1789 in terms of the social and political factors that contributed to their outbreaks.

ESSAY-WRITING TIPS: USING TRANSITIONAL EXPRESSIONS

Below is a by-no-means complete list of expressions that are helpful in writing. They guide the reader in terms of the mind-set of the author and the way she or he is organizing the essay. The writer uses transitional expressions to clarify relationships among the sentences in the essay. The expressions serve as connecting links in a narration. Some examples are listed here.

To clarify a sequence of events–*first, second, third, next, finally, last*

To show a similar relationship–*similarly, in like manner, likewise*

To point out a dissimilarity–*in opposition to, in contrast to, on the other hand, conversely*

To emphasize a point–*indeed, in fact, surely, certainly*

To show or point out a result–*consequently, as a result, therefore, hence, accordingly*

To summarize a position–*in summation, finally, in conclusion, in short*

To illustrate a point–*for example, by way of illustration, for instance*

To contrast a position–*on the other hand, however, but, yet, despite, although, nevertheless*

To record time–*now, gradually, later, eventually, immediately, at once, at this point, next, afterward, soon, then*

Now, compare the following brief paragraphs and their use of transitional phrases.

Paragraph A   Lenin modified Marxism in several ways. He posited a tightly organized cadre of committed revolutionaries in place of the proletariat. He telescoped the agrarian and industrial revolutions so that they could both take place in a limited time frame. With NEP he retreated on communism when expediency required that he make a partial regression. He was able to adapt Marxism to the unique conditions facing him in Russia. The November 1917 revolution and its success could not have been achieved without his revision.

Paragraph B   Lenin modified Marxism in several ways. First, he posited a tightly organized cadre of committed revolutionaries in place of the proletariat. Second, he telescoped the agrarian and industrial revolutions so that they could both take place within a limited time frame. And last, with NEP he retreated on communism when expediency required that he make a partial regression. In short, he was able to adapt Marxism to the unique conditions facing him in Russia. Without such adaptations, the November 1917 revolution and its success could not have been achieved.

Below is an essay on Russian women in the early twentieth century. However, transitional expressions have been omitted. Read the essay and fill in the blanks with appropriate expressions. Of course, more than one answer may be possible.

In the early twentieth century, educated Russian women, those who had studied abroad, formed a League for Women's Equality. Their goals were legal equality, education, employment, divorce reform, and birth control. In 1913, the Duma named International Women's Day, March 8, a national holiday. This International Women's Day recognition turned Lenin's attention to the Woman problem.

_____ Lenin and his Bolshevik party decided to accept the notion of communal child care centers, dining rooms, laundries, and dormitories in order to "separate the kitchen from marriage." _____, Lenin instituted a separate women's bureau in the party. _____ he went even further, and in December 1917 all the czarist marriage and divorce laws were repealed.

The newly instituted Family Code of 1918 stated that women were expected to work. _____ the wife could retain her own name, establish her own residence, and have equal access to family finances and property. In cases of divorce, men could qualify for alimony if they were disabled–otherwise, alimony was abolished.

_____, civil war wiped out the dreams of Russian feminists like Alexandra Kollantai. Anarchy replaced civilization. _____ half-educated Communists believed that the new law allowed them to have any woman they wished, since she was state property.

The bourgeois family was disintegrating, the socialist family held together by love had not materialized. A revised 1926 Family Code sanctioned common law marriages. _____ it instituted the "post-card divorce," allowing women to get support from men who had abandoned them. _____ the major concern for women like Kollantai was how to bring about the socialist state.

When Stalin came to power, in 1928, he incorporated women into his planned economy in several ways: _____ he recruited them for assembly line work in factories; _____ he employed them in digging ditches, maintaining roads, and building industrial plants; _____ he encouraged the upgrading of their skills for supervisory positions as managers on farms, brigade leaders, and tractor drivers.

_____ birthrates declined, and, in the mid-1930s, a sexual counterrevolution occurred. Childbearing became a social duty, and abortions were made criminal offenses. The post-1936 image of woman was a superwoman who made a home for her family *and* still performed on the job.

_____ under Stalin the choice was made to build up the industrial might of Russia. When necessity dictated cuts in the government budget, it was women's needs, such as length of maternity leave and child care centers, that were first affected. _____, under Stalin, the ideal of equality for women remained just that–an ideal.

IDENTIFICATIONS

Army Order no. 1–An order issued to the Russian military when the provisional government was formed. It deprived officers of their authority and placed power in elected committees of common soldiers. This led to the collapse of army discipline.

Bolsheviks–Left-wing, revolutionary Marxists headed by Lenin.

Cheka–The secret police under Lenin and his Communist Party.

Constitutional Democrats–Also known as the Cadets, the party of the liberal bourgeoisie in Russia.

Council of People's Commissars–The new government set up by Lenin following the Red Guard seizure of government buildings on November 6, 1917.

V. I. Lenin (1870-1924)–The Bolshevik leader who made the Marxist revolution in November 1917 and modified orthodox Marxism in doing so.

Mensheviks–Right-wing or moderate Marxists willing to cooperate with the bourgeoisie.

New Economic Policy (NEP)–Plan introduced by Lenin after the Russian civil war. Essentially it was a tactical retreat from war communism, allowing some private ownership among the peasants to stimulate agrarian production.

"Peace, land, and bread"–The promise Lenin made to his supporters on his arrival in April 1917 in Russia after his exile abroad.

Petrograd Soviet–The St. Petersburg, or Petrograd, council of workers, soldiers, and intellectuals who shared power with the provisional government.

provisional government–The temporary government established after the abdication of Nicholas II (1881-1970), from March until Lenin's takeover in November 1917.

Rasputin–An uneducated Siberian preacher (nicknamed Rasputin, the "Degenerate") who claimed to have mysterious healing powers. He could stop the bleeding of Czarina Alexandra's son–possibly through hypnosis–and was thus able to gain influence in the czar's court, much to the dismay of top ministers and aristocrats, who finally arranged for his murder. The czarina's relationship with Rasputin did much to discredit Czar Nicholas's rule.

Red Guards–The Bolshevik armed forces.

Treaty of Brest–Litovsk (March 1918)–Pact by which Lenin pulled Russia out of the war with Germany and gave up one third of the Russian population in the western territories.

Leon Trotsky (1879-1940)–Lenin's ally who organized and led the Bolshevik military takeover of the provisional government headed by Kerensky, in November 1917.

"Two Tactics for Social Democracy"–The 1905 essay in which Lenin argued that the agrarian and industrial revolutions could be telescoped. It was unnecessary for Russia to become an industrialized nation before the Marxist revolution.

war communism–The application of total war by the Bolsheviks to the civil war (1918-1920) at home–i.e, requisitioning grain, nationalizing banks and industries, and introducing rationing.

"What Is to Be Done?"–Essay written by Lenin in 1902 that outlined his plan for an elite revolutionary cadre to engineer the communist revolution in agrarian Russia.

Clara Zetkin (1857-1933)–German Marxist who focused on women's issues in the Communist Party.

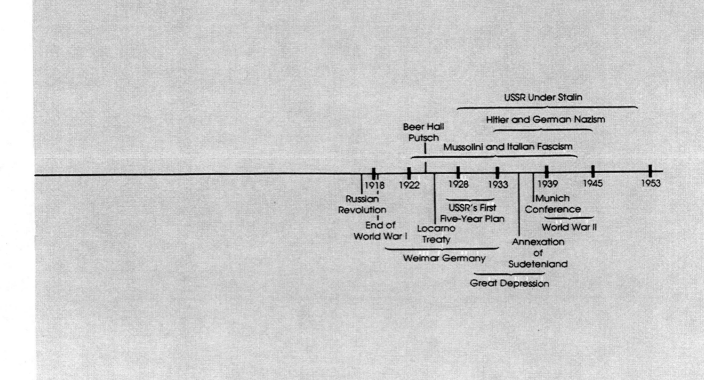

DEMOCRACY AND
DICTATORSHIP, 1919–1939

CHAPTER 14

GERMANY AFTER WORLD WAR I

The victory for the Allied forces in the First World War resulted in the abdication of Kaiser William II in 1918. The Social Democrats (a revisionist Marxist party) ascended to power in a provisional government and signed the armistice treaty, so humiliating to Germany. The Social Democrats, hereafter designated as the SPD, published decrees for the eight-hour working day, social security improvements, and freedom of speech. Yet the new government faced difficulties as rumors began to spread that the army had been stabbed in the back by radicals, ostensibly in the present government, at home. Left-wing Marxists (the **Spartacists**) who wanted to topple the new government and promote a proletarian revolution staged a coup. With the help of the army, the revolt was crushed and its principal leaders, Karl Liebknecht and Rosa Luxemburg, were shot.

The Weimar Republic

Soon after, elections were called for a Constituent Assembly to meet in the city of **Weimar**. The delegates elected were republicans–a coalition of Social and Liberal Democrats–who drafted a constitution establishing a democratic republic. The constitution embodied the principles of democracy–among them, universal suffrage (this included women), proportional representation, the **referendum**, and the recall. The president was to be elected for a seven-year term and would nominate the chancellor, who would have to be approved by the Reichstag, or lower house of Parliament. In short, the government would

161

be responsible to the Parliament, and the aristocracy would have no special privileges. The new Weimar Republic was Germany's first bona fide experiment in democracy. It has been noted that the republic was born in defeat, lived in turmoil, and died in disaster.

In spite of its promising beginnings, the new government faced continuing problems. Both the Left and the Right challenged its legitimacy. Strikes, **putsches** (illegal attempts to seize power), and assassinations threatened the stability of the government. Additionally unsettling was the runaway inflation tied into the government's attempt to meet its reparation payments with newly printed money that devalued the German mark and wiped out savings. Most humiliating was the French invasion of the Ruhr in 1923 for the failure of the Germans to meet their payments.

Assistance for Recovery and Peace Policies

Yet Germany did receive assistance in 1924 through the **Dawes Plan**, which provided U.S. loans to the Germans to help meet their reparation payments. Five years later, in 1929, the **Young Plan** set limits to Germany's reparation payments and arranged for an earlier than agreed-on end to the occupation of the Ruhr. In the mid-1920s, Germany was on a rocky road to recovery, a road paved with foreign loans and assistance.

In addition to the role that the League of Nations was to play in providing a location in Geneva where diplomats could settle international disputes, the European powers signed several agreements to further assure peace. In 1921, the **Washington Conference**, attended by major powers, reduced naval armaments. In 1925, the **Locarno Treaty** secured the frontier between Germany and France and contained Germany in the east as well. In 1928, a number of countries signed the **Kellogg-Briand Pact**, which denounced war as an instrument of national policy.

Political Opposition

Although support for the German republic continued to grow, there were political opponents on all sides. One such group was the **National Socialists** (Nazis) headed by **Adolf Hitler** (1889-1945) with the support of his **Brown Shirts**. He had attempted the **Beer Hall Putsch** in Munich in 1923. Arrested and jailed, he spent only nine months of his term, during which he wrote *Mein Kampf* (*My Struggle*), the outline of his theories and political program for the **Third Reich**.

FRANCE

For France and Great Britain following the First World War, the challenges were to restore their economies and promote social harmony. France had to rebuild its northern region devastated in the war; the government had to steer a cautious course between deficit spending and high taxes to avoid the inflation that had beset Germany. Even with its political uncertainties, Paris served as the magnet for artists and intellectuals from all over the world, among them Pablo Picasso, Ernest Hemingway, André Gide, Gertrude Stein, and the American singer Josephine Baker.

GREAT BRITAIN

In Great Britain the **Labor Party** replaced the Liberal Party and championed greater social equality for the working classes. During the 1920s, Britain, in an economic depression, faced heavy unemployment. The government expanded jobless benefits, including subsidized housing, medical aid, and increased old-age pensions. Gradualist democratic socialism prevented class warfare and pointed the way to the welfare state.

HITLER'S RISE TO POWER

The economic depression of 1929 is often cited as the reason for Hitler's accession to power. And although the worldwide depression created the conditions that correlate rising German unemployment with the increase in Nazi seats from less than 3 percent in the 1928 elections to 37 percent in 1932, other factors have been cited as well. They include (1) the national character of a people shaped by Martin Luther's justification of state power in the sixteenth century, Hegel's philosophic defense of the Prussian state in 1800, Bismarck's "blood and iron" method for unifying Germany, and the political anti-Semitism that flowered in 1870 and was endorsed by the composer Richard Wagner; (2) the harsh Treaty of Versailles, which stripped Germany of colonies, land, and industrial resources and left it with a small army and heavy reparation payments; (3) the charismatic personality of Hitler, whose diatribes against Communists, Jews, and republicans in a setting of bright lights and martial music soothed feelings of German inferiority with his talk of an Aryan super race; (4) Hitler's ruthless policies of intimidation, brutality, and terror that frightened his opposition. (Once he was in power, of course, there was no stopping him—e.g., the **Nuremberg Laws** and **Crystal Night**).

Hitler's Appointment as Chancellor

Yet two thirds of the German population did not vote for Hitler in the 1932 election. He came to power legally with his appointment as chancellor, on June 30, 1933, by the aging president, **Paul von Hindenburg** (1847-1934), who believed that the Conservatives in the government could control him. Hitler was able to use the Reichstag fire to blame the Communists and win Reichstag support for the **Enabling Act** that gave him dictatorial powers. Like his Italian counterpart, Mussolini, his accession to power was legitimate. His methods thereafter were not.

MUSSOLINI'S RISE TO POWER

Like Hitler, **Benito Mussolini** (1883-1945) used violence and terror to intimidate his opponents. Although Italy had fought on the side of the Allies in the First World War, its leaders desired more land than Trentino and Trieste, which it acquired. Workers and peasants clamored for social gains and land reform, which the Liberal Democratic government was unable to provide in the face of wartime debt and postwar depression. Although Mussolini started out as a Socialist, he shifted gears to beat up Socialists and convince his followers that his movement was a dynamic one to help the "little people." His private army of **Black Shirts** attacked and even murdered rival socialist opponents. Confident of his power, Mussolini and his Fascists marched to Rome in October 1922 to force **King Victor Emmanuel III** (1900-1946) to call on him to form a new cabinet. The king conceded, and Mussolini seized power "legally" with dictatorial authority for a year.

DOCUMENT-BASED QUESTION PRACTICE

Below is an excerpt of a speech given by Mussolini after he had come to power. After you have read the selection, evaluate the sentences that follow. Make a list of those sentences that represent the totalitarianism of Mussolini's *Fascism,* and a list of those sentences that represent the liberal point of view that he opposed.

FROM A SPEECH BY MUSSOLINI

The Fascist conception of the State is all-embracing; outside it no human or spiritual values can exist, much less have value . . . the State interprets, develops, potentiates the whole life of the people. . . .

War alone keys up all human energies to their maximum tension and sets the seal of nobility on those who have the courage to face it. . . . The Fascist accepts and loves life. . . . Life as he understands it means duty, elevation, conquest. . . .

Fascism denies that numbers, as such, can be the determining factors in human society; it denies the right of numbers to govern by means of periodical consultations; it asserts the . . . beneficent inequality of men who cannot be levelled by any such mechanical and extrinsic device as universal suffrage. . . .

This is the century of authority. . . . The key-stone of the Fascist doctrine is its conception of the State. For Fascism the State is absolute, individuals and groups relative. Individuals and groups are admissible in so far as they come within the State.

1. State power is limited.
2. The state takes over and controls the economic, social, intellectual, and cultural aspects of life.
3. The state protects the sacred rights of the individual.
4. The state stands for rationality, harmony, peaceful progress, and a strong middle class.
5. Ideology stresses willpower, preaches conflict, and worships violence.
6. Ideology promotes the belief that the individual is less valuable than the state.
7. Ideology espouses no lasting rights, only temporary rewards.
8. Ideology promotes a single powerful leader and a single political party to determine the destiny of the state.
9. Ideology derives from Enlightenment theory.
10. Ideology draws upon the Darwinian concept of the survival of the fittest.
11. Ideology asserts that there is a natural ranking of humans rather than an equality among them.
12. Ideology asserts that there must be some check on supreme authority.

Mussolini's Domestic Policies

After his accession to power, Mussolini imposed censorship of the press, ruled by decree, controlled the youth movement and the schools, and created Fascist labor unions. By 1926, Italy was a one-party dictatorship.

Pragmatically, he compromised with the old conservative classes. He left big business to regulate itself and did not pressure for land reform. To win the support of the Catholic church, he recognized the **Vatican** as a tiny independent state in the **Lateran Agreement** (1929). Concerned with a dynamic state and a population expansion, he abolished divorce, placing a special tax on bachelors. He limited women's access to high-paying jobs and encouraged women to bear children and maintain the home.

Both Germany and Italy under their leaders, Hitler and Mussolini, defied the efforts made in the 1920s to maintain international harmony and peace.

DOCUMENT-BASED ESSAY QUESTION

Below is a series of well-known historical events and also contemporary commentaries on those events. The passages illustrate the direction in which Europe was heading in the 1930s. Read them, and from the perspective of a liberal democrat, write an essay reacting to the events and the commentary.

ITALY'S INVASION OF ETHIOPIA

Italy invaded Ethiopia in October 1935. The League of Nations applied economic sanctions, but oil was omitted from the list of products. The French and British foreign ministers, Laval and Hoare, met in secret to discuss giving Ethiopia to Italy. When news of this meeting was leaked to the public, Laval was dismissed and Hoare resigned. In May 1936, Ethiopia capitulated.

Commentary by Haile Selassie, Emperor of Ethiopia, in a Speech to the League of Nations in Geneva

The problem . . . is much wider than merely a question of settlement of Italian aggression; it is collective security, it is the very existence of the League. . . . It is international morality that is at stake. . . .

SPANISH CIVIL WAR

In the Spanish civil war, a nationalist revolt led by the military and aided by Italian and German troops and planes fought and defeated Russian-supported Loyalists, comprising socialists, communists, anarchists, labor groups, and Catalan and Basque nationalists. The Basque town of Guernica (population 10,000) was destroyed by German bombers on April 26, 1937. In the spring of 1939, the Spanish republic fell to General Francisco Franco.

Commentary from *The Times* of London

Guernica, the most ancient town of the Basques and the centre of their cultural tradition, was completely destroyed yesterday afternoon by insurgent air-raiders. The bombardment of the open town far behind the lines occupied precisely three hours and a quarter, during which a powerful fleet of aeroplanes consisting of three German types, Junkers and Heinkel bombers and Heinkel fighters, did not cease unloading on the town bombs weighing from 1,000 lb. downwards. . . . The fighters meanwhile flew low from above the centre of the town to machine-gun those of the civilians who had taken refuge in the fields. The whole of Guernica was soon in flames except the historic Casa de Juntas. . . .

Commentary by Hermann Goering, Second in Command in Nazi Germany

. . . I sent a large part of my transport fleet and a number of experimental fighter units, bombers, and anti-aircraft guns, and in that way I had an opportunity to ascertain, under combat conditions, whether the matériel was equal to the task.

GERMANY'S ANNEXATION OF AUSTRIA

Hitler annexed Austria (**Anschluss**) in March 1938. The following September, he demanded the German-speaking section of Czechoslovakia (the Sudetenland). Prime Minister Neville Chamberlain of Great Britain flew to Germany for a series of conferences with Hitler.

Commentary by Neville Chamberlain, Following His Meeting with Hitler

I knew that his troops and tanks and guns and planes were ready to pounce, and only awaiting his word, and it was clear that rapid decisions must be taken if the situation was to be saved. . . . He . . . said if I could assure him that the British government accepted the principle of self-determination (which he had not invented), he was prepared to discuss ways and means. I said I could give no assurance without consultation . . . (then) meet him again. . . . I had established a certain confidence, which was my aim, and . . . I got the impression that here was a man who could be relied upon when he had given his word.

RUSSO-GERMAN NONAGGRESSION PACT

In the summer of 1939, Stalin and Hitler signed a nonaggression pact in which each leader agreed to remain neutral if the other became involved in war.

Commentary by William Shirer, an American Historian in Berlin at the Time (August 24, 1939), Written in His Diary

Everyone was reading the story in his newspaper. . . . you could see they (the Germans) like the news. Why? Because it means to them that the dreaded nightmare of encirclement—war on two fronts—apparently has been destroyed. Yesterday it was there. Today it is gone. There will be no long front against Russia to hold this time.

In summary, in spite of Western leaders' policies of **appeasement**, a series of acts of aggression by Hitler in Austria, in the Rhineland, in Czechoslovakia, and finally in Poland in September 1939 united Britain and France to declare war on Germany. The Second World War had begun.

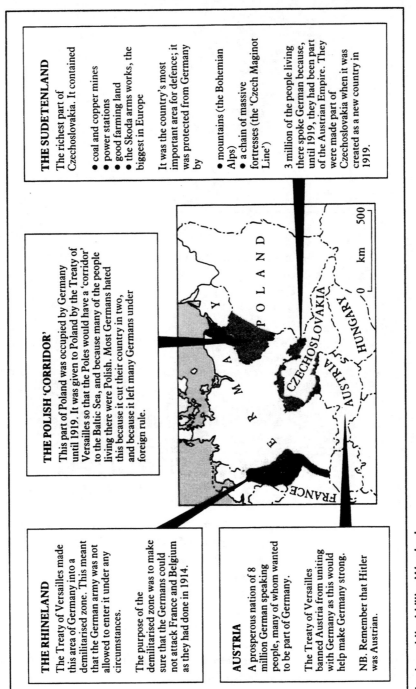

THE SUDETENLAND

The richest part of Czechoslovakia. It contained

- coal and copper mines
- power stations
- good farming land
- the Skoda arms works, the biggest in Europe

It was the country's most important area for defence; it was protected from Germany by

- mountains (the Bohemian Alps)
- a chain of massive fortresses (the 'Czech Maginot Line')

3 million of the people living there spoke German because, until 1919, they had been part of the Austrian Empire. They were made part of Czechoslovakia when it was created as a new country in 1919.

THE POLISH 'CORRIDOR'

This part of Poland was occupied by Germany until 1919. It was given to Poland by the Treaty of Versailles so that the Poles would have a 'corridor' to the Baltic Sea, and because many of the people living there were Polish. Most Germans hated this because it cut their country in two, and because it left many Germans under foreign rule.

THE RHINELAND

The Treaty of Versailles made this area of Germany into a demilitarised zone. This meant that the German army was not allowed to enter it under any circumstances.

The purpose of the demilitarised zone was to make sure that the Germans could not attack France and Belgium as they had done in 1914.

AUSTRIA

A prosperous nation of 8 million German speaking people, many of whom wanted to be part of Germany.

The Treaty of Versailles banned Austria from uniting with Germany as this would help make Germany strong.

NB. Remember that Hitler was Austrian.

The Land that Hitler Wanted

167

MULTIPLE-CHOICE QUESTIONS

1. This map represents the Continent of Europe in
   a. 1848
   b. 1870
   c. 1914
   d. 1919
   e. 1945

GERMAN TROOPS ENTER RHINELAND

2. This headline, from the London *Evening Standard*, marks Hitler's violation of which group of treaties and/or pacts?
   a. Rappalo and Nonaggression
   b. Versailles and Locarno
   c. Versailles and Munich
   d. Franco-Prussian and Kellogg-Briand
   e. Paris and Brest-Litovsk

3. The account below is an example of which of the following conditions in Germany in the interwar years?
   "May I give you some recollections of my own situation at that time? As soon as I received my salary I rushed out to buy the daily necessities. My daily salary, as editor of the magazine *Soziale Praxis*, was just enough to buy one loaf of bread and a small piece of cheese or oatmeal. I had to refuse to give a lecture at a Berlin city college because I could not be assured that my fee would cover the subway fare to the classroom, and it was too far to walk. . . .

"An acquaintance of mine, a clergyman, came to Berlin from a suburb with his monthly salary to buy a pair of shoes for his baby; he could only buy a cup of coffee."
   a. devaluation of the German mark
   b. *Weltpolitik*
   c. deficit financing
   d. hyperinflation
   e. *Lebensraum*

4. Which of the following was not a goal of Hitler?
   a. promoting a racial elite of Aryans
   b. expanding Germany to the south and east
   c. nationalizing the banks, railroads, and heavy industries
   d. implementing a policy of genocide against the Jews
   e. reducing unemployment through public works and rearmament

5. Mussolini won support for his Fascists by promoting his party as a bulwark against
   a. liberal democracy
   b. syndicalism
   c. capitalism
   d. Bolshevism
   e. nationalism

6. Fascist organizations tried to overthrow parliamentary government. As a result, Communists, Socialists, and the radicals allied to form a Popular Front to deal with the social and economic problems of the 1930s. The country in which this alliance succeeded is
   a. England
   b. France
   c. Czechoslovakia
   d. Germany
   e. Belgium

7. Which of the following was a weakness of the Dawes Plan?
   a. It discouraged foreign investments in Germany.
   b. It was used to support the growing private army of Hitler.
   c. It depended on continuous inflows of American capital.
   d. It heightened hyperinflation in Europe.
   e. It was rejected by the U.S. Senate.

8. He advocated large deficit financing in order to stimulate the economy and end the depression. His countercyclical policy was regarded as heresy by orthodox economic thinkers in the 1930s. This individual is
   a. Joseph Goebbels
   b. Stanley Baldwin
   c. Gustav Stresemann
   d. John Maynard Keynes
   e. Joseph Schumpeter

9. He painted *Guernica* to commemorate the bombing of a small town during the Spanish civil war (1937). Using techniques of cubism and expressionism, he protested the technology of modern war. This artist is
   a. Seurat   d. Chagall
   b. Renoir   e. Picasso
   c. Cézanne

10. The French postcard of 1939 above is critical of
    a. the Western policy of appeasement
    b. Wilson's Fourteen Points
    c. Article 48 of the Weimar constitution
    d. the Dawes Plan
    e. the Anschluss with Austria

PRACTICE ESSAY QUESTIONS

Use the questions below to practice essay writing. For each question write an essay that includes an introductory thesis, a body of supporting and/or illustrative data, and a conclusion.

1. Compare the ways in which Hitler and Mussolini came to power in Germany and Italy, respectively.

2. At what point, would you argue, did World War II become inevitable?
3. "Hitler's accession to power can be credited more to the Treaty of Versailles than to the Great Depression." Assess the validity of this statement.
4. How and in what ways was totalitarianism a repudiation of the Enlightenment?
5. Describe the efforts of Great Britain, France, and the United States to achieve international peace in the 1920s. What factors undermined their efforts?

ESSAY-WRITING TIPS: ORGANIZING FOR WRITING

Study Question 4—"How and in what ways was totalitarianism a repudiation of the Enlightenment?"—illustrates the importance of spending several minutes constructing an outline before attempting to write the essay. If an outline cannot be constructed, the essay choice is a poor one. For although one may have a "flash of an idea" in selecting an essay to write, the first flash may give way to total darkness and the writer is left struggling to develop a new thought as the clock ticks away.

An outline does not have to be overly detailed, but it should include the basics of the planned essay. For example,

Part A of the question: *How* did totalitarianism repudiate the Enlightenment?

Enlightenment—individual reason, natural law, and progress of humankind
Totalitarianism—exaltation of state over individual, disparagement of objective truth, virulent nationalism

Part B of the question: *In what ways* was totalitarianism a repudiation of the Enlightenment?

WAYS

- censorship, suppression of reason, manipulation of public opinion
- use of violence to repress opposition and destroy "deviants"
- the institution of youth movements to promote cults of virility

Before beginning to write the essay, even after the writer has formulated a brief outline, it is important to read the question again to mentally construct the overall framework and consider important elements that may not be jotted in the outline. For example,

- the definitions of *Enlightenment* and *totalitarianism*

- the historical time periods in which they develop

- key individuals who are connected with their development—Condorcet, Voltaire, Montesquieu, Rousseau, Stalin, Hitler, Mussolini

At this point, the writer should feel confident that she or he has enough material and ideas to answer the question and illustrate the response with supporting evidence. The following essay attempts to put the pieces together as an example of the use of a briefly constructed outline in essay writing.

Totalitarianism, in all its twentieth-century varieties—Fascism, Nazism, and communism—rejected the basic premise of eighteenth-century Enlightenment thought that humans, insofar as they are born with the capacity to reason, may discover natural laws and natural right. Societies could then be reconstructed in accord with these laws, resulting in progress for all humankind.

By exalting the *class*, in Stalin's case the proletariat, or the *nation*, as Hitler and Mussolini did, these leaders submerged the individual within the larger group and subjected him or her to the authority and decision making of the larger corporate body. Individual freedom was sacrificed.

Totalitarianism also undermined the Enlightenment notion of international harmony among all nations in their successive stages of progress. The French philosophe Condorcet best promoted this view when he wrote that "someday the sun will shine on free men who know no other master but their reason."

Nazism, in particular, elevated the concept of the German *volk*, described as a "blood-conditioned entity" that was historically destined for greatness. Hitler's nationalism was a virulent form that legitimated the destruction of other nations and the extermination of Jews and other "non-Aryan" types.

To promote the free flow of rational ideas, Voltaire, Montesquieu, Rousseau, and the other eighteenth-century philosophes had advocated freedom of speech, press, and religion. The famous dictum attributed to Voltaire—"I may not agree with you, but I will defend to the death your right to say it"—illustrates the Enlightenment view of personal freedom.

Yet totalitarian leaders—Stalin, Mussolini, and Hitler—all imposed strict censorship on individual expression. Through the press and radio, with loudspeakers, photographs, and commissioned paintings, they propagandized. They created the ideas that were to be regarded as truth. Dissidents were imprisoned, exiled, and shot. Brown Shirts, Black Shirts, and private police like the Cheka in the Soviet Union used violence and intimidation to suppress clear voices of reason.

Last, as a means to repudiate reason, the totalitarian leaders instituted youth movements that stressed body building, gymnastics, and breeding, and ignored the development of the mind and intellectual growth. No aspect of life was beyond the state's control.

Ironically, modern totalitarian dictatorships have claimed descent from one of the Enlightenment's greatest spokesmen—Rousseau. Totalitarian dictators have used his concept of the General Will to claim the right to interpret the common interest. But insofar as Rousseau equated the General Will with the sovereignty of the people, deriving from their individual participation in government, the use of the concept by totalitarian leaders to legitimate their unchallenged rule repudiates the freedom from arbitrary authority so central to Enlightenment thought.

ESSAY-WRITING ASSIGNMENT: ORGANIZING AN OUTLINE FOR AN ESSAY

Now choose another question from the Practice Essay Questions and construct an outline. After you have finished, write an essay, drawing from the outline of notes you have jotted down.

When you finish writing your essay, underline in red (or another appropriate color) the words, phrases, and ideas in your essay that came directly from your outline. In addition, note the time you spent working on the outline and compare it with the time you spent writing the essay. If your outline was fairly complete, the writing time for your essay should have been speedy.

IDENTIFICATIONS

Anschluss–The union of Austria with Germany, resulting from the occupation of Austria by the German army in 1938.

Appeasement–The making of concessions to an adversary in the hope of avoiding conflict. The term is most often used in reference to the meeting between Hitler and British prime minister Chamberlain in Munich, where agreement was made, in September 1938, to cede the Sudetenland (the German-speaking area of Czechosolvakia) to Germany.

Beer Hall Putsch–Hitler's attempt, in 1923, to overthrow the Weimar Republic when he fired his pistol in the ceiling of a Munich beer hall.

Black Shirts–The private army of Mussolini.

Brown Shirts–Hitler's private army of supporters, also known as the SA (Sturm Abteilung).

Crystal Night (Krystallnacht)–The November 1938 destruction, by Hitler's Brown Shirts and mobs, of Jewish shops, homes, and synagogues.

Dawes Plan (1924)–The provision of U.S. loans to Germany to help meet reparation payments, which were also reduced.

Enabling act–Article 48 of the Weimar constitution, which enabled Hitler to issue decrees carrying the force of law.

Fascism–The political and economic methods of Mussolini in Italy. The name comes from the *fasces*, or bundle of rods tied around an axe, the symbol of authority in ancient Rome.

Paul von Hindenburg (1847-1934)–President of Weimar Germany, who appointed Hitler chancellor in 1933; formerly a general in World War I.

Adolf Hitler (1889-1945)–The Nazi leader who came to power legally in Germany in 1933. He set up a totalitarian dictatorship and led Germany into World War II.

Kellogg-Briand Pact (1928)–Document, signed by fifteen countries, that "condemned and renounced war as an instrument of national policy."

Labor Party–The British party that replaced the Liberals in the early twentieth century and championed greater social equality for the working classes through the efforts of labor unions.

Lateran Agreement (1929)–Pact that provided recognition by Mussolini of the Vatican and a large sum of money to the church as well.

Locarno Treaty (1925)–Pact that secured the frontier between Germany and France and Germany and Belgium. It also provided for mutual assistance by France and Italy if Germany invaded its border countries.

Mein Kampf (*My Struggle*)–Work written by Hitler while in prison in 1923; the book outlines his policies for German expansion, war, and elimination of non-Aryans.

Benito Mussolini (1883-1945)–The founder and leader of the Italian Fascist Party.

National Socialists (Nazis)–The political party of Adolf Hitler.

Nuremberg Laws (1935)–Measures that excluded Jews from white-collar professions and from marriage and habitation with non-Jews.

Putsch–Forcible and illegitimate attempt to seize power.

Referendum–A plebiscite: the referring of a matter to the people for a decision.

Spartacists–Left-wing Marxists in Germany who hoped to bring about a proletarian revolution in 1919.

Sudetenland–German-speaking area of Czechoslovakia, ceded to Germany in the Hitler-Chamberlain Munich meeting (September 1938).

Third Reich–Name given to Germany during the Nazi regime, between 1933 and 1945. The First Reich (or empire) was from 963 to 1806 (the Holy Roman Empire); the second was from 1871 to 1917 (the reigns of William I and William II).

Totalitarianism–An attempt by government to control a society totally through a dictatorship that employs the modern methods of communication–press, radio, TV–to glorify the state over the individual. Its varieties are Fascism, Nazism, and communism.

Vatican–Independent sovereign state of the pope and the Catholic church, established in Rome in 1929.

Victor Emmanuel III (1900-1946)–King of Italy who asked Mussolini to form a cabinet in 1922, thus allowing Mussolini to take power legally.

Washington Conference (1921)–Conference of major powers to reduce naval armaments among Great Britain, Japan, France, Italy, and the United States.

Weimar–A reference to the republic of Germany that lasted from 1919 to 1933.

Young Plan (1929)–Schedule that set limits to Germany's reparation payments and reduced the agreed-on time for occupation of the Ruhr.

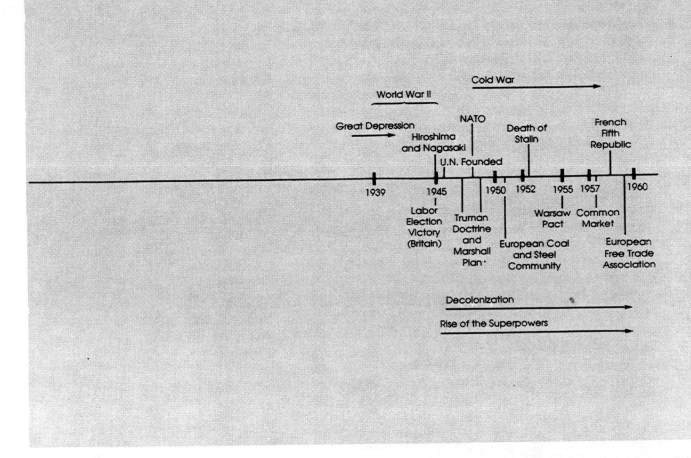

WORLD WAR II AND
ITS AFTERMATH

CHAPTER 15

EVENTS LEADING TO WORLD WAR II

1926	Germany joins the League of Nations
1928	Kellogg-Briand Pact renounces war as an instrument of international affairs
1929	Young Plan further reduces German reparations Crash of U.S. stock market
1929-1933	Depths of the Great Depression
1931	Japan invades Manchuria
1932	Nazis become the largest party in the Reichstag
January 1933	Hitler appointed chancellor
March 1933	Reichstag passes the Enabling Act, granting Hitler absolute dictatorial power
October 1933	Germany withdraws from the League of Nations
July 1934	Nazis murder Austrian chancellor
March 1935	Hitler announces German rearmament
June 1935	Anglo-German naval agreement
October 1935	Mussolini invades Ethiopia and receives Hitler's support
1935	Nuremberg Laws deprive Jews of all rights of citizenship
March 1936	German armies move unopposed into the demilitarized Rhineland
July 1936	Outbreak of civil war in Spain
1937	Japan invades China Rome-Berlin Axis
March 1938	Germany annexes Austria
September 1938	Munich Conference: Britain and France agree to German seizure of the Sudetenland from Czechoslovakia
March 1939	Germany occupies the rest of Czechoslovakia; the end of appeasement in Britain
August 1939	Russo-German Nonaggression Pact
September 1, 1939	Germany invades Poland
September 3, 1939	Britain and France declare war on Germany

WORLD WAR II

The German attack on Poland on September 1939 was a **blitzkreig**–i.e., a lightning war using planes, tanks, and artillery to deliver a swift knockout blow against Polish forces. There swiftly followed the invasion and defeat of Denmark, Norway, Belgium, Holland, Luxembourg, and France. The Axis powers of Germany and Italy, soon joined by Japan, were pitted against the Allied nations, which included Britain and France, later joined by the Soviet Union, the United States, China and forty-three other nations.

After France fell, Britain stood alone, but the development of radar and Britain's Royal Air Force thwarted German invasion of England and proved a setback for German forces. So too did Hitler's invasion of the Soviet Union.

Invasion of the Soviet Union   The **Nazi-Soviet Pact** (1939) did not lessen Hitler's hatred of communism nor weaken his desire to expand in the east. Believing that the Soviet Union could be crushed in eight weeks, Hitler invaded the country in June 1941. The obstacles were considerable—the vast territory, the industrial might, the patriotism that surfaced—and, in the end, Hitler, like Napoleon before him, suffered catastrophic defeat at the battle of Stalingrad, when Soviet reserves encircled the German Sixth Army of 300,000 men and forced their surrender.

The "Final Solution" Meanwhile, on the continent, Hitler's plans were officially formulated for the **"Final Solution,"** the genocide of six million Jews. Extermination facilities in the death camps of Europe gassed and burned women, men, and children and subjected others to slave labor or medical research. Historians have debated whether the Holocaust symbolizes the twentieth century gone awry or the supreme loss of the humane sensibilities of Hitler's supporters. Below are two arguments on the subject. The two documents take different positions on the uniqueness of the phenomenon.

DOCUMENT-BASED ESSAY QUESTION

Read the two arguments and compare in writing the nature of the differences in the viewpoints.

FROM C. LEONARD LUNDIN, "THE TWENTIETH CENTURY," IN *NEW PERSPECTIVES IN WORLD HISTORY*, ED. SHIRLEY H. ENGLE, 1964

But the cruelties were not all on Hitler's side. We all became fascists, in certain respects in the Second World War, and, indeed, in later, less extensive struggles such as the Korean War. We condemned vast numbers of personally innocent men, women, and children to horrible, flaming deaths, because they happened to be on the other side. The atomic bomb merely perfected a technique of mass slaughter with which we were already doing very well before that. . . .

The descriptions one could read in our newspapers during the Korean War of the effects of napalm bombs dropped on . . . villages inhabited by people whom the American aviators were professedly trying to liberate also gave rise to uncomfortable doubts about our virtue. It may be that historians of the future, if our hydrogen bombs leave any future for civilization, may consider Hitler the symbol of the twentieth century . . . and that we shall be lumped together with him in the minds of our descendants.

FROM EDWARD CRANKSHAW, *GESTAPO*, 1958

The dropping of atomic bombs (on Hiroshima and Nagasaki) without specific warning may have been inexcusable; but the decision to do so was taken by harassed men in the extremity of a life and death conflict. It aroused immediate feelings of revulsion. The mass murder of Jews . . . was a deliberate policy made possible by the war but had nothing to do with the winning of it. It was carried out systematically and in cold blood by men who knew what they were doing and watched their victims die.

We all have citizens who, given the necessary power and a total absence of restraint, would behave like S.S. Captain Kramer, "the Beast of Belsen (a concentration camp)." . . .

In all modern societies there are men and women who, released from all restraints, will behave like beasts towards their fellows. But in the twentieth century it has been only in Germany and in Russia that such men have been able to achieve absolute power; and it is only in Germany that they have deliberately delegated their power without reserve to psychopaths and the criminal riff-raff of their country, absolving them from all restraint.

UNITED STATES ENTERS THE WAR

During the early part of the war, the United States proclaimed neutrality. Yet secret agreements between President Roosevelt and Winston Churchill promoted their peace aims in the **Atlantic Charter** (1941), and Roosevelt backed up his support of the Allies with adoption of the Lend-Lease policy of providing army, raw materials, and food to countries at war with the Axis. The Japanese surprise attack on Pearl Harbor formally brought the United States into the war in December 1941. Roosevelt agreed with Stalin and Churchill that the war against Hitler should be their first priority. And the tide began to turn in 1942. There were U.S. victories in the Pacific. Anglo-American forces defeated the German General Rommel in Egypt and controlled the North African coast. Allied forces landed in Italy, where Mussolini was captured and executed. Massive air assaults against Germany led to invasion of the coast of Normandy on June 6, 1944. France was liberated and Russian, British, and American troops encircled Germany. Allied troops met in Berlin a few days following the suicide of Hitler, on April 30, 1945. The war continued in the Pacific until August and the dropping of the atomic bomb on the Japanese cities of **Hiroshima** and **Nagasaki**.

The Wartime Conferences

The war had lasted for six years. It was the second vast military conflagration in the century, made even more nightmarish than the first by the advanced technology with which it was waged. By early 1945, the time to attend to the peace had arrived, and the leaders of the Allies—Churchill, Roosevelt, and Stalin—held a series of wartime conferences expressing their goal of cooperating for world peace; the most famous was held at **Yalta** in February of that year, when defeat of the Axis seemed a reality.

The following were agreements reached at Yalta:

- Germany, after its defeat, would be divided into zones of occupation.
- A conference would be scheduled to prepare the United Nations Charter.
- The Soviet Union would go into the war against Japan for territorial concessions and railway rights in Manchuria.
- The Allies would sign the Declaration on Liberated Europe supporting "the right of all peoples to choose the form of government under which they live" through "democratic means" and "free elections."
- Stalin would hold "free and unfettered elections" in Poland, where the occupying Red Army had set up a provisional government.

Roosevelt died two months after Yalta; critics have held that he sold the freedom of Poland and Eastern Europe to the Soviet Union. Yet defenders of Roosevelt argue that Stalin had already taken Eastern Europe. The Red Army controlled Poland and was forty miles from Berlin while the Allies had not yet crossed the Rhine. And further, Roosevelt needed Stalin's help against Japan and Stalin's participation in the planned United Nations.

The free elections in Eastern Europe were never held. President Harry Truman, who replaced Roosevelt and had met Stalin at the **Potsdam Conference** (July–August 1945), cut off all aid to the Soviet Union. Winston Churchill pinpointed the **cold war** that had erupted between former allies when he told an American audience that "from Stettin in the Baltic to Trieste in the Adriatic, an iron curtain has descended across the Continent."

DOCUMENT-BASED QUESTION PRACTICE

Stalin reacted negatively to Churchill's famous "iron curtain" speech in Missouri, and other Soviet officials continued to denounce it. As the following two selections indicate, the Soviets attempted to justify their influence in Eastern and southeastern Europe. After you have read the selections, summarize in writing the major arguments used by the Soviet leaders in rebutting Churchill's claim that they were practicing expansionism.

STALIN'S RESPONSE PRINTED IN THE RUSSIAN NEWSPAPER *PRAVDA*, MARCH 1946

The following circumstances should not be forgotten. The Germans made their invasion of the USSR through Finland, Poland, Rumania, Bulgaria, and Hungary. The Germans were able to make their invasion through these countries because, at the time, governments hostile to the Soviet Union existed in these countries. As a result of the German invasion the Soviet Union has lost irretrievably in the fighting against the Germans, and also through the German occupation and the deportation of Soviet citizens to German servitude, a total of about seven million people. In other words, the Soviet Union's loss of life has been several times greater than that of Britain and the United States of America put together. Possibly in some quarters an inclination is felt to forget about these colossal sacrifices of the Soviet people which secured the liberation of Europe from Hitlerite yoke. But the Soviet Union cannot forget about them. And so what can there be surprising about the fact that the Soviet Union, anxious for its future safety, is trying to see to it that governments loyal in their attitude to the Soviet Union should exist in these countries? How can anyone, who has not taken leave of his senses, describe these peaceful aspirations of the Soviet Union as expansionist tendencies on the part of our state?

FROM AN OFFICIAL GOVERNMENT PUBLICATION OF THE SOVIET UNION BY B. N. PONOMARYON ET AL., *HISTORY OF THE COMMUNIST PARTY OF SOVIET UNION*, 1960

As a result of the war the capitalist system sustained enormous losses and became weaker. . . . Albania, Bulgaria, Eastern Germany, Hungary, Czechoslovakia, Poland, Rumania and Yugoslavia broke away from the system of capitalism. . . . The people's governments established in these countries carried out a number of important democratic reforms. . . . The rapid victories of the masses of the people in these countries over the bourgeolsie was achieved thanks to the correct policy of the Communist Parties and the leading role of the working class. A great factor in the liberation struggle of these peoples was the assistance rendered by the Soviet Union. . . .

The presence of the Soviet armed forces in the People's Democracies (that were set up) prevented domestic counter-revolution from unleashing a civil war and averted intervention. The Soviet Union paralysed the attempts of the foreign imperialists to interfere in the internal affairs of the democratic States.

U.S. POLICIES IN EUROPE

To counteract the Soviet influence in its satellite states of Poland, Czechoslovakia, Albania, Romania, Bulgaria, Hungary, and East Germany, where Stalin had installed puppet regimes, President Truman responded with the **Truman Doctrine,** the **Marshall Plan,** and the formation of the North Atlantic Treaty Organization (see below). In the effort to "contain" communism, the Truman Doctrine provided military aid to Greece and Turkey. The Marshall Plan expanded aid, offering assistance to all European nations to help them rebuild. Even the Soviet Union was offered help, which it rejected.

DOCUMENT-BASED QUESTION PRACTICE

When Soviet Foreign Minister Molotov turned down the offer of economic aid under the Marshall Plan, Eastern European states controlled by the Soviets followed suit. Examine the sources below, which deal with the reactions of the Soviets and their satellites, and answer in writing the question that follows each document.

FROM SOVIET DEPUTY FOREIGN MINISTER ANDREI VYSHINSKY, IN A SPEECH AT THE UNITED NATIONS, SEPTEMBER 1947

. . . the Marshall Plan constitutes in essence merely a variant of the Truman Doctrine adapted to the conditions of postwar Europe. In bringing forward this plan, the United States Government apparently counted on the cooperation of the Governments of the United Kingdom and France to confront the European countries in need of relief with the necessity of renouncing their inalienable right to dispose of their economic resources and to plan their national economy in their own way. The United States also counted on making all these countries directly dependent on the interests of American monopolies, which are striving to avert the approaching depression by an accelerated export of commodities and capital to Europe. . . .

It is becoming more and more evident to everyone that the implementation of the Marshall Plan will mean placing European countries under the economic and political control of the United States and direct interference by the latter in the internal affairs of those countries. (It) is an attempt to split Europe into two camps . . . to complete the formation of a *bloc* of several European countries hostile to the interests of the democratic countries of Eastern Europe and most particularly to the interests of the Soviet Union.

George Marshall stated that his plan was "not directed against any country or doctrine, but against hunger, poverty, desperation and chaos." What did the Soviet foreign ministry claim was the *real* purpose of the Marshall Plan and the actual intention of the United States in European affairs?

A BRITISH CARTOON BY DAVID LOW, JULY 1947

In the cartoon below, Madame Molotov is commanding her satellite charges to keep their "noses left." According to Low, how would the satellites of the Soviet Union have liked to respond to the Marshall Plan offer of grants? What forces or factors prevented them from doing so?

Noses Left

© *Evening Standard/Solo, London*

EUROPEAN EFFORTS TO REBUILD

The satellites of the Soviet Union were forced to reject the assistance that the Western European countries accepted to rebuild their cities and industries and hasten their recovery after World War II. Other designs contributed to the Western European "economic miracle," among them the creation of the **Schuman Plan**, or European Coal and Steel Community, integrating the coal and steel production of West Germany, Italy, Belgium, the Netherlands, Luxembourg, and France. These same nations also created the **European Economic Community**, known as the **Common Market**, in 1957. They reduced all their tariffs and created a free-trade area. A large unified market was established. The subsequent **Treaty of Rome** encouraged the free flow of capital and labor throughout the area. Nonmember states (Great Britain,

Denmark, Norway, Sweden, Switzerland, Austria, and Portugal) sought to copy the model and formed the **European Free Trade Association**. Stalin had countered early on by forcing the Soviet satellites to join the **Council for Mutual Economic Aid** (Comecon), which principally benefited the Soviet Union rather than the satellites, to their disappointment.

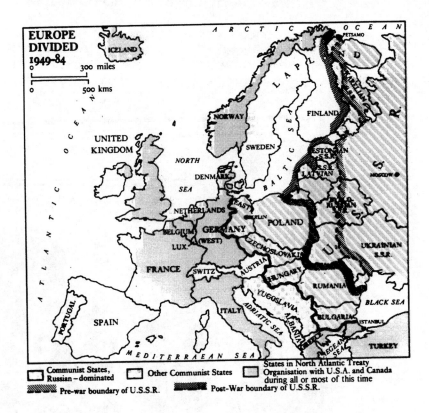

U.S.-SOVIET OPPOSITION

Meanwhile, in 1949 the United States spearheaded the creation of the **North Atlantic Treaty Organization** (NATO), an anti-Soviet military alliance of the Western European governments. Stalin reacted by uniting his satellites in the **Warsaw Pact**. In effect, the cold war brought economic and technological competition between the great superpowers with rival military alliances and economic organizations.

Even before NATO, conflicts had exacerbated tension between the rival blocs. The Soviets had blockaded land routes linking West Berlin to the West German zones, forcing American and British bombers to airlift supplies for almost a year until land access was restored. Both superpowers were testing ever-more destructive nuclear bombs as well as developing rocket missiles.

KHRUSHCHEV IN POWER

Stalin's death in 1953 brought a temporary "thaw" inside the Soviet Union as the new government head, **Nikita Khrushchev** (1894–1971), denounced Stalin's rule and the "cult of personality," in which the brutal leader had been glorified as a benevolent hero to the people. The de-Stalinization movement allowed some writers, such as **Boris Pasternak** (1890-1960), and **Alexander Solzhenitsyn** (1918-) to detail the grimness of life in the **gulag** under Stalin and even brought some relaxation in the political relationship with the United States. Khruschev's policy of **peaceful coexistence** helped ease the cold war tensions with the West and even with **Marshal Tito** (1892-1980), the leader of Yugoslavia, a Communist nation that had repeatedly asserted its independence from Soviet rule. But differences in philosophy remained that weakened the **détente** and created conflicts leading to the construction of the **Berlin Wall**.

The Hungarian Revolution

When Eastern European satellites sought greater liberty, they were stalled in their attempts and brutally put down. In 1956, the **Hungarian Revolt** proved unsuccessful. Soviet troops and tanks crushed the revolutionaries with force and speed.

DOCUMENT-BASED QUESTION PRACTICE

Below are a series of demands of the Hungarian reformers. Explain in a series of written sentences why Soviet Union political leaders would have opposed each of them.

We Hungarian writers have formulated in seven points the demands of the Hungarian nation:

1. We demand an independent national policy based on the principles of socialism. Our relations with all countries, particularly with the USSR and the People's Democracies, should be based on the principle of equality. . . .
2. We demand an end to the (present) policy on national minorities. . . .
3. We demand a clear disclosure of the country's economic situation.
4. Factories should be directed by workers and specialists. The present wage system should be reformed. . . . Trade unions should truly represent the interests of the Hungarian working class.
5. Peasants should be assured the right of free self-determination. . . . Our present agricultural policy should be established on new foundations.
6. Imre Nagy, the pure and courageous communist who enjoys the confidence of the Hungarian people . . . should be given a suitable post. At the same time, a resolute stand must be taken against all counter-revolutionary attempts and aspirations.
7. The development of the situation demands that the Patriotic People's Front should assume political representation of the working classes of Hungarian society. Our electoral system should correspond to the demands of Socialist democracy. The people should elect, by secret ballot, the representatives of parliament and to all the autonomous organs of our administration.

Other Satellite Revolts

Other satellites that attempted independence were crushed by the Soviet leaders. A liberal regime in Czechoslovakia was put down, and trade union independence and agitation for reforms in Poland were suppressed. The new Soviet leader, **Leonid Brezhnev** (1907-1982), who had helped to oust

Khrushchev in the 1964 quiet palace revolution, had formulated a hard-line doctrine. The Soviet Union, he asserted, had the right to prevent a satellite from deviating from Marxist-Leninist principles. The **Brezhnev Doctrine** had been enunciated in 1968 to justify the Soviet Union's military intervention in Czechoslovakia to put down the so-called **Prague Spring**, the movement for democratic socialism.

GREAT BRITAIN AFTER THE WAR

As international tensions alternately abated and heightened between East and West in the 1945-1970 period, the countries of Western Europe proceeded on the course of economic and political recovery. In Great Britain, the Labor Party developed a wide range of health care, education, and other social programs. Major industries were nationalized—coal, steel, electricity, and public transport. The Labor Party sought to create a welfare state, a goal that shifted the electoral successes of the Conservative and Labor parties back and forth in the post-World War II period. Inflation at home and a declining balance of trade brought high unemployment; harsh measures of austerity and foreign loans were required in order to counteract the economic ills.

FRANCE AFTER THE WAR

After the war, France established the Fourth Republic, which lasted until 1958, when the **Fifth Republic** was set up with a new constitution that gave greater powers to the president. The leader promoting this change was **Charles de Gaulle** (1890-1970), who, as head of the **Free French** movement during World War II, had fought the Axis from abroad. As first president of the Fifth Republic, he sought to make France the leading nation of Europe. In the postwar period of **decolonization**, de Gaulle granted independence to France's former colony Algeria following the breakout of a war for independence by the **Algerian Liberation Movement**. De Gaulle resented U.S. influence in Western Europe and took his French military forces out of NATO in 1967, even though he stayed within the alliance itself. He served as presidential dictator until his resignation in 1969. Before leaving office, he had to face the unrest, demonstrations, and strikes by university students calling for dramatic changes in school curriculums and a greater voice in university administration. In 1968, students were joined by rank-and-file industrial workers, who led a general strike across France. De Gaulle was forced to promise wage increases and educational reforms to quell the outbreak.

ITALY AFTER THE WAR

In Italy, **Alcide de Gasperi** (1881-1954) ran the country from 1946 to 1953. As a Christian Democrat and in the context of the cold war, he refused Communists a seat on his cabinet. However, after 1953 and a succession of prime ministers, the Communists, stating their independence from the Soviet Union, gained political strength. And in spite of the economic problems of the largely preindustrial south, with its high unemployment and stream of workers migrating to the north in search of jobs, Italy enjoyed industrial growth and economic expansion.

By 1963, however, the boom was collapsing as inflation and a trade deficit brought labor discontent and economic instability. The Communist Party, the largest in Western Europe, sought reconciliation with the Christian Democratic Party and the other non-communist political parties. They merged their interests to control political turmoil and condemn the terrorism of groups like the **Red Brigade**, which had kidnapped and murdered **Aldo Moro**, the former premier of Italy and leader of the Christian Democratic Party in 1978.

GERMANY AFTER THE WAR

As for Germany, the Western allies allowed formation of the Federal Republic in 1949 and ended their occupation in 1955. That year, too, the Soviets halted their occupation of eastern Germany, which became the German Democratic Republic. The early years witnessed the **Nuremberg war crimes trials**. The Allied nations brought to trial German military and civilian leaders for crimes against the peace and against humanity. In spite of defenses that they were "only following orders," those convicted were sentenced to death. Each of the Allied powers tried the war criminals in its own occupation zones.

Konrad Adenauer (1876-1967) was the first chancellor of West Germany, the seat of the economic miracle. Even at the center of the cold war, industrial production skyrocketed and unemployment vanished. By 1955, West Germany was a partner in NATO, and in 1957 a member of the European Economic Community. Adenauer and a later successor, **Willy Brandt** (1913–), continued to seek reunification with the German Democratic Republic (a goal finally achieved in 1990).

INTELLECTUAL CURRENTS

In spite of economic advances and material prosperity that did come to many in Western Europe in the postwar years, disillusionment with the war and the disquiet that remained contributed to the spiritual crisis in which the philosophy of **existentialism** thrived. Although there were forerunners like Nietzsche in the nineteenth century, the movement grew from the writings of the German **Karl Jaspers** (1883-1969) and the French **Jean-Paul Sartre** (1905-1980), **Albert Camus** (1913-1960), and **Simone de Beauvoir** (1908-1986). Critics have argued that existentialism is not a philosophy but rather a label for several widely different revolts against traditional philosophy, and that the key words distinguishing existentialist writings are *choice, freedom, decision, commitment,* and *anguish.*

DOCUMENT-BASED QUESTION PRACTICE

Using the excerpts below from the major writers, write a paragraph constructing a definition of existentialism.

FROM JEAN-PAUL SARTRE

Man is free; he stands alone in the universe, responsible for his condition, likely to remain in a lowly state but free to reach above the stars.

In fashioning myself, I fashion man.

Man is nothing else but what he purposes. He exists only in so far as he realizes himself, he is nothing else but the sum of his actions, nothing else but what his life is. . . . man is no other (but) a series of undertakings . . . he is the sum, the set of relations that constitute these undertakings.

FROM ALBERT CAMUS

What happens is that the scenery crumbles. Get up, streetcar, four hours at the office or factory, eat, streetcar, four hours of work, eat, sleep, and Monday, Tuesday, Wednesday, Thursday, Friday, and Saturday with the same myths. . . . But one day the "why" arises and everything begins with this fatigue colored by surprise.

But what is absurd is the confrontation of this irrational world and of the desperate desire for clarity whose call echoes in the human heart.

The world's order is ambiguous.

FROM KARL JASPERS

There exists a solidarity among men as human beings that makes each co-responsible for every wrong and every injustice in the world, essentially for crimes committed in his presence or with his knowledge. If I fail to do whatever I can to prevent them, I, too, am guilty.

True philosophizing must well up from men's individual existence and address itself to other individuals to help them to achieve a true existence.

It is never simply true that orders are orders.

The Literary and Visual Arts

In literature and the arts, as well as in philosophy, there were voices charting new courses. The trends of abstract expressionism evident in many of Henry Moore's massive sculptures, the music of the Beatles, and the films of Fellini and Ingmar Bergman are cited as examples of the varied directions of creative expression in the postwar world. Other voices were raised, insistent on equality–political, economic, legal, religious, and gender–in the aftermath. In the quest for human freedom, these voices called upon the liberal traditions of the Western past, a continuing source for regeneration, even in our own times.

MULTIPLE-CHOICE QUESTIONS

1. The 1945 wartime conference at Yalta was the scene of efforts to
   a. coordinate Western defense measures
   b. provide economic aid to Britain and France
   c. divide Germany into occupation zones
   d. plan for a nuclear attack on Japan
   e. create a Jewish state in Israel

2. "We shall fight on the beaches . . . we shall fight in the fields and in the streets, we shall fight in the hills; we shall never surrender."These famous and decisive words of encouragement were spoken during World War II by
   a. Benito Mussolini
   b. Charles de Gaulle
   c. Franklin D. Roosevelt
   d. Adolf Hitler
   e. Winston Churchill

3. Which of the following was a primary goal of Charles de Gaulle as French president?
   a. refuse independence for Algeria
   b. enlist the support of Great Britain in forming the Common Market
   c. coordinate the French military in the NATO superstructure
   d. strengthen the presidency and weaken political instability in France
   e. create "cradle to grave" security in a French welfare state

©Evening Standard/Solo, London.

4. The cartoon above suggests that
   a. each of the Allied nations in World War II had a preferred national sport
   b. each of the Allied leaders had a different political agenda
   c. the French were more interested in independence than in team cooperation
   d. the rules of the United Nations mandated majority decision making
   e. Leisure activities replaced the work of war following Allied victory in World War II

5. The policy of "de-Stalinization" under Khrushchev permitted all the following EXCEPT
   a. greater literary freedom for political dissidents
   b. the removal of Stalin's body from Lenin's tomb
   c. the renaming of Stalingrad to Volgograd
   d. opposition candidates on political ballots
   e. a shift of some production from military to consumer goods

6. The invasion and occupation of Czechoslovakia by Soviet troops in 1968 was legitimated by the
   a. Nazi-Soviet Nonaggression Pact
   b. Brezhnev Doctrine
   c. Warsaw Pact
   d. re-Stalinization of Soviet Russia
   e. Potsdam Agreement

7. In the *Second Sex*, published in France in 1949, she stressed that women were often required to take a position in society subordinate to men, to take the role of the "other." The author referred to is
   a. Christabel Pankhurst
   b. Simone de Beauvoir
   c. Flora Tristan
   d. Doris Lessing
   e. Germaine Greer

8. • Giacometti
   • Brancusi
   • Arp
   • Kandinsky
   The artists listed are practitioners of the style known as
   a. impressionism
   b. neoclassicism
   c. abstract expressionism
   d. realism
   e. pointillism

9. "As a result of the [Second World] war, the capitalist system sustained enormous losses and became weaker . . . manifesting itself chiefly in a new wave of revolutions. Albania, Bulgaria, Eastern Germany, Hungary, Czechoslovakia, Poland, Rumania and Yugoslavia broke away from the system of capitalism. . . . the people acquired extensive democratic rights and liberties. . . . property rights were abolished and the peasants were given land." This interpretation was most likely written by a
   a. liberal democrat
   b. Fascist
   c. Marxian communist
   d. nihilist
   e. utopian socialist

10. A social historian would be most likely interested in researching which of the following topics related to World War II?
    a. the confrontations that exacerbated the cold war

b. the creation and structure of the United Nations
c. women's participation in the labor force during the war
d. the diplomatic correspondence between Churchill and Roosevelt
e. Allied troop landings on the coast of Normandy on D-Day

PRACTICE ESSAY QUESTIONS

Use the questions below to practice essay writing. For each question write an essay that includes an introductory thesis, a body of supporting and/or illustrative data, and a conclusion.

1. Describe and analyze the factors that contributed to the "economic miracle" of Western Europe after World War II.
2. Was the cold war inevitable? Describe the individuals and incidents that were crucial to its emergence.
3. How and to what extent did the Holocaust influence existentialism after World War II?
4. "The artist is a barometer of the general mood of his or her time." Assess the validity of this statement with reference to the visual and literary arts after World War II.
5. "World War II and its aftermath totally discredited the Enlightenment." Support or refute this statement.

ESSAY-WRITING TIPS: BEING YOUR OWN HISTORIAN

The study questions throughout this guide, like AP essays, are open-ended. They ask the writer to

- take a position
- support the position with illustrative evidence and data
- reach a conclusion based on the developing argument

The strength of an essay derives from the clarity of its thesis and the breadth of its perspective—i.e., consider the *range* of factors that contributed to the "economic miracle" of Western Europe after World War II (Study Question 1). The student who goes beyond the political and economic, and brings in technological and social factors, like gender, in her or his analysis is imposing an interpretation on the past. The student is writing history.

The student who states that Yalta made the cold war inevitable (Study Question 2) is writing history. So, too, is the student who argues that there was no inevitability but that a series of events heightened the tensions that might have been reduced through diplomatic talks and correspondence. Both writers, with opposing viewpoints, could make a compelling argument for her or his position. Both essays could illuminate our understanding and make us wonder which was "right."

The history writer creates patterns of understanding using examples to make those patterns clear. But patterns can be challenged and revised as evidence warrants. Being your own historian means exercising your historical imagination to put the pieces of the historical puzzle together according to your conception of the "fit." The exercise is grounded to a degree in reality–i.e., in human events and persons–but the flight of imaginative creation lifts it from the banality of chronicle, where one event follows another, to a height where *meaning* for us is clear.

IDENTIFICATIONS

Konrad Adenauer (1876-1967)–The first chancellor of West Germany; he was able to establish a stable democratic government.

Algerian Liberation Movement–An eight-year struggle by Algeria to secure independence from French colonial control; the goal was finally achieved in 1962.

Atlantic Charter–The joint declaration, in August 1941, by Roosevelt and Churchill, stating common principles for the free world: self-determination, free choice of government, equal opportunities for all nations for trade, permanent system of general security and disarmament.

Simone de Beauvoir (1908-1986)–Existentialist and feminist who has written on the psychology and social position of women.

Berlin Wall–Concrete barrier constructed by the Soviets in August 1961 between West Berlin and East Berlin to prevent East Germans from fleeing to the West. (In 1990, the wall was torn down.)

Blitzkreig–A lightning war using planes, tanks, artillery, and mechanized infantry to knock out the opponent swiftly.

Willy Brandt (1913-)–Chancellor of West Germany in the late 1960s; he sought to improve relations with the states of Eastern Europe.

Leonid Brezhnev (1907-1982)–Soviet leader who helped oust and then replace Khrushchev.

Brezhnev Doctrine–Policy proclaimed in 1968 and declaring that the Soviet Union had the right to intervene in any Socialist country whenever it determined there was a need.

Albert Camus (1913-1960)–French existentialist who stated that in spite of the general absurdity of human life, individuals could make rational sense out of their own existence through meaningful personal decision making.

Cold war–An intense conflict between the superpowers using all means short of military might to achieve their respective ends.

Common Market–Another name for the European Economic Community, which created a free-trade area among the Western European countries.

Council for Mutual Economic Aid (Comecon)–An economic alliance, founded in 1949, to coordinate the economic affairs of the Soviet Union and its satellite countries.

Decolonization–The collapse of colonial empires. Between 1947 and 1962, practically all former colonies in Asia and Africa gained independence.

Détente–Reference to the period of relaxation or thaw in relations between the superpowers during Khrushchev's rule in the Soviet Union.

European Economic Community (Common Market)–Organization, begun on January 1, 1958, including France, German Federal Republic, Italy, and the Benelux nations (Belgium, Netherlands, and Luxembourg). By 1966 the Common

Market would eliminate all customs barriers between the countries, would set up a common tariff policy on imports, and would gradually remove all restrictions on the movement of workers and capital.

European Free Trade Association–An association of Western European nations agreeing to favor each other in respect to tariffs. Members were Denmark, Norway, Sweden, Austria, Portugal, Switzerland, and Great Britain. Sometimes referred to as the Outer Seven–i.e., outside the Common Market; formed in 1959.

Existentialism–A label for widely different revolts against traditional philosophy, stressing choice, freedom, decision, and anguish, and emerging strongly during and after the World War II years.

Fifth Republic–Government established in France in October 1958. The First Republic lasted from 1793 to 1804; the Second, from 1848 to 1852; the Third, from 1875 to 1945; and the Fourth, from 1946 to 1958.

Final Solution–Hitler's policy of virulent anti-Semitism, culminating in the Holocaust, the genocide of six million Jews.

Free French–Supporters of General de Gaulle who refused to acknowledge the French armistice in 1940. In 1944, de Gaulle's Committee of National Liberation was proclaimed and recognized as the French provisional government.

Alcide de Gasperi (1881-1954)–The leader of the Christian Democrats in Italy, he was committed to democracy and moderate social reform.

Charles de Gaulle (1890-1970)–First president of the French Fifth Republic and former head of the Free French movement in World War II.

Gulag–Forced labor camps set up by Stalin for political dissidents.

Hiroshima–Japanese city on which the United States dropped an atomic bomb on August 6, 1945.

Hungarian Revolt (1956)–Attempt by students and workers to liberalize the Communist regime and break off military alliance with the Soviet Union.

Karl Jaspers (1883-1969)–German existentialist seeing all people as equally co-responsible for the terrors and injustices of the world.

Nikita Khrushchev (1894-1971)–Soviet leader who denounced Stalin's rule and brought a temporary thaw in the superpowers' relations.

Marshall Plan–Program that advanced more than $11 billion for European recovery to sixteen Western nations from 1947 to 1953; the final cost to the United States was $20 billion.

Aldo Moro–Former premier of Italy and leader of the Christian Democratic Party who was assassinated by a terrorist group in 1978.

Nagasaki–Japanese city on which the United States dropped an atomic bomb on August 9, 1945, bringing the Japanese surrender and an end to World War II.

Nazi-Soviet Pact (1939)–An agreement between Hitler and Stalin to remain neutral if the other went to war; also, German acknowledgment of Russia's sphere of influence in the Baltics and a secret clause agreeing to the division and takeover of Poland.

North Atlantic Treaty Organization (NATO)–Military alliance founded in 1949, between the United States and Great Britain, France, Belgium, the Netherlands, Luxembourg, Canada, Norway, Iceland, Denmark, Portugal, and Italy; later, Greece, Turkey, and West Germany joined.

Nuremberg War Crimes trials–Proceedings held after 1945 to convict German military and civilian leaders of "crimes against humanity" for their role in the extermination of the Jews and other peoples.

Boris Pasternak (1890-1960)–Russian author of *Dr. Zhivago*, a novel condemning the brutality of the Stalin era.

Peaceful coexistence–The thaw in cold war tensions between the superpowers.

Potsdam Conference–The July-August 1945 meeting of Truman, Stalin, and Clement Atlee of Great Britain, at which disagreements arose over the permanent borders of Germany and free elections in East European countries. Stalin refused to hold free elections, in fear of anti-Soviet governments.

Prague Spring–The liberal reforms introduced by Alexander Dubček, the Czechoslovak Communist Party secretary. On August 20, 1968, twenty thousand troops from the Soviet Union and its satellite countries occupied Prague to undo the reforms.

Red Brigade–Terrorist group committed to radical political and social change that claimed responsibility for the assassination of former Italian premier Aldo Moro in 1978.

Jean-Paul Sartre (1905-1980)–French existentialist most famous for his statement that "existence precedes essence"–i.e., first we exist and then our decisions and choices shape our character or essence.

Schuman Plan–An international organization set up in 1952 to control and integrate all European coal and steel production; also known as the European Coal and Steel Community.

Alexander Solzhenitsyn (1918-)–Russian author of *One Day in the Life of Ivan Denisovich*, a novel detailing life in a Stalinist concentration camp.

Marshal Tito (1892-1980)–Communist chief of Yugoslavia who proclaimed independence of his country from Soviet influence.

Treaty of Rome–Pact, created in 1957, that set up the European Economic Community (also known as the Common Market).

Truman Doctrine–Policy providing military aid to Greece and Turkey in an effort to contain Communism (1947-1948).

Warsaw Pact–A military alliance, formed in 1955, of the Soviet Union and its Eastern European satellite nations.

Yalta–The wartime meeting of Roosevelt, Churchill, and Stalin in February 1945 to discuss military strategy and postwar plans.

APPENDIX A

RULERS AND REGIMES

ENGLAND

Houses of Lancaster and York

Henry IV	1399–1413
Henry V	1413–1422
Henry VI	1422–1461
Edward IV	1461–1483
Edward V	1483
Richard III	1483–1485

Tudors

Henry VII	1485–1509
Henry VIII	1509–1547
Edward VI	1547–1553
Mary I	1553–1558
Elizabeth I	1558–1603

Stuarts

James I	1603–1625
Charles I	1625–1649
Interregnum	1649–1660
Charles II	1660–1685
James II	1685–1688
William III and Mary II	1689–1694
William III alone	1694–1702
Anne	1702–1714

**Hanoverians
(from 1917, Windsors)**

George I	1714–1727
George II	1727–1760
George III	1760–1820
George IV	1820–1830
William IV	1830–1837
Victoria	1837–1901
Edward VII	1901–1910
George V	1910–1936
Edward VIII	1936
George VI	1936–1952
Elizabeth II	1952–

FRANCE

Valois

Philip VI	1328-1350
John	1350-1364
Charles V	1364-1380
Charles VI	1380-1422
Charles VII	1422-1461
Louis XI	1461-1483
Charles VIII	1483-1498
Louis XII	1498-1515
Francis I	1515-1547
Henry II	1547-1559
Francis II	1559-1560
Charles IX	1560-1574
Henry III	1574-1589

Bourbons

Henry IV	1589-1610
Louis XIII	1610-1643
Louis XIV	1643-1715
Louis XV	1715-1774
Louis XVI	1774-1792

Post-1792

Napoleon I, Emperor	1804-1814
Louis XVIII (*Bourbon*)	1814-1824
Charles X (*Bourbon*)	1824-1830
Louis Philippe (*Bourbon-Orléans*)	1830-1848
Napoleon III, Emperor	1851-1870

SPAIN

Ferdinand and	1479-1516
Isabella	1479-1504

Hapsburgs

Philip I	1504-1506
Charles I (Holy Roman Emperor as Charles V)	1506-1556
Philip II	1556-1598
Philip III	1598-1621
Philip IV	1621-1665
Charles II	1665-1700
Philip V	1700-1746
Ferdinand VI	1746-1759
Charles III	1759-1788
Charles IV	1788-1808
Ferdinand VII	1808
Joseph Bonaparte	1808-1813

Bourbons

Ferdinand VII (restored)	1814-1833
Isabella II	1833-1868
Amadeo	1870-1873
Alfonso XII	1874-1885
Alfonso XIII	1886-1931
Juan Carlos I	1975-

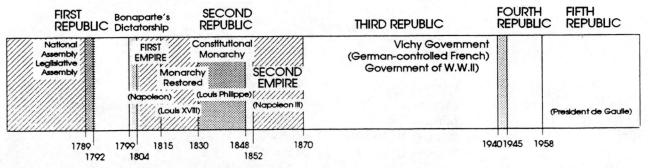

The Changing Forms of the French Government

AUSTRIA AND AUSTRIA-HUNGARY

(Until 1806 all except Maria Theresa were also Holy Roman Emperors.)

Maximilian I, Archduke	1493-1519	Leopold I	1658-1705
Charles I (Emperor as Charles V)	1519-1556	Joseph I	1705-1711
		Charles VI	1711-1740
Ferdinand I	1556-1564	Maria Theresa	1740-1780
Maximilian II	1564-1576	Joseph II	1780-1790
Rudolf II	1576-1612	Leopold II	1790-1792
Matthias	1612-1619	Francis II	1792-1835
Ferdinand II	1619-1637	Ferdinand I	1835-1848
Ferdinand III	1637-1657	Francis Joseph	1848-1916
		Charles I	1916-1918

PRUSSIA AND GERMANY

Hohenzollerns

Frederick William the Great Elector	1640-1688	Frederick William III	1797-1840
		Frederick William IV	1840-1861
Frederick I	1701-1713	William I	1861-1888
Frederick William I	1713-1740	Frederick III	1888
Frederick II the Great	1740-1786	William II	1888-1918
Frederick William II	1786-1797		

RUSSIA

Ivan III	1462-1505	
Basil III	1505-1533	**Romanovs**
Ivan IV the Terrible	1533-1584	
Theodore I	1584-1598	Elizabeth — 1741-1762
Boris Godunov	1598-1605	Peter III — 1762
Theodore II	1605	Catherine II the Great — 1762-1796
Basil IV	1606-1610	Paul — 1796-1801
Michael	1613-1645	Alexander I — 1801-1825
Alexius	1645-1676	Nicholas I — 1825-1855
Theodore III	1676-1682	Alexander II — 1855-1881
Ivan IV and Peter I	1682-1689	Alexander III — 1881-1894
Peter I the Great alone	1689-1725	Nicholas II — 1894-1917
Catherine I	1725-1727	Provisional Government 1917
Peter II	1727-1730	Communist Revolution 1917
Anna	1730-1740	Union of Soviet Socialist Republics — 1922-1991
Ivan VI	1740-1741	

ITALY

Victor Emmanuel II	1861-1878	Victor Emmanuel III	1900-1946
Humbert I	1878-1900	Humbert II	1946

HOLY ROMAN EMPIRE

Hapsburgs

Frederick III	1440–1493
Maximilian I	1493–1519
Charles V	1519–1556
Ferdinand I	1556–1564
Maximilian II	1564–1576
Rudolf II	1576–1612
Matthias	1612–1619
Ferdinand II	1619–1637
Ferdinand III	1637–1657
Leopold I	1658–1705
Joseph I	1705–1711
Charles VI	1711–1740
Charles VII	1742–1745
Francis I	1745–1765
Joseph II	1765–1790
Leopold II	1790–1792
Francis II	1792–1806

THE PAPACY

Nicholas V	1447–1455
Pius II	1458–1464
Alexander VI	1492–1503
Julius II	1503–1513
Leo X	1513–1521
Adrian VI	1522–1523
Clement VII	1523–1534
Paul III	1534–1549
Paul IV	1555–1559
Pius V	1566–1572
Gregory XIII	1572–1585
Pius VII	1800–1823
Gregory XVI	1831–1846
Pius IX	1846–1878
Leo XIII	1878–1903
Pius X	1903–1914
Benedict XV	1914–1922
Pius XI	1922–1939
Pius XII	1939–1958
John XXIII	1958–1963
Paul VI	1963–1978
John Paul I	1978
John Paul II	1978–

Guernica; Braque, *The Table*). Value: a new way of seeing; a view of the world as a mosaic of multiple relationships; reality as interaction. Nonrepresentational art; no climaxes; flattened-out planes and values; the real appearance of forms in nature is subordinated to an aesthetic concept of form composed of shapes, lines, and colors (Moore, *Reclining Figure*; Giacometti, *Man Pointing*; Rothko, *Ochre on Red*). Value: personal and subjective interpretation.

A P P E N D I X B

WESTERN ART THROUGH THE AGES— CHARACTERISTICS, VALUES, AND REPRESENTATIVE ARTISTS OF DOMINANT STYLES

Medieval	Byzantine style dominates; religious scenes with stiff, one-dimensional figures associated with the priestly functions of the church; backgrounds generally in gold to provide illumination in the church (Berlinghieri, *St. Francis altarpiece*). Values: religious, transcendental, otherworldly.
Renaissance	An art of line and edges; figures from the bible, classical history, and mythology; commissioned portraits; use of perspective, *chiaroscuro* (light and dark) to achieve rounded effect; secular backgrounds and material splendor (Botticelli, *Birth of Venus*; Fra Filippo Lippi, *Mother and Child*; Raphael, *School of Athens*; Michelangelo, *David* and *Creation of Adam*; Bronzino, *Portrait of a Young Man*). Values: secularism, individualism, *virtu* (excellence), balance, order, passivity, and calm.
Baroque (Counter-Reformation)	Art style that is florid, more colorful, richer in texture and decoration, more light and shade—apparently less control. Scenes embody mystery and drama, violence and spectacle, suggesting a deliberate striving after effect; the Catholic church commissions artists to stir religious emotions and win back defectors (Bernini, *The Ecstasy of St. Theresa*; Artemisia Gentileschi, *Judith and Holofernes*; Caravaggio, *The Conversion of St. Paul*; El Greco, *The*

Burial of Count Orgaz; Rembrandt, *Supper at Emmaus*; Rubens, *The Elevation of the Cross*). Values: sensualism, dynamism, emotion.

**Northern Realism
Seventeenth Century**

Genre or everyday scenes exhibit mathematical and geometric values of seventeenth-century science. Middle-class Dutch patrons commissioned secular works: portraits, still-lifes; landscapes, and genre paintings (Vermeer, *Woman with a Water Jug*; van Ruisdael, *View of Haarlem*; Rembrandt, *The Anatomy Lesson of Dr. Tulp*). Values: quiet opulence, comfortable domesticity, realism.

**Rococo
Eighteenth Century**

Art of the French aristocracy portraying nobility in sylvan settings or ornate interiors; Venuses and Cupids abound; ladies wear silk finery alongside similarly dressed cavaliers (Boucher, *Cupid a Captive*; Fragonard, *The Swing*; Watteau, *Return from Cythera*). Rococo art is "candy-box" art—saccharine, frivolous, delicate. Values: ornamentation, elegance, sweetness.

**Neoclassicism
Eighteenth Century**

A return to classical antiquity for inspiration; scenes are historical and mythological; figures appear to be sculpted; the appeal is to the intellect, not the heart; emotions are restrained, and balance is achieved (David, *Socrates Taking the Hemlock*; Ingres, *Oedipus and the Sphinx*; David, *The Death of Marat*). Values: reason, order, balance, reverence for antiquity.

**Romanticism
Nineteenth Century**

A reaction against the "cold and unfeeling" reason of the Enlightenment and against the destruction of nature resulting from the Industrial Revolution. Stress is on light, color, and self-expression, in opposition to the emphasis on line and firm modeling typical of neoclassical art (Géricault, *Raft of the Medusa*; Delacroix, *Liberty Leading the People*; J. M. W. Turner, *The Slave Ship*; Goya, *The Third of May*). Values: emotion, feeling, morbidity, exoticism, mystery.

**Impressionism
Nineteenth Century**

An attempt to portray the fleeting and transitory world of sense impressions based on scientific studies of light; forms are bathed in light and atmosphere; colors are juxtaposed for the eye to fuse from a distance; short, choppy brush strokes to catch the vibrating quality of light (Monet, *Rouen Cathedral*; Renoir, *Le Moulin de la Galette*; Degas, *Ballet Rehearsal*; Seurat, *Sunday Afternoon on the Island of La Grande Jatte*). Values: the immediate, accidental, and transitory.

**Expressionism
Nineteenth and
Twentieth Centuries**

Indebted to Freud; art tries to penetrate the façade of bourgeois superficiality and probe the psyche, that which lurks beneath an individual's calm and artificial posture (Munch, *The Scream*; Kirchner, *The Red Cocotte*; Kokoschka, *The Tempest*; Beckmann, *The Night*; van Gogh, *Starry Night* and *Self-Portrait*). Values: subliminal anxiety; dissonance in color and perspective; pictorial violence—manifest and latent.

**Surrealism
Nineteenth and
Twentieth Centuries**

Also indebted to Freud; explores the dream world, a world without logic, reason, or meaning; fascination with mystery, the strange encounters between objects, and incongruity; subjects are often indecipherable in their strangeness; the beautiful is the quality of chance association (de Chirico, *Nostalgia of the Infinite*; Dali, *The Persistence of Memory*; Ernst, *Two Children Are Menaced by a Nightingale*; Miró, *Dog Barking at the Moon*; Chagall, *Self-Portrait with Seven Fingers*). Values: the dream sequence; illogic; fantasy.

**Cubism
Twentieth Century**

No single point of view; no continuity or simultaneity of image contour; all possible views of the subject are compressed into one synthesized view of top, sides, front, and back; picture becomes a multifaceted view of objects with angular, interlocking planes (Picasso, *Les Demoiselles d'Avignon* and

Abstract
Expressionism
Twentieth Century

Guernica; Braque, *The Table*). Value: a new way of seeing; a view of the world as a mosaic of multiple relationships; reality as interaction. Nonrepresentational art; no climaxes; flattened-out planes and values; the real appearance of forms in nature is subordinated to an aesthetic concept of form composed of shapes, lines, and colors (Moore, *Reclining Figure*; Giacometti, *Man Pointing*; Rothko, *Ochre on Red*). Value: personal and subjective interpretation.

ANSWER KEY–
MULTIPLE-CHOICE QUESTIONS

Chapter 1	Chapter 3	Chapter 5	Chapter 7
1. e	1. b	1. a	1. a
2. d	2. c	2. c	2. b
3. a	3. d	3. b	3. d
4. d	4. b	4. d	4. d
5. a	5. d	5. b	5. c
6. d	6. e	6. c	6. e
7. e	7. a	7. c	7. d
8. c	8. c	8. a	8. a
9. b	9. c	9. c	9. a
10. d	10. b	10. c	10. c

Chapter 2	Chapter 4	Chapter 6	Chapter 8
1. e	1. b	1. b	1. b
2. c	2. a	2. a	2. c
3. b	3. c	3. c	3. c
4. c	4. e	4. c	4. d
5. e	5. c	5. d	5. c
6. a	6. d	6. a	6. d
7. d	7. d	7. d	7. b
8. d	8. a	8. a	8. a
9. a	9. b	9. a	9. c
10. c	10. c	10. d	10. e

Chapter 9	Chapter 11	Chapter 13	Chapter 15
1. a	1. d	1. b	1. c
2. c	2. b	2. c	2. e
3. d	3. b	3. d	3. d
4. e	4. a	4. a	4. b
5. d	5. e	5. b	5. d
6. c	6. b	6. e	6. b
7. b	7. b	7. d	7. b
8. b	8. b	8. b	8. c
	9. c		9. c
Chapter 10	10. b	Chapter 14	10. c
1. d		1. d	
2. c	Chapter 12	2. b	
3. d		3. d	
4. a	1. e	4. c	
5. d	2. c	5. d	
6. b	3. c	6. a	
7. e	4. a	7. c	
8. d	5. b	8. d	
	6. b	9. e	
	7. d	10. b	
	8. d		
	9. a		
	10. b		

GLOSSARY*

Absolutism–The theory that the monarch is supreme and can exercise full and complete power unilaterally.

Konrad Adenauer (1876-1967)–The first chancellor of West Germany; he was able to establish a stable democratic government.

Gustavus Adolphus (1594-1632)–Swedish Lutheran king who won victories for the German Protestants in the Thirty Years' War and lost his life in one of the battles.

Alexander II (1855-1881)–Reforming czar who emancipated the serfs and introduced some measure of representative local government.

Alexander III (1881-1894)–Politically reactionary czar who promoted economic modernization of Russia.

Algerian Liberation movement–An eight-year struggle by Algeria to secure independence from French colonial control; the goal was finally achieved in 1962.

Duke of Alva (1508-1582)–Military leader sent by Philip II to pacify the Low Countries.

Ancien régime (Old Regime)–France prior to the French Revolution.

Anschluss–The union of Austria with Germany, resulting from the occupation of Austria by the German army in 1938.

Appeasement–The making of concessions to an adversary in the hope of avoiding conflict. The term is most often used in reference to the meeting between Hitler and British prime minister Chamberlain in Munich, where agreement was made, in September 1938, to cede the Sudetenland (the German-speaking area of Czechoslovakia) to Germany.

Aristotelian-Ptolemaic cosmology–The geocentric view of the universe that prevailed from the fourth century B.C. to the sixteenth and seventeenth centuries and accorded with church teachings and Scriptures.

Armada (1588)–Spanish vessels defeated in the English Channel by an English fleet, thus preventing Philip II's invasion of England.

---

*Dates for monarchs are of reigns, not birth and deaths.

Army Order no. 1–An order issued to the Russian military when the provisional government was formed in March 1917. It deprived officers of their authority and placed power in elected committees of common soldiers. This led to the collapse of army discipline.

Article 231–Provision of the Versailles Treaty that blamed Germany for World War I.

Atlantic Charter–The joint declaration, in August 1941, by Roosevelt and Churchill, stating common principles for the Free World: self-determination, free choice of government; equal opportunities for all nations for trade, permanent system of general security and disarmament.

Francis Bacon (1561-1626)–Inductive thinker who stressed experimentation in arriving at truth.

Vasco de Balboa–First European to reach the Pacific Ocean.

Banalités–Fees that French peasants were obligated to pay landlords for the use of the village mill, bakeshop, and winepress.

Baroque–The sensuous and dynamic style of art of the Counter-Reformation. (See Appendix B.)

Bastille–The political prison and armory stormed on July 14, 1789, by Parisian city workers alarmed by the king's concentration of troops at Versailles.

Simone de Beauvoir (1908-1986)–An existentialist and feminist who has written on the psychology and social position of women.

Cesare Beccaria–Author of *Of Crime and Punishment*.

Beer Hall Putsch–Hitler's attempt, in 1923, to overthrow the Weimar Republic when he fired his pistol in the ceiling of a Munich beer hall.

Jeremy Bentham (1748-1832)–British theorist and philosopher who proposed utilitarianism–the principle that governments should operate on the basis of utility, or the greatest good for the greatest number.

Berlin Wall–Concrete barrier constructed by the Soviets in August 1961 between West Berlin and East Berlin to prevent East Germans from fleeing to the West.

Eduard Bernstein (1850-1932)–Revisionist German Social Democrat who favored socialist revolution by the ballot rather than the bullet–i.e., by cooperating with the bourgeois members of Parliament and securing electoral victories for his party (the SDP).

Bill of Rights (1689)–Document declaring that sovereignty resided with the Parliament.

Otto von Bismarck (1815-1898)–Prussian chancellor who engineered a series of wars to unify Germany under his authoritarian rule.

Black Death–The bubonic plague that struck Europe in the mid-fourteenth century and killed from one third to one half of the population before it ran its course after 1600.

Black Hand–The Serbian secret society alleged to be responsible for assassinating Archduke Francis Ferdinand.

Black Shirts–The private army of Mussolini.

Blank check–Reference to the full support provided by William II to Austria-Hungary in its conflict with Serbia.

Blitzkreig–A lightning war using planes, tanks, artillery, and mechanized infantry to knock out the opponent swiftly.

Bolsheviks–Left-wing, revolutionary Marxists headed by Lenin.

Boyar–Russian noble.

Willy Brandt (1913-)–Chancellor of West Germany in the late 1960s; he sought to improve relations with the states of Eastern Europe.

Brethren of the Common Life–Pious laypeople in sixteenth-century Holland who initiated a religious revival in their model of Christian living.

Leonid Brezhnev (1907-1982)–Soviet leader who helped oust and then replace Khrushchev.

Brezhnev Doctrine–Policy proclaimed in 1968 and declaring that the Soviet Union had the right to intervene in any Socialist country whenever it determined there was a need.

Brown Shirts–Hitler's private army of supporters, also known as the SA (Sturm Abteilung).

Bundesrat–The upper house, or Federal Council, of the German Diet (the legislature).

Edmund Burke (1729-1797)–Member of British Parliament and author of *Reflections on the Revolution in France* (1790), which criticized the underlying principles of the French Revolution and argued conservative thought.

Burschenschaften–Politically active students around 1815 in the German states proposing unification and democratic principles.

Cahier de doléances–List of grievances that each Estate drew up in preparation for the summoning of the Estates-General in 1789.

John Calvin (1509-1564)–A French theologian who established a theocracy in Geneva and is best known for his theory of predestination.

Albert Camus (1913-1960)–French existentialist who stated that in spite of the general absurdity of human life, individuals could make rational sense out of their own existence through meaningful personal decision making.

Carbonari–Italian secret societies calling for a unified Italy and republicanism after 1815.

Carlsbad Decrees (1819)–Repressive laws in the German states limiting freedom of speech and dissemination of liberal ideas in the universities.

Cat and Mouse Act (1913)–Law that released suffragettes on hunger strikes from jail and then rearrested and jailed them again.

Catherine de Médicis (1547-1589)–The wife of Henry II (1547-1559) of France, who exercised political influence after the death of her husband and during the rule of her weak sons.

Catherine the Great (1762-1796)–An "enlightened despot" of Russia whose policies of reform were aborted under pressure of rebellion by serfs.

Catholic Emancipation Bill (1829)–Act enabling Catholics to hold public office for the first time in England.

Count Cavour (1810-1861)–Italian statesman from Sardinia who used diplomacy to help achieve unification of Italy.

Benvenuto Cellini (1500-1571)–A goldsmith and sculptor who wrote an autobiography, famous for its arrogance and immodest self-praise.

Charles I (1625-1649)–Stuart king who brought conflict with Parliament to a head and was subsequently executed.

Charles II (1660-1685)–Stuart king during the Restoration, following Cromwell's Interregnum.

Charles V (1519-1556)–Hapsburg dynastic ruler of the Holy Roman Empire and of extensive territories in Spain and the Netherlands.

Cheka–The secret police under Lenin and his Communist Party.

Church Statute of 1721–A Holy Synod that replaced the office of patriarch. All of its members (lay and religious) had to swear allegiance to the czar.

Classical liberalism–A middle-class (bourgeois) doctrine indebted to the writings of the philosophes, the French Revolution, and the popularization of the Scientific Revolution. Its goals were self-government, a written constitution, natural rights, limited suffrage, and a laissez-faire economy.

Code Napoléon–The codification and condensation of laws assuring legal equality and uniformity in France.

Colbert (1619-1683)–The financial minister under the French king Louis XIV who promoted mercantilist policies.

Cold war–An intense conflict between the superpowers using all means short of military might to achieve their respective ends.

Christopher Columbus (1446-1506)–First European to sail to the West Indies, 1492.

Committee of Public Safety–The leaders under Robespierre who organized the defenses of France, conducted foreign policy, and centralized authority during the period 1792-1795.

Common Market–Another name for the European Economic Community, which created a free-trade area among the Western European countries.

Concordat (1801)–Napoleon's arrangement with Pope Pius VII to heal religious division in France with a united Catholic church under bishops appointed by the government.

Concordat of Bologna (1516)–Treaty under which the French Crown recognized the supremacy of the pope over a council and obtained the right for the government to nominate all French bishops and abbots.

Condorcet–Author of *Sketch of the Progress of the Human Mind.*

Condottiere–A mercenary soldier of a political ruler.

Conservative Party–Formerly the Tory Party, headed by Disraeli in the nineteenth century.

Constitutional Democrats–Also known as the Cadets, the party of the liberal bourgeoisie in Russia.

Constitutionalism–The theory that power should be shared between rulers and their subjects, and the state governed according to laws.

Continental System–Napoleon's efforts to block foreign trade with England by forbidding importation of British goods into Europe.

Nicolaus Copernicus (1473-1543)–Polish astronomer who posited a heliocentric universe in place of a geocentric universe.

Corn Laws–Legislation enacted in 1815 that imposed a tariff on imported grain and was a symbolic protection of aristocratic landholdings. They were repealed in 1846.

Hernando Cortez–Conqueror of the Aztecs, 1519-1521.

Corvées–Road work; obligation of French peasants to landowners.

Council for Mutual Economic Aid (Comecon)–An economic alliance, founded in 1949, to coordinate the economic affairs of the Soviet Union and its satellite countries.

Council of People's Commissars–The new government set up by Lenin following the Red Guard seizure of government buildings on November 1917.

Council of Trent–The congress of learned Roman Catholic authorities that met intermittently from 1545 to 1563 to reform abusive church practices and reconcile with the Protestants.

Coup d'état–Overthrow of those in power.

Crimean War (1853-1856)–Conflict between Russia and Turkey ostensibly waged by Russia to protect Orthodox Christians in the Ottoman Empire; in actuality, to gain a foothold in the Black Sea. Turks, Britain, and France forced Russia to sue for peace. The Treaty of Paris (1856) forfeited Russia's right to maintain a war fleet in the Black Sea. Russia also lost the principalities of Wallachia and Moldavia.

Oliver Cromwell (1559-1658)–The principal leader and a gentry member of the Puritans in Parliament.

Crystal Night (Krystallnacht)–The November 1938 destruction, by Hitler's Brown Shirts and mobs, of Jewish shops, homes, and synagogues.

Charles Darwin (1809-1882)–British scientist whose *Origin of Species* (1859) proposed the theory of evolution based on his biological research.

Dawes Plan (1924)–The provision of U.S. loans to Germany to help meet reparation payments, which were also reduced.

Decembrists–Russian revolutionaries calling for constitutional reform in the early nineteenth century.

Decembrist revolt–The 1825 plot by liberals (upper-class intelligentsia) to set up a constitutional monarchy or a republic. The plot failed, but the ideal remained.

Declaration of the Rights of Man and Citizen (August 27, 1789)–Document that embodied the liberal revolutionary ideals and general principles of the philosophes' writings.

Decolonization–The collapse of colonial empires. Between 1947 and 1962, practically all former colonies in Asia and Africa gained independence.

Defenestration of Prague–The hurling, by Protestants, of Catholic officials from a castle window in Prague, setting off the Thirty Years' War.

Deism–The belief that God has created the universe and set it in motion to operate like clockwork. God is literally in the wings watching the show go on as humans forge their own destiny.

René Descartes (1596-1650)–Deductive thinker whose famous saying *cogito, ergo sum* ("I think, therefore I am") challenged the notion of truth as being derived from tradition and Scriptures.

Détente–Reference to the period of relaxation or thaw in relations between the superpowers during Khrushchev's rule in the Soviet Union.

Dialectical materialism–The idea, according to Karl Marx, that change and development in history result from the conflict between social classes. Economic forces impel human beings to behave in socially determined ways.

Bartholomew Diaz–First European to reach the southern tip of Africa, 1487-1488.

Denis Diderot–One of the authors of the *Encyclopedia*.

Diggers and **Levellers**–Radical groups in England in the 1650s who called for the abolition of private ownership and extension of the franchise.

Directory (1795-1799)–The five-man executive committee that ruled France in its own interests as a republic after Robespierre's execution and prior to Napoleon's coming to power.

Benjamin Disraeli–Leader of the British Tory Party who engineered the Reform Bill of 1867, which extended the franchise to the working class.

Divine-right monarchy–The belief that the monarch's power derives from God and represents Him on earth.

Domestic system–The manufacture of goods in the household setting, a production system that gave way to the factory system.

Dreadnought–A battleship with increased speed and power over conventional warships, developed by both Germany and Great Britain to increase their naval arsenals.

Alfred Dreyfus (1859-1935)–French and Jewish army captain unfairly convicted of espionage in a case that lasted from 1894 to 1906.

Dual Monarchy–An 1867 compromise between the Germans of Austria-Bohemia and the Magyars of Germany to resolve the nationalities problem by creating the empire of Austria and the kingdom of Hungary, with a common ministry for finance, foreign affairs, and war.

Duma–Russian national legislature.

Dutch East India Company–Government-chartered joint-stock company organized in 1602 that controlled the spice trades in the East Indies.

Edict of Nantes (1598)–The edict of Henry IV that granted Huguenots the rights of public worship and religious toleration in France.

Elizabeth I (1558-1603)–Protestant ruler of England who helped stabilize religious tensions by subordinating theological issues to political considerations.

Emancipation Edict (1861)–The imperial law that abolished serfdom in Russia and, on paper, freed the peasants. In actuality they were collectively responsible for redemption payments to the government for a number of years.

Ems telegram–The carefully edited dispatch by Bismarck to the French ambassador that appeared to be insulting and thus requiring retaliation by France for the seeming affront to French honor in 1870.

Enabling Act–Article 48 of the Weimar constitution, which enabled Hitler to issue decrees carrying the force of law.

Encirclement–Before both world wars, the policy of other European countries that, Germany claimed, prevented German expansion, denying it the right to acquire "living room" (*lebensraum*).

Friedrich Engels (1820-1895)–Collaborator with Karl Marx. Engels was a textile factory owner and supplied Marx with the hard data for his economic writings, notably *Das Kapital* (1867).

Enlightenment–The intellectual revolution of the eighteenth century in which the philosophes stressed reason, natural law, and progress in their criticism of prevailing social injustices.

Entente Cordiale–The 1904 "gentleman's agreement" between France and Britain, establishing a close understanding.

Estates-General–The French national assembly summoned in 1789 to remedy the financial crisis and correct abuses of the *ancien régime*.

European Economic Community (Common Market)–Organization, begun on January 1, 1958, including France, the German Federal Republic, Italy, and the Benelus nations (Belgium, Netherlands, and Luxembourg). By 1966 according to the treaty establishing it, the Common Market would eliminate all customs barriers between the countries, would set up a common tariff policy on imports, and would gradually remove all restrictions on the movement of workers and capital.

European Free Trade Association–An association of Western European nations agreeing to favor each other in respect to tariffs. Members were Denmark, Norway, Sweden, Austria, Portugal, Switzerland, and Great Britain. Sometimes referred to as the Outer Seven–i.e., outside the Common Market; formed in 1959.

Existentialism–A label for widely different revolts against traditional philosophy, stressing choice, freedom, decision, and anguish, and emerging strongly during and after the World War II years.

Fabian Society–Group of English socialists, including George Bernard Shaw, who advocated electoral victories, rather than violent revolutions, to bring about social change.

Factory Act (1833)–Limited children's and adolescents' workweek in textile factories in England.

Fascism–The political and economic methods of Mussolini in Italy. The name comes from the fasces, or bundle of rods tied around an axe, the symbol of authority in ancient Rome.

Feudalism–A decentralized political system in which lords and their vassals, both members of the aristocracy, allied to fight wars and defend territorial gains.

J. G. Fichte (1762-1814)–German writer who believed that the German spirit was nobler and purer than that of other peoples.

Fifth Republic–Government established in France in October 1958. The First Republic lasted from 1792 to 1804; the Second, from 1848 to 1852; the Third, from 1870 to 1940; and the Fourth, from 1945 to 1958.

Final Solution–Hitler's policy of virulent anti-Semitism, culminating in the Holocaust, the genocide of six million Jews and other peoples.

Charles Fourier (1772-1837)–A leading utopian socialist who envisaged small communal societies in which men and women cooperated in agriculture and industry, abolishing private property and monogamous marriage as well.

Fourteen Points–Wilson's peace plans after World War I calling for freedom of the seas, arms reduction, and the right of self-determination for ethnic groups.

Frederick the Great (1740-1786)–The Prussian ruler who expanded his territory by invading the duchy of Silesia and defeating Maria Theresa of Austria.

Frederick William (1640-1688)–The "Soldier's King," who built a strong Prussian army and infused military values into Prussian society.

Frederick William IV (1840-1861)–King of Prussia who promised and later reneged on his promises for constitutional reforms in 1848.

Free French–Supporters of General de Gaulle who refused to acknowledge the French armistice in 1940. In 1944, de Gaulle's Committee of National Liberation was proclaimed and recognized as the French provisional government.

Free trade–An economic theory or policy of the absence of restrictions or tariffs on goods imported into a country. There is no "protection" in the form of tariffs against foreign competition.

French Academy of Sciences–Organized body for scientific study, founded in the 1600s.

French classicism–The style in seventeenth-century art and literature stressing discipline, balance, and restraint and thus resembling the arts in the ancient world and in the Renaissance–e.g., the works of Poussin, Molière, and Racine.

Sigmund Freud (1856-1939)–Viennese psychoanalyst whose theory of human personality based on sexual drives shocked Victorian sensibilities.

Fronde–The last aristocratic revolt against a French monarch, specifically nobility-led riots against the monarchy between 1648 and 1660.

Galileo (1564-1642)–Italian scientist who formulated terrestrial laws and the modern law of inertia; he also provided evidence for the Copernican hypothesis.

Father Gapon (1870-1906)–Leader of the factory workers who assembled before the czar's palace to petition him on January 1905 (Bloody Sunday) for social and political reforms.

Giuseppe Garibaldi (1807-1882)–Soldier of fortune who amassed his "red shirt" army to bring Naples and Sicily into a unified Italy.

Alcide de Gasperi (1881-1954)–The leader of the Christian Democrats in Italy; he was committed to democracy and moderate social reform.

Charles de Gaulle (1890-1970)–First president of the French Fifth Republic and former head of the Free French movement in World War II.

William Gladstone (1809-1898)–British Liberal Party leader and prime minister, a chief rival of Disraeli. Gladstone's ministry included reforms in public education, civil service exams, and secret balloting.

Glorious Revolution–A reference to the political events of 1688-1689 when James II abdicated his throne and was replaced by his daughter Mary and her husband, Prince William of Orange.

Great Fear–The panic and insecurity that struck French peasants in the summer of 1789 and led to their widespread destruction of manor houses and archives.

François Guizot (1787-1874)–Chief minister under Louis Philippe. Guizot's repressive policies led to the revolution of 1848.

Gulag–Forced labor camps set up by Stalin for political dissidents.

Habeas corpus–The legal protection that prohibits the imprisonment of a subject without demonstrated cause.

Hegelian dialectic–The idea, according to G. W. F. Hegel, that social change results from the conflict of opposite ideas. The thesis is confronted by the antithesis, resulting in a synthesis, which then becomes a new thesis in this evolutionary process.

Prince Henry the Navigator–Sponsor of voyages along West African coasts, 1418.

Henry IV (1589-1610)–Formerly Henry of Navarre; ascended the French throne as a convert to Catholicism.

J. G. Herder (1774-1803)–Forerunner of the German Romantic movement who believed that each people shared a national character, or *Volksgeist*.

Paul von Hindenburg (1847-1934)–President of Weimar Germany, who appointed Hitler chancellor in 1933; formerly a general in World War I.

Hiroshima–Japanese city on which the United States dropped an atomic bomb on August 6, 1945.

Adolf Hitler (1889-1945)–The Nazi leader who came to power legally in Germany in 1933, set up a totalitarian dictatorship, led Germany into World War II.

Thomas Hobbes (1588-1679)–Political theorist advocating absolute monarchy based on his concept of an anarchic state of nature.

Holy Alliance–An alliance dreamed up by Alexander I of Russia by which those in power were asked to rule in accord with Christian principles.

House of Savoy–The Italian dynasty ruling the independent state of Piedmont-Sardinia. Its head was King Victor Emmanuel II.

Huguenots–French Calvinists.

Humanism–The recovery and study of classical authors and writings.

David Hume–Author of *An Inquiry Concerning Human Understanding*.

Hungarian Revolt (1956)–Attempt by students and workers to liberalize the Communist regime and break off military alliance with the Soviet Union.

John Huss (1369-1415)–Czech priest who was burned at the stake for rejecting and questioning certain church doctrines, such as transubstantiation.

Imperialism–The acquisition and administration of colonial areas, usually in the interests of the administering country.

Indemnities–Financial demands placed on loser nations.

Indemnity bill (1867)–The bill passed by the German Reichstag that legitimated Bismarck's unconstitutional collection of taxes to modernize the army in 1863.

Index–A list of books that Catholics were forbidden to read.

Individualism–The emphasis on the unique and creative personality.

Indulgence–Papal pardon for remission of sins.

Inquisition–A religious committee of six Roman cardinals that tried heretics and punished the guilty by imprisonment and execution.

Interregnum–The period of Cromwellian rule (1649-1660), between the Stuart dynastic rules of Charles I and Charles II.

Jacobins–The dominant group in the National Convention in 1793 who replaced the Girondins. It was headed by Robespierre.

James I (1603-1625)–Stuart monarch who ignored constitutional principles and asserted the divine right of kings.

James II (1685-1688)–Final Stuart ruler; he was forced to abdicate in favor of William and Mary, who agreed to the Bill of Rights, guaranteeing parliamentary supremacy.

Karl Jaspers (1883-1969)–German existentialist seeing all people as equally co-responsible for the terrors and injustices of the world.

Jean Jaurès (1859-1914)–French revisionist socialist who was assassinated for his pacifist ideals at the start of World War I.

Jesuits–Also known as the Society of Jesus; founded by Ignatius Loyola (1491-1556) as a teaching and missionary order to resist the spread of Protestantism.

Kellogg-Briand Pact (1928)–Document, signed by fifteen countries, that "condemned and renounced war as an instrument of national policy."

Nikita Khrushchev (1894-1971)–Soviet leader who denounced Stalin's rule and brought a temporary thaw in the superpowers' relations.

John Knox (1505-1572)–Calvinist leader in sixteenth-century Scotland.

Kulak–An independent and propertied Russian farmer.

Kulturkampf–Bismarck's anticlerical campaign to expel Jesuits from Germany and break off relations with the Vatican. Eventually, after little success, Bismarck halted these policies.

Labor Party–The British party that replaced the Liberals in the early twentieth century and championed greater social equality for the working classes through the efforts of labor unions.

Laissez-faire–The economic concept of the Scottish philosophe Adam Smith (1723-1790). In opposition to mercantilism, the government's role in the economy was one of non-interference.

Ferdinand Lassalle (1825-1864)–Leader of the revisionist socialists, who hoped to achieve socialism through the ballot rather than the bullet. Revisionists agreed to work within the framework of the existing government.

Lateran Agreement (1929)–Pact that provided recognition by Mussolini of the Vatican and a large sum of money to the church as well.

Law of the maximum–The fixing of prices on bread and other essentials under Robespierre's rule.

League of Nations–A proposal included in Wilson's Fourteen Points to establish an international organization to settle disputes and avoid future wars.

V. I. Lenin (1870-1924)–The Bolshevik leader who made the Marxist revolution in November 1917 and modified orthodox Marxism in doing so.

Levée en masse–The creation, under the Jacobins, of a citizen army with support from young and old, heralding the emergence of modern warfare.

Liberal Party–Formerly the Whig Party, headed by Gladstone in the nineteenth century.

Locarno Treaty (1925)–Pact that secured the frontier between Germany and France and Germany and Belgium. It also provided for mutual assistance by France and Italy if Germany invaded its border countries.

John Locke (1632-1704)–Political theorist who defended the Glorious Revolution with the argument that all people are born with certain natural rights to life, liberty, and property. His most important works are *Two Treatises on Government* and *Essay on Human Understanding*.

Louis XIV (1643-1715)–Also known as the "Sun King"; the ruler of France who established the supremacy of absolutism in seventeenth-century Europe.

Louis Napoleon Bonaparte (1808-1873)–Nephew of Napoleon I; he came to power as president of the Second French Republic in 1848.

Lusitania–The British merchant liner carrying ammunition and passengers that was sunk by a German U-boat in 1915. The loss of 139 American lives on board was a factor bringing the United States into World War I.

Martin Luther (1483-1546)–German theologian who challenged the church's practice of selling indulgences, a challenge that ultimately led to the destruction of the unity of Roman Catholic world.

Ferdinand Magellan–Circumnavigator of the globe, 1519-1522.

Thomas Malthus (1776-1834)–English parson whose *Essay on Population* (1798) argued that population would always increase faster than the food supply.

Manorialism–The economic base of feudalism; in brief, the economic system in which the serfs worked the fields of the manorial lord and provided the material wherewithal to support the noble class.

Maria Theresa (1740-1780)–Archduchess of Austria, queen of Hungary, who lost the Hapsburg possession of Silesia to Frederick the Great but was able to keep her other Austrian territories.

Marshall Plan–Program that advanced more than $11 billion dollars for European recovery to sixteen Western nations from 1947 to 1953; the final cost to the United States was $20 billion.

Karl Marx (1818-1883)–German philosopher and founder of Marxism, the theory that class conflict is the motor force driving historical change and development.

Giuseppe Mazzini (1805-1872)–Idealistic patriot devoted to the principle of united and republican Italy in a world of free states.

Mein Kampf (My Struggle)–Work written by Hitler while in prison in 1923; the book outlines his policies for German expansion, war, and elimination of non-Aryans.

Mensheviks–Right-wing or moderate Russian Marxists willing to cooperate with the bourgeoisie.

Mercantilism–Governmental policies by which the state regulates the economy, through taxes, tariffs, subsidies, laws.

Prince Klemens von Metternich (1773-1859)–Austrian member of the nobility and chief architect of conservative policy at the Congress of Vienna.

John Stuart Mill (1806-1873)–British philosopher who published *On Liberty* (1859), advocating individual rights against government intrusion, and *The Subjection of Women* (1869), on the cause of women's rights.

Mir–A village commune where the emancipated serfs lived and worked collectively in order to meet redemption payments to the government.

Montesquieu–Author of *Spirit of the Laws* and *Persian Letters* .

Sir Thomas More (1478-1535)–Renaissance humanist and chancellor of England, executed by Henry VIII for his refusal to acknowledge publicly his king as Supreme Head of the Church Clergy of England.

Aldo Moro–Former premier of Italy and leader of the Christian Democratic Party who was assassinated by a terrorist group in 1978.

Moroccan crises–Confrontations in 1906 and 1911 between Germany and the nations of France and England over William II's interest in colonial gains in Africa.

Benito Mussolini (1883-1945)–The founder and leader of the Italian Fascist Party.

Nagasaki–Japanese city on which the United States dropped an atomic bomb on August 9, 1945, bringing the Japanese surrender and an end to World War II.

Napoleon Bonaparte (1769-1821)–Consul and later emperor of France (1799-1815), who established several of the reforms (Code Napoléon) of the French Revolution during his dictatorial rule.

Napoleon III (1852-1870)–The former Louis Napoleon, who became president of the Second Republic of France in 1848 and engineered a coup d'état, ultimately making himself head of the Second Empire.

National Socialists (Nazis)–The political party of Adolf Hitler.

Nationalism–The shared traditions and common loyalties uniting peoples, speaking a similar language (there may be dialect differences).

Nazi-Soviet Pact (1939)–An agreement between Hitler and Stalin to remain neutral if the other went to war; also, German acknowledgment of Russia's sphere of influence in the Baltics and a secret clause agreeing to the division and takeover of Poland.

Nepotism–The practice of rewarding relatives with church positions.

New Economic Policy (NEP)–Plan introduced by Lenin after the Russian civil war. Essentially it was a retreat from war communism, allowing some private ownership among the peasants to stimulate agrarian production.

New Model Army–The disciplined fighting force of Protestants led by Oliver Cromwell in the English civil war.

New Monarchs–The term applied to Louis XI of France, Henry VII of England, and Ferdinand and Isabella of Spain, who strengthened their monarchical authority, often by Machiavellian means.

Isaac Newton (1642-1727)–English scientist who formulated the law of gravitation that posited a universe operating in accord with natural law.

Friedrich Nietzsche (1844-1900)–German philosopher and forerunner of the modern existentialist movement; he stressed the role of the *Übermensch*, or "Superman," who would rise above the common herd of mediocrity.

Nicholas II (1894-1917)–The last czar of the Romanov dynasty, whose government collapsed under the pressure of World War I.

Night of August 4, 1789–Date of the declaration by the more liberal aristocrats and bourgeoisie of the National Assembly at a secret meeting to abolish the feudal regime in France.

North Atlantic Treaty Organization (NATO)–Military alliance founded in 1949, between the United States and Great Britain, France, Belgium, the Netherlands, Luxembourg, Canada, Norway, Iceland, Denmark, Portugal, and Italy; later, Greece, Turkey, and West Germany joined.

Caroline Norton (1808-1877)–British feminist whose legal persistence resulted in the Married Women's Property Act (1883), which gave married women the same property rights as unmarried women.

Nuremberg Laws (1935)–Measures enacted in Nazi Germany tht excluded Jews from white-collar professions and from marriage and habitation with non-Jews.

Nuremburg War Crimes trials–Proceedings held after 1945 to convict German military and civilian leaders of "crimes against humanity" for their role in the extermination of the Jews and other peoples.

Emmeline Pankhurst (1858-1928)–British suffragette and founder of the Women's Social and Political Union.

Pan-Slavism–A movement to unite Slavs in the Balkans.

Paris Commune–The revolutionary municipal council, led by radicals, that engaged in a civil war (March-May 1871) with the newly elected National Assembly set up at Versailles after the defeat of Napoleon III in the Franco-Prussian War.

Parlement–French law court staffed by nobles that could register or refuse to register a king's edict in Old Regime France.

Parliament Act of 1911–Legislation that deprived the House of Lords of veto power in all money matters.

Boris Pasternak (1890-1960)–Russian author of *Dr. Zhivago*, a novel condemning the brutality of the Stalin era.

Peace of Westphalia (1648)–The treaty ending the Thirty Years' War in Germany; it allowed each prince–whether Lutheran, Catholic, or Calvinist–to choose the established creed of his territory.

Peace of Augsburg (1555)–Document in which Charles V officially recognized Lutheranism as a religion in the Holy Roman Empire that a ruler or free city had the liberty to choose for all subjects in the region.

Peace of Utrecht (1713)–The pact concluding the War of Spanish Succession, forbidding the union of France, and conferring control of Gibraltar on England.

"Peace, land, and bread"–The promise Lenin made to his supporters on his arrival in April 1917 in Russia after his exile abroad.

Peaceful coexistence–The thaw in cold war tensions between the superpowers.

Peninsular War (1808-1813)–Napoleon's long-drawn-out war with Spain.

Sofia Perovskaia–The first woman to be executed for a political crime in Russia. She was a member of a militant movement that assassinated Czar Alexander II in 1881.

Peter the Great (1682-1725)–The Romanov czar who initiated the westernization of Russian society by traveling to the West and incorporating techniques of manufacturing as well as manners and dress.

Petition of Right (1628)–Parliamentary document that restricted the king's power. Most notably, it called for recognition of the writ of habeas corpus and held that only Parliament could impose taxes.

Petrograd Soviet–The St. Petersburg, or Petrograd, council of workers, soldiers, and intellectuals who shared power with the provisional government in 1917.

Philip II (1556-1598)–Son and successor to Charles V, ruling Spain and the Low Countries.

Philosophes–Social critics of the eighteenth century who subjected social institutions and practices to the test of reason and critical analysis.

Francisco Pizarro–Conqueror of Peru, 1532-1533.

Pluralism–The holding of several benefices, or church offices.

Poor Law of 1834–British legislation that restricted the number of poverty-stricken eligible for aid.

Potsdam conference–The July-August 1945 meeting of Truman, Stalin, and Clement Atlee of Great Britain, at which disagreements arose over the permanent borders of Germany and free elections in East European countries. Stalin refused to hold free elections, in fear of anti-Soviet governments.

Prague Spring–The liberal reforms introduced by Alexander Dubček, the Czechoslovak Communist Party secretary. On August 20, 1968, twenty thousand troops from the Soviet Union and its satellite countries occupied Prague to undo the reforms.

Provisional government–The temporary government established after the abdication of Nicholas II, from March until Lenin's takeover in November 1917.

Pugachev (1726-1775)–Head of the bloody peasant revolt in 1773 that convinced Catherine the Great to throw her support to the nobles and cease internal reforms.

Puritan Revolution–A reference to the English civil war (1642-1646), waged to determine whether sovereignty would reside in the monarch or in Parliament.

Puritans–Protestant sect in England hoping to "purify" the Anglican church of Roman Catholic traces in practice and organization.

Putsch–A forcible and illegitimate attempt to seize power.

Quadruple Alliance–Organization, made up of Austria, Britain, Prussia, and Russia, to preserve the peace settlement of 1815; France joined in 1818.

Rasputin–An uneducated Siberian preacher (nicknamed Rasputin, the "Degenerate") who claimed to have mysterious healing powers. He could stop the bleeding of Czarina Alexandra's son–possibly through hypnosis–and was thus able to gain influence in the czar's court, much to the dismay of top ministers and aristocrats, who finally arranged for his murder. The czarina's relationship with Rasputin did much to discredit the rule of Czar Nicholas II.

Rationalism–The application and use of reason in understanding and explaining events.

Realpolitik–The "politics of reality," i.e., the use of practical means to achieve political ends. Bismarck was a practitioner.

Red Brigade–A terrorist group committed to radical political and social change that claimed responsibility for the assassination of former Italian premier Aldo Moro in 1978.

Red Guards–The Bolshevik armed forces.

Red Shirts–Volunteers in Garibaldi's army.

Referendum–A plebiscite: the referring of a matter to the people for a decision.

Reform Bill of 1832–Act that allowed the middle class to obtain political influence. It gave the vote to all men in England who paid ten pounds rent a year and it also eliminated the rotten boroughs.

Reichstag–The lower house of the German Diet, or legislature.

Renaissance–The period from 1400 to 1600 that witnessed the birth and transformation of cultural and intellectual values from primarily Christian to classical or secular ones in northern Italy, and that spread to the rest of Europe.

Rerum Novarum (1891)–Papal encyclical of Leo XIII (1878-1903) that upheld the right of private property but criticized the inequities of capitalism. It recommended that Catholics form political parties and trade unions to redress the poverty and insecurity fostered under capitalism.

Restoration—The return of the Stuart monarchy (1660) after the period of republican government under Cromwell which was, in fact, a military dictatorship.

Revanche—The French desire for revenge against Germany for the loss of Alsace and Lorraine in the Franco-Prussian War (1870).

Revisionists—Marxists who believed that workers empowered to vote could obtain their ends through democratic means without revolution and the dictatorship of the proletariat, known as revisionism.

David Ricardo (1772-1823)—English economist who formulated the "iron law of wages," according to which wages would always remain at the subsistence level for the workers because of population growth.

Risorgimento—Italian drive and desire for unity and resurrection of Italian glory of ancient times and the Renaissance.

Rotten boroughs—Depopulated areas of England that nevertheless sent representatives to Parliament. The 1832 Reform Bill abolished them.

Jean-Jacques Rousseau—Author of *The Social Contract* and *Emile*.

Royal Society of London—Organized body for scientific study, founded in the 1600s.

Sans-culottes—A reference to Parisian workers who wore loose-fitting trousers rather than the tight-fitting breeches worn by aristocratic men.

Sarajevo—The Balkan town in the Austro-Hungarian province of Bosnia where Gavrilo Princip assassinated the Archduke Franz Ferdinand, heir to the throne.

John-Paul Sartre (1905-1980)—French existentialist most famous for his statement that "existence precedes essence," i.e., first we exist and then our moral decisions and choices shape our character or essence.

Schlieffen Plan—Top-secret German strategy to fight a two-front war against Russia and France during World War I. The idea was to invade neutral Belgium for a quick victory against France, and then direct German forces against a more slowly mobilizing Russia.

Schuman Plan—An international organization set up in 1952 to control and integrate all European coal and steel production; also known as the European Coal and Steel Community.

SDP—The Social Democratic Party in Germany, based on Marx's ideology.

Secularism—The emphasis on the here-and-now rather than on the spiritual and otherworldly.

Self-determination—The ability of an ethnic group to decide how it wishes to be governed, as an independent nation or as part of another country.

Siege of Paris—The four-month Prussian assault on the French capital after Napoleon III's surrender in 1870.

Simony—The selling of church offices.

Adam Smith—Author of *Wealth of Nations*.

Social Darwinism—The belief that only the fittest survive in human political and economic struggle.

Alexander Solzhenitsyn (1918-)—Russian author of *One Day in the Life of Ivan Denisovich*, a novel detailing life in a Stalinist concentration camp.

Spartacists—Left-wing Marxists in Germany who hoped to bring about a proletarian revolution in 1919.

Herbert Spencer (1820-1903)—English philosopher who argued that in the difficult economic struggle for existence, only the "fittest" would survive. This concept is usually termed *social Darwinism*.

St. Bartholemew's Day Massacre (August 24, 1572)—Catholic attack on Calvinists on the marriage day of Margaret of Valois to Henry of Navarre (later Henry IV).

Peter Stolypin (1862-1911)—Russian minister under Nicholas II who encouraged the growth of private farmers and improved education for enterprising peasants.

Sudetenland—German-speaking area of Czechoslovakia, ceded to Germany in the Hitler-Chamberlain Munich meeting (September 1938).

Syllabus of Errors (1864)—Doctrine of Pope Pius IX (1846-1878) that denounced belief in reason and science and attacked ''progress, liberalism, and modern civilization''

Syndicalism–The French trade-unionist belief that unions would become the governmental power through a general strike that would paralyze society.

Syndicats–French trade unions.

Tabula rasa–John Locke's concept of the mind as a blank sheet ultimately bombarded by sense impressions that, aided by human reasoning, formulate ideas.

Taille–A direct tax from which most French nobles were exempt.

Tennis Court oath (June 20, 1789)–Declaration mainly by members of the Third Estate not to disband until they had drafted a constitution for France.

Test Act (1673)–British law prohibiting Catholics and dissenters from holding political office.

Theocracy–A community, such as Calvin's Geneva, in which the state is subordinate to the church.

Third Reich–The name given to Germany during the Nazi regime, between 1933 and 1945. The First Reich (or empire) was from 963 to 1806 (the Holy Roman Empire); the second was from 1871 to 1917 (the reigns of William I and William II).

Three Emperors' League–The 1873 alliance between Germany, Austria, and Russia.

Marshal Tito (1892-1980)–Communist chief of Yugoslavia who proclaimed Communist independence of his country from Soviet influence.

Totalitarianism–An attempt by government to control a society totally through a dictatorship that employs the modern methods of communication–press, TV, radio–to glorify the state over the individual.

Treaty of Brest-Litovsk (March 1918)–Pact by which Lenin pulled Russia out of the war with Germany and gave up one third of the Russian population in the western territories of Poland, the Baltic states, and the Ukraine.

Treaty of Frankfurt (1871)–The end of the Franco-Prussian War, which ceded the territories of Alsace and Lorraine to Germany.

Treaty of Rome–Pact, created in 1957, that set up the European Economic Community (also known as the Common Market).

Treaty of Tilst (1807)–Agreement between Napoleon and Czar Alexander I in which Russia became an ally of France and Napoleon took over the lands of Prussia west of the Elbe as well as the Polish provinces.

Triple Alliance–The 1882 alliance between Germany, Austria, and Italy.

Triple Entente–After 1907, the alliance between England, France, and Russia.

Flora Tristan (1803-1844)–Socialist and feminist who called for working women's social and political rights.

Leon Trotsky (1879-1940)–Lenin's ally who organized and led the Bolshevik military takeover of the provisional government headed by Kerensky, in November 1917.

Truman Doctrine–Policy providing military aid to Greece and Turkey in an effort to contain Communism (1947-1948).

"Two Tactics for Social Democracy"–The 1905 essay in which Lenin argued that the agrarian and industrial revolutions could be telescoped. It was unnecessary for Russia to become an industrialized nation before the Marxist revolution.

Usury–The practice of lending money for interest.

Lorenzo Valla (1407-1457)–A humanist who used historical criticism to discredit an eighth-century document giving the papacy jurisdiction over Western lands.

Vatican–The independent sovereign state of the pope and the Catholic church, established in Rome in 1929.

Vatican Council of 1870–Gathering of Catholic church leaders that proclaimed the doctrine of papal infallibility.

Versailles–Palace constructed by Louis XIV outside of Paris to glorify his rule and subdue the nobility.

Victor Emmanuel III (1900-1946)–King of Italy who asked Mussolini to form a cabinet in 1922, thus allowing Mussolini to take power legally.

Virtu–The striving for personal excellence.

Voltaire–Author of *Philosophical Letters* and *Candide*.

War communism–The application of total war by the Bolsheviks to the civil war (1918-1920) at home–i.e., requisitioning grain, nationalizing banks and industries, and introducing rationing.

War of the Spanish Succession (1701-1713)–The last of Louis XIV's wars involving the issue of succession to the Spanish throne and culminating in the Peace of Utrecht.

Warsaw Pact–A military alliance, formed in 1955, of the Soviet Union and its Eastern European satellite nations.

Washington Conference (1921)–Conference of major powers to reduce naval armaments among Great Britain, Japan, France, Italy, and the United States.

Weimar–A reference to the republic of Germany that lasted from 1919 to 1933.

Weltpolitik ("world politics")–The policy of making Germany a major global power through an expanding navy and the acquisition of colonies–the dream of William II.

"What Is to Be Done?"–Essay written by Lenin in 1902 that outlined his plan for an elite revolutionary cadre to engineer the communist revolution in agrarian Russia.

William of Orange (1672-1702)–Dutch prince and foe of Louis XIV who became king of England in 1689.

Woodrow Wilson (1856-1924)–President of the United States and key figure in the peace conferences following World War I intending to make the world "safe for democracy."

Sergei Witte (1849-1915)–Finance minister under whom Russia industrialized and began a program of economic modernization.

Mary Wollstonecraft–Author of *A Vindication of the Rights of Woman*.

John Wycliffe (c. 1320-1384)–English theologian who wrote that Scriptures alone, not papal claims, should be the standard of Christian belief and practice.

Yalta–The wartime meeting of Roosevelt, Churchill, and Stalin in February 1945 to discuss military strategy and postwar plans.

Young Italy–An association under the leadership of Mazzini that urged the unification of the country.

Young Plan (1929)–Schedule that set limits to Germany's reparation payments and reduced the agreed-on time for occupation of the Ruhr.

Zemstvo–A type of Russian local government with powers to tax and make laws; essentially, a training ground for democracy, dominated by the property-owning class when established in 1864.

Clara Zetkin (1857-1933)–German Marxist who focused on women's issues in the Communist Party.

Zimmermann telegram–A secret German message to Mexico supporting the Mexican government in regaining Arizona and Texas if the Mexicans declared war on the United States–another factor propelling the United States into World War I in April 1917.

Zollverein–Economic customs union of German states established in 1818 by Prussia and including almost all German-speaking states except Austria by 1844.

ABOUT THE AUTHOR

Mildred Alpern teaches Advanced Placement European History at Spring Valley (New York) Senior High School, in the East Ramapo Central School District. She graduated Phi Beta Kappa, summa cum laude, from Boston University and received a master's degree from Columbia University Teachers College.

She has served as a reader and as a table leader at the AP national examination reading. In addition, she is a former member of the AP European History Test Development Committee, as well as a former chair of that committee. In 1987 she received the Advanced Placement Recognition Award, and the following year she was selected as one of the top five teachers in New York State. Alpern has chaired the College Board History and Social Science Advisory Committee and the College Board Academic Advisory Committee. Currently the author serves as a consultant for the College Board in Advanced Placement.

In addition to teaching at Spring Valley Senior High School, Alpern has been an instructor in the teaching of Advanced Placement European History at Manhattan College and at La Salle University. She has also taught a methods course in the teaching of social studies at Columbia University Teachers College and was designated a "Master Teacher" at a Sarah Lawrence College summer institute.

A former coeditor of "Teaching History Today"–a regular column in *Perspectives*, a newsletter of the American Historical Association–Alpern has written articles on advanced placement and teaching for *Social Education*, *Women's Studies Quarterly*, and *The History Teacher*, among other publications.

The author is the recipient of several NEH grants and a Fulbright scholarship and is listed in the *Directory of American Scholars* (History and Literature) and *Who's Who of American Women*.